Critical Multiculturalism

D0218403

Critical multiculturalism has emerged over the last decade as a direct challenge to liberal or benevolent forms of multicultural education. By integrating and advancing various critical theoretical threads such as antiracist education, critical race theory, and critical pedagogy, critical multiculturalism has offered a fuller analysis of oppression and the institutionalization of unequal power relations in education. But what do these powerful theories really mean for classroom practice and specific disciplines?

Edited by two leading authorities on multicultural education, *Critical Multiculturalism: Theory and Praxis* brings together international scholars of critical multiculturalism to directly and illustratively address what a transformed critical multicultural approach to education might mean for teacher education and classroom practice. Providing both contextual background and curriculum specific subject coverage ranging from language arts and mathematics to science and technology, each chapter shows how critical multiculturalism relates to praxis. As a watershed in the further development of critical multicultural approaches to education, this timely collection will be required reading for all scholars, educators, and practitioners of multicultural education.

Stephen May is Professor of Education in the School of Critical Studies in Education, Faculty of Education, University of Auckland, New Zealand.

Christine E. Sleeter is Professor Emerita in the College of Professional Studies at California State University, Monterey Bay.

Critical Multiculturalism

Theory and Praxis

Edited by

Stephen May
Christine E. Sleeter

Routledge
Taylor & Francis Group

NEW YORK AND LONDON

The cover picture is from an acrylic painting "*Te Kaha o te Mahi*" by Donn Ratana (copyright D. K. Ratana, 2009). The painting depicts the *mangopare* (hammer head shark) moving around the different currents of the ocean. It emphasizes blazing trails, new adventures and different pathways.

First published 2010
by Routledge
270 Madison Avenue, New York, NY 10016

Simultaneously published in the UK
by Routledge
2 Park Square, Milton Park, Abingdon, Oxon OX14 4RN

Routledge is an imprint of the Taylor & Francis Group, an informa business

Transferred to Digital Printing 2010

© 2010 Taylor & Francis

Typeset in Minion by Book Now Ltd, London

Library of Congress Cataloging-in-Publication Data
Critical multiculturalism: theory and praxis/editors, Stephen May, Christine E. Sleeter.
    p. cm.
Includes bibliographical references and index.
1. Multicultural education. 2. Multiculturalism. 3. Critical pedagogy. I. May, Stephen, 1962– II. Sleeter, Christine E., 1948–
LC1099.C746 2010
370.117—dc22   2009050288

ISBN10: 0–415–80284–9 (hbk)
ISBN10: 0–415–80285–7 (pbk)
ISBN10: 0–203–85805–0 (ebk)

ISBN13: 978–0–415–80284–0 (hbk)
ISBN13: 978–0–415–80285–7 (pbk)
ISBN13: 978–0–203–85805–9 (ebk)

Contents

Part III
Critical Multiculturalism in Mathematics/Sciences

Part IV
Critical Multiculturalism in Humanities and Social Science

Introduction
Critical Multiculturalism: Theory and Praxis

STEPHEN MAY AND CHRISTINE E. SLEETER

A little more than a decade ago, it seemed that multicultural education would become common practice in schools. After all, advocacy for it had by that time—in the 1990s—a history of 30–40 years in Western countries such as the United States, Canada, the United Kingdom, New Zealand, and Australia. Its core tenets seemed both obvious and unproblematic—at least, that is, with respect to its most popular variant, liberal multiculturalism. What could be wrong, surely, with recognizing, respecting, and including cultural differences as the basis for teaching and learning, as liberal multiculturalism averred? Wasn't fostering intercultural respect and engagement among both students and teachers a worthy and important goal? Why couldn't we all just get along better, recognizing and celebrating our ethnic and cultural differences in the classroom, and beyond?

You might well ask these questions—since in the last decade, we have seen a major retrenchment of the principles of multiculturalism, in both education and wider public policy. In the United States, a rapidly growing standards and testing movement has replaced earlier attention to racial and ethnic diversity. Beginnings of this shift were visible in the report *A Nation at Risk* (National Commission on Excellence in Education, 1983), which warned that U.S. international preeminence was being eroded by the mediocre performance of its educational institutions. A system of setting standards and measuring student performance based on them was cemented by passage of the *No Child Left Behind Act* in 2001, leading to pressure to raise test scores, which has turned the work of teachers into that of standardized curriculum technicians and test managers (Valli, Croninger, & Chambliss, 2008). In this context, despite emphasis on efforts to close the "achievement gap," multicultural education has all but disappeared.

This move towards a standardized curriculum was also framed within a wider, growing skepticism of the merits of diversity per se, particularly, after 9/11. For many, ethnic, linguistic, and cultural diversity are no longer something to be celebrated, but rather feared. Bellicose U.S. critics of multiculturalism, such as Barry (2000) and Huntingdon (2005), argue that ongoing ethnic, cultural,

1

linguistic, and religious differences are simply no longer to be tolerated if nation-states are to continue to make their way safely in the world. And the role of multicultural education is often at the center of such attacks.

As a result of such visceral critiques of multiculturalism, and their prominence in political and media commentary, wider multicultural policies and practices that seemed well accepted have simply unraveled. For example, decades of affirmative action and related civil rights advances for African Americans have been dismantled, most notably in relation to access to higher education (Kellough, 2006). The provision of bilingual education, particularly for Latino/a Americans, has also been severely circumscribed, and in some U.S. states actually proscribed, by legislation promoting a monolingual English language philosophy as a prerequisite for U.S. citizenship (May, 2008). Meanwhile, across Europe, multiculturalism as public policy is in apparent full retreat, as European states increasingly assert that minority groups "integrate" or accept dominant social, cultural linguistic and (especially) religious mores as the price of ongoing citizenship (Modood, 2007). The obvious target here, as Modood argues, are Muslims and Islam (see also Rhedding-Jones, this volume), who have regularly been both homogenized and demonized in the post-9/11 environment, a position represented most clearly in the former U.S. President George W. Bush's irresponsible and reductionist phrase "axis of evil."

And if that were not all, there is neoliberal economic philosophy, with its emphasis on laissez-faire economics, the "free" (read: unregulated) market, and individualistic opportunism, as the key drivers of late capitalism. This philosophy, the implosion of the 2009 U.S. economic market aside, dominates the social and economic policies of modern nation-states, as well as those powerful supranational organizations, such as the World Bank and the International Monetary Fund (IMF) who control the provision of funds to the developing world. In the process, neoliberalism has entrenched, rather than ameliorated, differences in access and opportunity between the already privileged and the marginalized and disempowered. In many nations, such as the United Kingdom, as neoliberalism has shifted education from a "democratic right" to a "prize to be competitively sought," the "haves" increasingly resist sharing social resources, leading to a rewidening of gaps (Tomlinson, 2001). Not surprisingly, this also corresponds closely with established racial, ethnic, and gender hierarchies (Giroux, 2008).

Even here, not all is what it seems. Critics of multiculturalism, for example, increasingly construct middle-class whites, white men, and/or monolingual English speakers as the "new minority," the newly disadvantaged (see, e.g., Barry, 2000; cf. Vavrus, this volume). It is almost as if, in Kozol's (1992) wry observation, having monopolized power and privilege, such groups now wish to monopolize misery! And yet, the ongoing social and economic realities for indigenous, black and other marginalized groups continue to tell quite a different story—often, a disturbingly tragic one. Residential taxation formulas in the United States consistently privilege wealthy white communities and their schools at the expense of poorer black, Latino, and Native American communities and schools (Kozol, 1992; Pollock, 2008). Exclusions disproportionately target

African American males and male black British students in the United States and Britain respectively (Gillborn, 2008). Non-white and/or English language learners have likewise been consistently overrepresented in special education classes, particularly in the United States (Menken, 2008). Teachers still too often construct indigenous and other minoritized students in deficit terms, with inevitable negative consequences for their longer-term academic success (Shields, Bishop, & Mazawi, 2005; see Bishop, this volume). All these trends are the result of longstanding racialized institutional policies and practices that consistently disadvantage minoritized students.

Meanwhile, contra the multicultural critics, the wider distribution of social, economic, and cultural capital also clearly continues to favor those whom it always has. Take the relationship between racialization and wealth. In the United States, even when white and black families are on similar incomes, their respective net worth still differs markedly. Fewer black families own their homes, for example, and more are likely to live in minority neighborhoods, where house values appreciate more slowly (Guinier & Torres, 2002). As Guinier and Torres argue, these differences in family wealth have demonstrable intergenerational consequences, particularly when one recognizes the close relationship, highlighted by Kozol above, between wealth and educational access and opportunity in the United States. Guinier and Torres conclude: "Race in this society [the United States] tracks wealth, wealth tracks education, and education tracks access to power" (p. 48).

Why do these structural inequalities continue to persist? And why is it that multiculturalism has apparently been so easily rebuffed as a potential answer, both within and beyond education? The next sections will explore this conundrum in two ways. First, we will highlight, ironically, a key weakness of liberal multiculturalism—its inability to tackle seriously and systematically these structural inequalities, such as racism, institutionalized poverty, and discrimination, as a result of its continued use of the affirmational and politically muted discourses of "culture" and cultural recognition. Second, we explore how more critical educational conceptions—notably, antiracist education, critical race theory, critical pedagogy, and critical multiculturalism—too often fail in turn to provide actual examples of transformed and/or emancipatory pedagogy and practice. Indeed, as we shall see, a key focus of this volume is to do precisely the latter, for both teachers and teacher educators. By this, we aim to make clearer and more consistent links *across* the various critical paradigms, in ways that complement and extend them, rather than entrench them in their own disciplinary orbits.

The Limits of Liberal Multiculturalism

Let us begin here with a vignette. Picture a predominantly white, affluent school somewhere in the United States that has begun to experience a gradual diversification of its student population, as a few middle-class African American students and a small but growing population of Mexican immigrant students from low-income homes began to attend. As a result, two people at the school independently contacted Christine. One, a Mexican immigrant parent, was concerned about teachers' low expectations for Mexican students' learning, and the school's inability to communicate with Spanish-speaking parents. She wanted Christine to talk with the teachers about their expectations and attitudes. The other, a white administrator, believed the main problem was that students called each other derogatory names, some of them race-related; he wanted to develop a "few activities" to build better cross-group relationships among the students. Both had defined the school's immediate "multicultural problem" quite differently. The parent was concerned about teachers' racial prejudice while the administrator was concerned about prejudices he believed students brought from home. But both saw the solution as building cross-cultural understanding, through either a workshop for teachers or human relations activities for students.

This is the nub of liberal multiculturalism. The focus is on getting along better, primarily via a greater recognition of, and respect for, ethnic, cultural, and/or linguistic differences, while the approach adopted is a problem-solving one. In some ways, this is not surprising. Although multicultural education in the United States initially grew out of civil rights struggles and was connected with challenges to racism in education, it has been widely filtered through people's interpretations of ethnicity. Practitioners, confronted with a myriad of human problems every day, usually interpret and respond to them through their implicit understandings of difference and equity, generally with a focus on how to fix them. This is why multicultural education initially gained such traction in schools—it seemed a ready, and readily implementable, answer to "the problem" of ethnic and cultural diversity.

But this is also its major weakness. Liberal multicultural education may be easy to implement but this is only so because it abdicates any corresponding recognition of unequal, and often untidy, power relations that underpin inequality and limit cultural interaction, however well meaning. Indeed, it seems that the less substantively a set of practices challenges power relations, the more likely they are to be taken up in schools!

In practice then, multicultural education commonly takes forms reflected in this vignette, in which the root of conflict is viewed as misunderstanding of differences rather than inequitable power relations. Culture, often equated or elided with ethnicity, is seen as a characteristic of individuals, and as a set of stable practices that can be described and taught. For example, in a recent Google search, the first website to appear for "multicultural education in schools" explained that its goals are:

(1) to remedy ethnocentrism in the traditional curriculum; (2) to build understanding among racial and cultural groups and appreciation of different cultures; (3) to defuse intergroup tensions and conflicts; and (4) to make the curricula relevant to the experiences, cultural traditions, and historical contributions of the nation's diverse population.

(Webb, 2003–2005)

These goals are to be addressed by developing awareness of multiple ethnic cultural histories, contributions, and points of view, which can be organized into forms ranging from discrete lessons to wholesale curricular revision. Lesson plans based on this view, which teach about visible cultural differences, are easily available for teachers.

Viewing culture as a set of concrete practices is reminiscent of an outdated colonial view that dominated the work of anthropologists until about 40 years ago. As Geertz (1995) put it, this stance is one of "they have a culture out there and your job is to come back and tell us what it is" (p. 43). The classroom parallel is that "other people" have culture out there, and our job is to study it through its artifacts. But doing so ends up constructing imagined cultures that romanticize difference and create fiction, a process that can happen even when narrators are members of the ethnic group they are describing (Ortiz, 2008).

A more complex view of culture sees it as "intelligent attempts to make a viable existence for human beings in the midst of the very considerable limitations that are endemic to human life" (Nussbaum, 1997, p. 138). Individuals live within multiple collectivities that share existence: families, communities, gender groups, and so forth. How people define particular dimensions of their cultural identity is refracted through multiple communal experiences, such as social class, religion, and ethnicity (e.g., Kirmani, 2008; Soudien, 2001). Schools can be understood as cultural sites, and everyone in the classroom as culturally constructed through participation in multiple cultural communities. From the point of view of multicultural education theorists, examining culture should begin with peeling back the layers of identity, practice, and existence of inhabitants of a classroom. This is more complicated than studying cultural artifacts or the practices of others, and it requires a depth of understanding of culture that most educators have not developed.

But locating multicultural education praxis in culture is also problematic because it continues to reflect assumptions that are rooted in political liberalism. Liberalism, with its emphasis on individualism and rationality, focuses on the relationship between individuals and nation-states. Liberal multiculturalism adds identification with culture and community in a way that attempts to link unity with diversity. For example, in a discussion of multicultural democracy and education, Gutmann (2004) argues that "individuals should be treated and treat one another as equal citizens, regardless of their gender, race, ethnicity, ... or religion" (p. 71). Rather than ignoring differences, education should teach tolerance and understanding of "the role that cultural differences have played in shaping society and the world in which children live" (p. 71). But framing everyone as "equal citizens" directs attention away from material inequalities, and framing people as individuals first and foremost directs attention away from power relationships among groups.

Likewise, the notion of multiple identities championed by cosmopolitan theorists such as Nussbaum (1997), and allied postmodern advocates of hybridity, such as Bhabha (1994) and Gilroy (2000), presumes that everyone has an equal opportunity to pick and choose freely from the mélange of identities available to them.

But this is simply not the case. Rather, identity choices are inevitably shaped and constrained by one's position(ing) in the wider society, a product in turn of power relations. Taking ethnicity as an example, a white American may have a wide range of ethnic options from which to choose on the basis of ancestry—both hyphenated (e.g., Italian American) and hybrid. African Americans, in contrast, are confronted with essentially one ethnic choice—black; irrespective of any preferred ethnic (or, for that matter, other) alternatives they might wish to employ.

Similarly, cosmopolitan advocates, like Nussbaum (1997), who champion a new deracinated global identity of "citizen of the world" and who argue that this global identity will quickly replace more localized ethnic and cultural ones, consistently underestimate both the enduring nature of the latter and, once again, the issue of choice and constraint. As Calhoun argues, in his compelling critique of cosmopolitanism, these ideas

> reflect the attractive illusion of escaping from social determinations into a realm of greater freedom, and of cultural partiality into greater universalism. But they are remarkably unrealistic, and so abstract as to provide little purchase on what the next steps of actual social action might be for real people who are necessarily situated in particular webs of belonging, with access to particular others but not humanity in general. Treating ethnicity as essentially a choice of identifications, [cosmopolitan theorists] neglect the omnipresence of ascription (and discrimination) as determinations of social identities.
>
> (2003, p. 536)

In short, identities, ethnic or otherwise, are not—indeed, *cannot*—be freely chosen and to suggest otherwise is to adopt an ahistorical approach which reduces life to the level of "a market, or cafeteria" (Worsley, 1984, p. 246). Rather, as McLaren (1997) asserts, identity choices are structured by class, ethnic, and gender stratification, objective constraints, and historical determinations. Put another way, individuals and groups are inevitably located, and often *differentially* constrained, by wider structural forces such as capitalism, racism, colonialism, and sexism. As George Orwell observed satirically in his famous allegorical and dystopian novel, *Animal Farm*: "all animals are equal, but some animals are more equal than others."

Multicultural educational approaches that both essentialize and depoliticize culture—treating culture as a thing, while at the same time ignoring the wider social and political context—are thus inherently delimited. As Kincheloe and Steinberg (1997) comment, a key problem is their failure "to see the power-grounded relationships among identity construction, cultural representations and struggles over resources." Rather, such approaches engage "in [a] celebration of difference when the most important issues to those who fall outside the white, male and middle class norm often involve powerlessness, violence and poverty" (p. 17). It is this key issue that antiracist education, critical race theory, critical pedagogy and critical multiculturalism have variously tried to address in their own extensive critiques of liberal multiculturalism. It is to these critical variants that we now briefly turn.

Critical Responses to Multiculturalism

The limitations of liberal multicultural education have long been recognized, even by its proponents. A quarter century ago, Banks (1984) argued that while multicultural education is part of larger movement by excluded ethnic groups to attain social equality, it is frequently trivialized, taking the form of practices like those above, such as holiday celebrations or lessons focusing on self-esteem.

These self-reflective criticisms by advocates of multicultural education have been much more trenchantly applied, and extended, by critical scholars. Antiracist education scholars, initially writing in a British context and from an overtly neo-Marxist perspective, were among the first to dismiss the culturalist emphases of multicultural education as both naïve and actively counterproductive to its espoused social justice aims. They argued that multicultural education overemphasized the impact of curricular change and underemphasized, or simply ignored, the wider structural constraints, such as racism, sexism, and discrimination, which affected minoritized students' lives. The late Barry Troyna (1987, 1993) argued that liberal multiculturalism—termed "benevolent multiculturalism" in these British antiracist critiques—constituted an irredeemably "deracialized" discourse, an approach which reified culture and cultural difference, and which failed to address adequately, if at all, material issues of racism and disadvantage, and related forms of discrimination and inequality. This acerbic dismissal of multicultural education is encapsulated by another British antiracist educator Richard Hatcher's (1987) observation that while

> culture is the central concept around which [this] multiculturalism is constructed, the concept is given only a taken-for-granted common sense meaning, impoverished both theoretically and in terms of concrete lived experience. It is a concept of culture innocent of class.
>
> (p. 188)

Hatcher's dismissive assessment formed part of a sustained assault by British antiracist theorists throughout the 1980s and 1990s (see May, 1994 for an overview), an assault that extended to Canada (see, e.g., Dei, 1996) and, eventually, to the United States. In the United States, however, a distinct critique of multicultural education has been framed within a related critical paradigm—critical race theory. Critical race theory had its origins in critical legal studies, but it has since been taken up widely within education (e.g., Delgado Bernal, 2002; Ladson-Billings, 1998; Ladson-Billings & Tate, 1995; Milner, 2008). It is predominantly a U.S.-based theoretical discourse, reflecting the sometimes-hermetic nature of national academic debates. However, British antiracist educators such as Gillborn (2008) and Preston (2007) have recently (re-)applied critical race theory to the British context.

Like antiracist education, critical race theory sees problems with multicultural education. In the article that is credited with establishing critical race theory in education, Gloria Ladson-Billings and William Tate argue:

> We assert that the ever-expanding multicultural paradigm follows the traditions of liberalism—allowing a proliferation of difference. Unfortunately, the tensions between and among these differences are rarely interrogated [critically]… the current multicultural paradigm is mired in liberal ideology that offers no radical change in the current order …
>
> (1995, p. 62)

Such was the impact of this article that, ten years later, Ladson-Billings (2005) could observe that while the literature on critical race theory and education still remained "in its infancy," it is also "a theoretical treasure—a new scholarly covenant, if you will, that we as scholars are still parsing and moving towards new exegesis" (p. 119). In the intervening period, and since, critical race theory has consistently examined the structural roots of racism and the persistence of collective white control over power and material resources, articulating a theory of race and racism that "allows us to better understand how racial power can be produced even from within a liberal discourse that is relatively autonomous from organized vectors of racial power" (Crenshaw, Gotanda, Peller, & Thomas, 1995, p. xxv; see also Delgado & Stefancic, 2001; Dixson & Rousseau, 2006; Taylor, Gillborn, & Ladson-Billings, 2009). This critical analysis includes, among other things, an emphasis on the notion of "political race." This notion reframes race as a concept that denotes both social location and political commitment, and is also used as a basis for building inclusive agendas that begin with the issues and concerns of communities of color, but which are also expanded, *at least potentially*, to address class, gender, and other inequalities (Guinier & Torres, 2002). A key part of this process methodologically is the use of "counter-storytelling," a form of "writing back" that aims to give minoritized students voice by highlighting their experiences of discrimination (Dixson & Rousseau, 2006; cf. Bishop, this volume).

The above caveat with respect to "political race"—"at least potentially"—is important here. Guinier and Torres (2002) argue that while efforts for social change must address centrally the needs of communities of color, they cannot end there. While some critical race theorists link racism with other forms of oppression (e.g., Delgado Bernal, 2002), others do not, which can limit engagement with the much wider manifestations of racism that extend beyond color, at least in the ways they are *expressed*. An obvious example of these "new racisms" is the construction of Muslims and Islam, post 9/11, as a homogeneous collective threat to western nations and, individually, as representing and/or practicing an antediluvian, illiberal, religious identity. This reductionist construction of Muslims may simply talk of cultural or religious differences (and not mention color at all), but it is clearly racialized nonetheless (Modood, 2007).

As Darder and Torres (2002, pp. 246, 260) argue, in their sometimes critical discussion of critical race theory, what is needed instead is "a critical language and conceptual apparatus" that, while still foregrounding racism and racial inequality, simultaneously encompasses "multiple social expressions of racism." This challenge can also be applied to other critical work, since there is an inevitable tendency to privilege one's principal point of focus. Thus, class analyses of oppression found in critical and Marxist theories tend to privilege class as the primary axis of oppression (e.g., Hill, 2009). Critical feminism tends to privilege gender (e.g., Brady & Kanpol, 2000); critical disability theory tends to privilege disability (e.g., Pothier & Devlin, 2006). Some view postcolonial theory as offering a space where these various forms of oppression can be interrogated and connected (e.g., Asher, 2005), while others see critical pedagogy as more encompassing or inclusive, although even this too has its limits.

Critical pedagogy emphasizes such concepts as voice, dialog, power, and social class that multicultural education too often either under-utilizes or ignores, particularly as it is taken up in schools. For example, Paulo Freire's notion of dialogical communication rejects both authoritarian imposition of knowledge and also the idea that everyone's beliefs are equal (Freire, 1998). Freire (1970) rejected a "banking" form of pedagogy "in which students are the depositories and the teacher is the depositor" (p. 53), viewing empowering pedagogy not as delivery of a multiculturalized curriculum, but rather as a dialogical process in which the teacher, acting as a partner with students, helps them to examine the world critically and politically, using a problem-posing process that begins with their own experience and historical location (Giroux, 1988; hooks, 1994; see also Gutstein, McShay, this volume).

Many critical pedagogues critique multicultural education for its tendency to reify culture as a fixed "thing" to teach about, its muted attention to complexities of identity and power in the classroom, and its inattention to social class and global capitalism (e.g., McCarthy, 1998). While multicultural education grew primarily out of racial and ethnic struggle, critical pedagogy grew primarily out of class struggle. Freire's work in Latin America was grounded in an analysis of class relations—an analysis extended to the United States in the 1980s by educators such as Giroux and McLaren. This was a welcome development, since in the United States, particularly, class tends to be under-theorized, partially because of the myth that the United States is a "classless" society, which leads to a general refusal to examine class relations critically. But critical pedagogy's "racial blindspots" (Lynn, 2004, p. 153) also sometimes privilege concepts and assumptions that clash with or mute those of racialized groups. Grande (2000), for example, argued that critical pedagogy's critique of essentialized identities and its interest in border crossing ignores the history of border crossing and cultural blending (read: appropriation) that indigenous peoples have experienced. To indigenous peoples, border crossing has meant "whitestream America . . . appropriating Native lands, culture, spiritual practices, history and literature" (p. 481; cf. Bishop; Stewart, this volume).

Thus, while the various critiques of multicultural education are instructive and offer important conceptual ground to guide praxis, no single critique simultaneously takes up the range of concerns that multiculturalism seeks to address. To that we now turn.

Critical Multiculturalism

From our point of view, critical multiculturalism provides the best means by which to integrate and advance these various critical theoretical threads (see May, 1999, 2009; Sleeter & Delgado Bernal, 2004). Each theoretical analysis of oppression usefully unpacks the workings and institutionalization of unequal power relations, although focusing on one axis of oppression offers only a partial analysis. We need to learn to build solidarity across diverse communities, both academically and professionally, which can only happen when all of us learn to embrace struggles against oppression that others of us face. This also centrally includes locating ourselves, and our own individual and collective histories, critically and reflectively in these wider discourses, and their associated power relations.

Why is critical multiculturalism a useful way forward? As with antiracist education and critical race theory, rather than prioritizing culture, critical multiculturalism gives priority to structural analysis of unequal power relationships, analyzing the role of institutionalized inequities, including *but not necessarily limited to* racism. As Berlak and Moyenda (2001) argue: "central to critical multiculturalism is naming and actively challenging racism and other forms of injustice, not simply recognizing and celebrating differences and reducing prejudice" (p. 92).

The implication of this kind of structural analysis is that challenging power relations requires understanding how power is used and institutionalized, and taking collective action to bring about change. If one assumes that schools are organized in ways that embody existing power and material disparities, teaching students and teachers about cultural differences, as in liberal or benevolent multicultural educational approaches, is likely to have, at best, only a mild and temporary effect. More helpful is learning to identify the material, political, and ideological underpinnings of inequality, analyses that are articulated by communities that experience oppression directly, and understanding how specific forms of inequality have been successfully challenged in the past (Dei, 1996). And, as Banks (2006) points out, "both cultural knowledge and knowledge about why many ethnic groups are victimized by institutional racism and class stratification are needed" (p. 95).

A structural analysis via critical multiculturalism frames culture in the context of how unequal power relations, lived out in daily interactions, contribute toward its production, rather than framing it primarily as an artifact of the past. Culture and identity are understood here as multilayered, fluid, complex, and encompassing multiple social categories, and at the same time as being continually reconstructed through participation in social situations. For example, popular culture that youth create in peer groups and share through media is a profound source of identity and meaning (e.g., Perry, 2007; Price, 2005). From this, popular culture also operates as a site in which youth contest the power of the dominant society (McCarthy, 1998). Such a positive, dynamic conception of culture continues to recognize, however, "that all speak from a particular place, out of a particular history, out of a particular experience, a particular culture, *without being contained by that position*" (Hall, 1992; p. 258, emphasis added). In other words, the recognition of our cultural and historical situatedness should not set the limits of ethnicity and culture, nor act to undermine the legitimacy of other, equally valid forms of identity.

This critical multicultural understanding of identity provides the opportunity to analyze the normative nature of whiteness and the processes of racialization that critical race theory so clearly highlights as well. By grounding multiple identities in their material contexts, critical multiculturalism also usefully avoids the vacuous deracinated, apolitical celebration of hybridity or cosmopolitanism, discussed in the previous section. As May (2009) puts it:

> A critical multicultural approach can thus foreground sociological understandings of identity—the multiple, complex strands and influences that make up who we *are*—alongside a critical analysis of the structural inequalities that still impact differentially on so many minority groups— in other words, what such groups *face* or *experience*.
>
> (p. 42, emphasis in original)

Critical multiculturalism's interdisciplinary strengths in sociology, anthropology and political studies, alongside education, allow for this level of critical engagement, while also usefully complementing and extending the legal/educational axis of critical race theory.

An additional advantage of critical multiculturalism is its internationalism. An overarching characteristic of debates on racism, culture, and schooling over the years has been a largely unquestioned and unexamined framing of these debates *within* national contexts. Until the recent extension of critical race theory to the British context, U.S. debates on multicultural education seldom extended much beyond their borders, international codicils in major handbooks of multicultural education being the usual form of engagement.[1] Likewise, British debates, particularly in the 1980s and 1990s, were almost wholly consumed by an often-visceral internal struggle between multicultural and antiracist educators, with little reference to wider debates (May, 1994). Engaging more closely and directly with and across a wider range of national contexts helps us to become more aware of our own normative assumptions as these have developed within our own particular educational and wider societal contexts, along with the institutional practices that characterize them.

Theory and Praxis

Although critical work—which may draw on a range of theories—is conceptually rich, it has paid relatively little attention to how such critiques can be applied to classroom practices. This is true also for critical multiculturalism, which, as with critical race theory, has tended to focus on the theoretical parameters of the debate rather than their actual application. There have been some notable exceptions to this general trend (e.g., Bigelow & Peterson, 2002; Gutstein & Peterson, 2005; May, 1994; Mayo, 1999; Shor, 1992, 1996; Sleeter, 1995). For example, Morrell (2002) has designed and taught high-school English in a way that works with urban youth's hip-hop culture, popular films, and television, to expand students' ability to critically analyze media and learn to use relevant theoretical texts as tools for unpacking how their everyday lives are constructed by racism and other injustices (cf. Sharma, this volume).

But, be that as it may, practitioners are still more likely to struggle with critical multiculturalism than with liberal multiculturalism, for several reasons. First, liberalism is far more prominent in mainstream ideology than critical perspectives, particularly in advanced capitalist societies (Barry, 2000). As such, educators tend not to question assumptions of liberal multiculturalism, or recognize these as questionable. Second, as noted above, much of the theoretical work in critical multiculturalism, as with other critical work, is conceptually dense, with relatively few illustrations of what this looks like in practice. Third, as institutions, schools often resist critical multicultural approaches, deeming them to be too destabilizing. For example, in a study of new teachers whose teacher preparation had been from a critical multicultural perspective, Flores (2007) found that schools pressured them away from it, through various forms: what veteran teacher colleagues modeled and espoused, the standardization of school curricula and testing, and the institutionalized model of a "good student."

A central purpose of this volume, then, is to show *how* critical multiculturalism relates to praxis, through examples that both teachers and teacher educators can readily identify with. Chapters are organized into four parts. The five chapters in Part I speak to the preparation and professional development of teachers. Michael Vavrus examines the contested nature of multiculturalism in higher education, focusing particularly on teacher education in the United States; he examines the institutionalization of non-critical forms of multiculturalism, arguing for "a *deep* critical pedagogy that supports critical multiculturalism." Virginia Lea provides an example of a teacher education Social Foundations course in which preservice teachers engage in working with families from historically marginalized communities, while in the context of critically interrogating dominant ideologies. Lilia Bartolomé provides a detailed discussion of how teacher education programs for English-language teachers can be developed that incorporate the central tenets of critical multiculturalism, including explicit study of the role of ideology in shaping the curriculum, and in the often asymmetrical power relations between English-language teachers and their predominantly minoritized students. Russell Bishop, after analyzing theories that draw from "culturalist" or "structuralist" discourses to address educational disparities that afflict indigenous and other minoritized peoples, proposes relational discourses as useful, offering critical implications for education and teacher professional development. Jeanette Rhedding-Jones considers implications of critical multiculturalism for early childhood education, providing illustrations from her work with Muslim immigrant families and their children in Norway.

Part II applies critical multiculturalism to language and language arts. Terry Locke considers various paradigms for responding to diversity in English classes, showing how they are limited in relationship to critical multiculturalism. Ryuko Kubota examines race and racism in the context of English as a Second Language/English as a Foreign Language instruction, exploring implications of critical multiculturalism for language education. Sanjay Sharma applies critical multiculturalism to media studies, where he argues that teachers can use popular media to activate students' agency, encouraging them to explore and to make creative connections that push the boundaries of their everyday experiences and knowledge.

Part III takes up implications of critical multiculturalism for math, science and technology. Eric Gutstein applies Paulo Freire's work to mathematics, illustrating how to teach students to "read the world" through mathematics with his work with urban U.S. youth. James McShay illustrates critical multiculturalism in technology by also applying a Freirian lens to the creation and use of digital stories. Georgina Stewart applies a postcolonial perspective to science, first by critically examining how theorists have conceptualized use of indigenous knowledge, then illustrating use of local indigenous knowledge in *Pūtaiao*, an indigenous science curriculum in New Zealand.

Part IV applies critical multiculturalism to the humanities and social science. Jill Flynn shows what critical multiculturalism looks like "in action" in a U.S. middle-school social studies class through a case study of a teacher, focusing on how he scaffolded students' learning to engage in "hot lava" topics, particularly race and racism. Katie Fitzpatrick discusses the implications of critical multiculturalism for physical education, particularly, the racialized constructions of thin, white bodies, and analyzes a case study of a critical physical education teacher, focusing on five key aspects of his teaching that embody critical multiculturalism. Mary Stone Hanley discusses the transformative power of arts for enabling students to imagine other experiences and social relations, illustrating with various arts genres. Finally, Charlene Morton examines music, critiquing Eurocentric structures and assumptions that are embodied in school music programs, even as they add in multiculturalism, while urging us to rethink taken-for-granted assumptions about culture, power, and music.

All of these chapters have as their central concern the elaboration of explicitly critical multicultural principles to educational policy and practice, addressing a key lacuna in writing on critical education more generally. In so doing, each addresses directly and illustratively what a transformed critical multicultural approach to education might mean for teacher education and/or classroom practice. Each chapter makes links, where appropriate, with the complementary critical approaches highlighted in this introduction, building disciplinary bridges, and making connections within as well as across these key critical education paradigms. And each chapter, while focusing principally on the national context of the author, makes connections *across* contexts, addressing the nationally bounded nature of much previous academic commentary in the area, as well as the normative assumptions that inevitably frame national debates on multicultural education. For all these reasons, we believe that this volume will mark a watershed in the further development of critical multicultural approaches to education.

Note

1 For a notable recent exception, see Banks (2009).

References

Asher, N. (2005). At the interstices: Engaging postcolonial and feminist perspectives for a multicultural education pedagogy in the South. *Teachers College Record, 107*(5), 1079–1106.

Banks, J. A. (1984). Multicultural education and its critics: Britain and the United States. *The New Era, 65*(3), 58–65.

Banks, J. A. (2006). *Race, culture and education.* New York: Routledge.

Banks, J. A. (Ed.). (2009). *The Routledge international companion to multicultural education.* New York: Routledge.

Barry, B. (2000). *Culture and equality: An egalitarian critique of multiculturalism.* Cambridge, MA: Harvard University Press.

Berlak, A., & Moyenda, S. (2001). *Taking it personally.* Philadelphia: Temple University Press.

Bhabha, H. (1994). *The location of culture.* London: Routledge.

Bigelow, B., & Peterson, B. (2002). *Rethinking globalization.* Milwaukee, WI: Rethinking Schools, Ltd.

Brady, J. F., & Kanpol, B. (2000). The role of critical multicultural education and feminist critical thought in teacher education: Putting theory into practice. *Educational Foundations, 14*(3), 39–50.

Calhoun, C. (2003). Belonging in the cosmopolitan imaginary. *Ethnicities, 3*(3), 531–553.

Crenshaw, K., Gotanda, N., Peller, G., & Thomas, K. (Eds.). (1995). *Critical race theory: The key writings that formed the movement.* New York: The New Press.

Darder, A., & Torres, R. (2002). Shattering the 'race' lens: Towards a critical theory of racism. In A. Darder, R. Torres, & M. Baltodano (Eds.), *The critical pedagogy reader* (pp. 245–261). New York: Routledge/Falmer.

Dei, G. S. (1996). *Anti-racism education: Theory and practice.* Black Point, NS: Fernwood Publishing Co.

Delgado, R., & Stefancic, J. (Eds.). (2001). *Critical race theory: The cutting edge* (2nd ed.). Philadelphia: Temple University Press.

Delgado Bernal, D. (2002). Critical race theory, Latino critical theory, and critical raced-gendered epistemologies. *Qualitative Inquiry, 8*(1), 105–126.

Dixson, A. D., & Rousseau, C. K. (Eds.). (2006). *Critical race theory in education: All God's children got a song.* New York: Routledge.

Flores, M. T. (2007). Navigating contradictory communities of practice in learning to teach for social justice. *Anthropology and Education Quarterly, 38*(4), 380–404.

Freire, P. (1970). *Pedagogy of the oppressed.* New York: Seabury Press.

Freire, P. (1998). *Pedagogy of freedom.* Boulder, CO: Rowman & Littlefield.

Geertz, C. (1995). *After the fact: Two countries, four decades, one anthropologist.* Cambridge, MA: Harvard University Press.

Gillborn, D. (2008). *Racism and education: Coincidence or conspiracy?* London; Routledge.

Gilroy, P. (2000). *Between camps: Nations, cultures and the allure of race.* London: Allen Lane/Penguin Press.

Giroux, H. A. (1988). Literacy and the pedagogy of voice and political empowerment. *Educational Theory, 38*(1), 61–75.

Giroux, H. A. (2008). *Against the terror of neoliberalism: Politics beyond the age of greed.* Boulder, CO: Paradigm Publishers.

Grande, S. M. A. (2000). American Indian geographies of identity and power. *Harvard Educational Review, 70*(4), 467–498.

Guinier, L., & Torres, G. (2002). *The miner's canary: Enlisting race, resisting power, transforming democracy.* Cambridge, MA.: Harvard University Press.

Gutmann, A. (2004). Unity and diversity in democratic multicultural education. In J. A. Banks (Ed.), *Diversity and citizenship education: Global perspectives* (pp. 71–96). San Francisco, CA: Jossey-Bass.

Gutstein, E., & Peterson, B. (2005). *Rethinking mathematics.* Milwaukee, WI: Rethinking Schools, Ltd.

Hall, S. (1992). New ethnicities. In J. Donald & A. Rattansi (Eds.), *'Race', culture and difference* (pp. 252–259). London: Sage.

Hatcher, R. (1987). Race and education: Two perspectives for change. In B. Troyna (Ed.), *Racial inequality in education* (pp. 184–200). London: Tavistock.

Hill, D. (Ed.). (2009). *Contesting neoliberal education: Public resistance and collective advance.* London: Routledge.

hooks, b. (1994). *Teaching to transgress: Education as the practice of freedom.* New York: Routledge.

Huntingdon, S. (2005). *Who are we? America's great debate.* New York: Free Press.

Kellough, J. (2006). *Understanding affirmative action: Politics, discrimination, and the search for justice.* Washington, DC: Georgetown University Press.

Kincheloe, J., & Steinberg, S. (1997). *Changing multiculturalism.* Buckingham, England: Open University Press.

Kirmani, N. (2008). Competing constructions of "Muslim-ness" in the South Delhi neighborhood of Zakir Nagar. *Journal of Muslim Minority Affairs, 28*(3), 355–370.

Kozol, J. (1992). *Savage inequalities: Children in America's schools.* New York: HarperPerennial.

Ladson-Billings, G. (1998). Just what is critical race theory and what is it doing in a *nice* field like education? *International Journal of Qualitative Studies in Education, 11*, 7–24.

Ladson-Billings, G. (2005). The evolving role of critical race theory in educational scholarship. *Race, Ethnicity and Education, 8*(1), 115–119.

Ladson-Billings, G., & Tate, W. (1995). Towards a critical race theory of education. *Teachers College Record, 97*, 47–68.

Lynn, M. (2004). Inserting the "race" into critical pedagogy: An analysis of "race-based epistemologies." *Educational Philosophy and Theory, 36*(2), 153–165.

May, S. (1994). *Making multicultural education work.* Clevedon, England: Multilingual Matters.

May, S. (Ed.). (1999). *Critical multiculturalism: Rethinking multicultural and antiracist education.* London: RoutledgeFalmer.

May, S. (2008). Bilingual/immersion education: What the research tells us. In J. Cummins & N. Hornberger (Eds.), *Bilingual education: The encyclopedia of language and education,* 2nd ed., Vol. 5 (pp. 19–34). New York: Springer.

May, S. (2009). Critical multiculturalism and education. In J. A. Banks (Ed.), *The Routledge international companion to multicultural education* (pp. 33–48). New York: Routledge.

Mayo, P. (1999). *Gramsci, Freire and adult education: Possibilities for transformative action.* London: Zed Books.

McCarthy, C. (1998). *The uses of culture: Education and the limits of ethnic affiliation.* New York: Routledge.

McLaren, P. (1997). *Revolutionary multiculturalism: Pedagogies of dissent for the new millennium.* Boulder, CO: Westview Press.

Menken, K. (2008). *English language learners left behind: Standardized testing as language policy.* Clevedon, England: Multilingual Matters.

Milner, H. R. (2008). Critical race theory and interest convergence as analytic tools in teacher education policies and practices. *Journal of Teacher Education, 59*(4), 332–346.

Modood, T. (2007). *Multiculturalism: A civic idea.* Cambridge, England: Polity Press.

Morrell, E. (2002). Toward a critical pedagogy of popular culture: Literacy development among urban youth. *Journal of Adolescent & Adult Literacy, 46*(1), 72–77.

National Commission on Excellence in Education. (1983). *A Nation at risk: The imperative for educational reform.* Washington, DC: U.S. Department of Education.

Nussbaum, M. C. (1997). *Cultivating humanity.* Cambridge, MA: Harvard University Press.

Ortiz, W. P. (2008). Fictionalized history in the Philippines: Five narratives of collective amnesia. *Children's Literature in Education, 39,* 269–280.

Perry, L. (2007). Queering teen culture: All-American boys and same-sex desire in film and television. *Journal of Popular Culture, 40*(5), 898–900.

Pollock, L. (2008). *Because of race: How Americans debate harm and opportunity in our schools.* Princeton, NJ: Princeton University Press.

Pothier, D., & Devlin, R. (Eds.) (2006). *Critical disability theory.* Vancouver, BC: University of British Columbia Press.

Preston, J. (2007). *Whiteness and class in education.* Dordrecht, The Netherlands: Springer.

Price, R. J. (2005). Hegemony, hope, and the Harlem renaissance: Taking hip-hop culture seriously. *Convergence, 38*(2), 55–64.

Shields, C., Bishop, R., & Mazawi, A. (2005). *Pathologizing practices: The impact of deficit thinking on education.* New York: Peter Lang.

Shor, I. (1992) *Empowering education: Critical teaching for social change.* Chicago: University of Chicago Press.

Shor, I. (1996). *When students have power.* Chicago: University of Chicago Press.

Sleeter, C. (1995). Reflections on my use of multicultural and critical pedagogy when students are white. In C. E. Sleeter & P. L. McLaren (Eds.), *Multicultural education, critical pedagogy and the politics of difference* (pp. 415–438). Albany: SUNY Press.

Sleeter, C. E., & Delgado Bernal, D. (2004). Critical pedagogy, critical race theory, and antiracist education: Their implications for multicultural education. In J. A. Banks & C. M. Banks (Eds.), *Handbook of Research on Multicultural Education,* 2nd ed. (pp. 240–260). San Francisco, CA: Jossey Bass.

Soudien, C. (2001). Certainty and ambiguity in youth identities in South Africa: Discourses in transition. *Discourse: Studies in the Cultural Politics of Education, 22*(3), 311–326.

Taylor, E., Gillborn, D., & Ladson-Billings, G. (Eds.). (2009). *Foundations of critical race theory in education.* New York: Routledge.

Tomlinson, S. (2001). *Education in a post-welfare society.* Buckingham, England: Open University Press.

Troyna, B. (Ed.). (1987). *Racial inequality in education.* London: Tavistock.

Troyna, B. (1993). *Racism and education.* Buckingham, England: Open University Press.

Valli, L., Croninger, R. G., & Chambliss, M. J. (2008). *Test driven: High-stakes accountability in elementary schools.* New York: Teachers College Press.

Webb, M. (2003–2005). Multicultural education in elementary and secondary schools. ERIC Digest Number 76. Retrieved December 9, 2008 from http://www.ericdigests.org/pre-9218/secondary.htm

Worsley, P. (1984). *The three worlds: Culture and world development.* London: Weidenfeld & Nicholson.

I
Critical Multiculturalism
and Teachers

1

Critical Multiculturalism and Higher Education

Resistance and Possibilities Within Teacher Education

MICHAEL VAVRUS

Contemporary multiculturalism in higher education emerged during the 1960s and 1970s. It was a result of uprisings against colonial regimes globally and activism for civil rights in the United States when the effects of racism and economic dependency were identified as central political reasons for emancipatory social action by historically marginalized and oppressed groups. From this cauldron of international movements for fundamental civil rights, multicultural education as a reform movement materialized. The struggle to incorporate multicultural perspectives into the higher education curriculum, including teacher education, was met with stiff resistance from Eurocentric privileging of access and knowledge. The fight for academic studies with explicit counter-hegemonic content such as Black, Chicano, and Indigenous studies paved the way for eventual calls for inclusion of multiculturalism in higher education.

Despite these initial inroads, what appears to take place in higher education today generally reflects normative sentiments of the nation-state as a monocultural, equal-opportunity entity for all individuals, whereas group identity discrimination is viewed as an aberration rather than a structural practice. Hierarchical group rankings along the lines of race, gender, and religion, however, "are both worldwide and local, and ... have enormous consequences in the lives of people and in the operation of the capitalist world-economy" that result in local nationalized interpretations as to "who would be considered 'true' nationals" (Wallerstein, 2004, p. 39). Hence, consistently denied by monocultural nationalists are pervasive racialized "societies in which economic, political, social, and ideological levels are partially structured by the placement of actors in racial categories or races" (Bonilla-Silva, 2005, p. 11).

Since World War II the United States, along with the United Kingdom, has exported an educational model based on universalistic meritocratic assumptions that mask the realities of a political economy of racialized hierarchies globally. This imperial model ignores the demoralizing poverty perpetuated through the political role of international monetary organizations that negatively affect life opportunities for millions, including access to even elementary education in a political environment where tax bases for public services are sacrificed to prop up finance capital for the upper classes (Foster, 2007; Wroughton, 2008). Correspondingly, access to higher education internationally in the last quarter of the twentieth century witnessed an affirmative action rise and a corresponding twenty-first century retreat for historically subordinated people. Even where equitable access to higher education is a stated goal for a nation like Brazil, inadequate secondary education has limited the success of traditionally subordinated populations (Canen, 2005). Tomasevski (2003) explained that globally,

> the laissez-faire regime for universities has led to private universities being operated as commercial companies whose shares are quoted on stock exchanges .... A blend of deregulation and privatization has created fertile ground for the mushrooming of private universities. The cost has been removed from the public to the private realm, to individual students, to their families and to corporate sponsorship.
>
> (p. 115)

Furthermore, as demand for higher education increased internationally, public expenditures have declined relative to public funding (Gordon, 2007). Hence, as education entered international trade law as a commodity in the 1990s, access to higher education by low-income and poor students significantly decreased (Tomasevski, 2003).

Because the state—and hence public primary, secondary, and higher education—depends on significant revenues from corporate capitalism, state institutions behave accordingly through selections and exclusions, including ideological orientations, that can in turn service capital. This dependency on capital filters into universities and public schools through rules and regulations that influence and often set educational expectations that can be contrary to multiculturalism. In this climate, Mahalingam and McCarthy (2000) warn about "the need to rescue the best intuitions in multiculturalism from a full-scale corruption and incorporation by the interests of global capitalism" (p. 6).

Placed within this international political and economic environment, this chapter uses teacher education as a key example of the contested nature of multiculturalism in higher education. First, an overview is presented of the disjunctive nature of teacher education programs that claim a vision of multiculturalism yet evidence practices absent of a critical perspective. Next examined for their effect on multiculturalism are higher education accreditation standards to which teacher education programs in the United States are expected to demonstrate an adherence. This analysis of accreditation standards focuses on the problematic construction of multicultural and social justice discourse. Following this is a case study of the response and resistance of a local state government and its teacher education institutions within the U.S. state of Washington to efforts to incorporate critical multiculturalism into their programs for preservice teachers. The chapter concludes with a discussion of promising critical multicultural perspectives and practices in teacher education.

Locating the *Critical* in Multicultural Teacher Education

Today, multicultural education in higher education is explicitly located within academic studies orientated toward prospective and current primary and secondary school teachers. As an interdisciplinary field of study, multicultural education draws from such disciplines as sociology, history, legal studies, economics, political science, social philosophy, social psychology, and communications studies. Within teacher preparation programs, multicultural education is often located programmatically under the umbrella of the social foundations of education and marginally, if at all, infused across the curriculum.

By the beginning of the twenty-first century, the growing consensus among internationally recognized multicultural scholars (see Vavrus, 2002, pp. 2–6) was for an emancipatory conception of multicultural education as the best possibility to transform social relations and institutions in order to overcome discriminatory schooling and societal conditions. Sleeter and Bernal (2004) highlight how drawing from critical pedagogy, critical race theory, and antiracist education, a critical multiculturalism can "steer the course of transforming education more strongly" (p. 252). Yet, as Sleeter and Bernal aptly observe, this theoretical consensus for a critical multiculturalism should not be confused with actual higher education practices.

In effect, the response has generally been tepid to multicultural incorporation into teacher education programs. Overall, for the past 40 years teacher education in the United States has successfully managed multicultural expressions and commitments so that individualistic psychological and technical orientations remain the central curricular focus of these programs. In a comprehensive review of higher education programs, Cochran-Smith, Davis, and Fries (2004) poignantly observe:

> Although a "new multicultural teacher education" may indeed be envisioned as the way to meet the needs of students and families in the real world, it is far removed from the demands and traditions of another real world: the institutional reality of colleges and universities, which supports and maintains the status quo.
>
> (p. 954)

Isolated praiseworthy programmatic and individual faculty efforts aside, the tendency in teacher education is to exclude social, economic, and political factors that affect student learning: "many of the fundamental assumptions about the purposes of schooling and the meritocratic nature of American society that have long been implicitly in teacher education remain unchallenged and undermined by the other aspects of preparation" (p. 964). Faculty and programs who make multicultural commitments face a double bind in that this status quo orientation spills over even more dramatically from higher education to primary and secondary government-supported schools, the public spaces in which their graduates work.

This disjunctive condition between critical multicultural advocacy and higher education's too-often status quo position should not be entirely surprising. The roots of critical multiculturalism developed from the ways in which critical theory "problematizes the structures of history that embody who we are and have become" (Popkewitz, 1999, p. 3). Embedded within this critical perspective is the development of a critical consciousness cognizant of unjust social systems that can lead to a sense of agency where mainstream conditions are perceived as capable of being transformed (Freire, 1970). Clearly, critical multiculturalism can strike at the heart of hegemonic positions both inside and outside of higher education and faces, therefore, waves of opposition.

Higher Education Accreditation Standards

In the United States, higher education state and national accreditation standards serve to set multicultural and "diversity" expectations and parameters along with a normative climate for teacher education. The following sections examine from a critical multicultural perspective the accreditation standards of the influential National Council for the Accreditation of Teacher Education (NCATE) that determine "which schools, colleges, and departments of education meet rigorous national standards in preparing teachers and other school specialists for the classroom" (NCATE, 2008c). As of 2006, NCATE had accredited 632 institutions with another 100 colleges and universities in the process of seeking governmental approval for their teacher education programs (NCATE, 2006). Following this is a case study of a state of Washington effort to create a critical, performance-based pedagogical assessment instrument for preservice teachers in its 21 higher education institutions. Revealed in analyses of both of these cases is a resistance to naming a "master narrative" (Huggins, 1991) that demands institutional incorporation of a history of European colonialism, white supremacy, and the implications of this history for the schooling and eventual economic and political opportunities for historically marginalized populations.

NCATE's Vague Multicultural Advocacy

By the use of the term *diversity* in the absence of any mention of *multicultural,* turn-of-the-century NCATE (2001) standards advanced an assimilationist assessment ideology upon state-level accrediting requirements that drive higher education teacher education practices. A critique of those standards and accompanying assessment rubrics revealed an absence of transformative knowledge grounded in historical foundations of white privilege, property rights, and color blindness (Vavrus, 2002). Seven years later NCATE (2008b) tinkered with diversity expectations that remain in effect until 2015.

Multicultural and Global Perspectives

Just one use of the term multicultural is found in the primary text of current NCATE higher education accreditation standards (2008b) by mentioning the importance of "educators who can reflect *multicultural* and *global perspectives* that draw on the histories, experiences, and representations of students and families from diverse populations" (emphasis added) (p. 36). NCATE's glossary defines a "multicultural perspective" as "an understanding of the social, political, economic, academic, and historical constructs of ethnicity, race, socioeconomic status, gender, exceptionalities, language, religion, sexual orientation, and geographical area" (p. 87). The glossary definition is the one place where higher education could be held to a critical perspective. Yet, given the master narrative that surrounds these named historical constructs and the ways in which they continue to be conservatively expressed across the vast majority of preparation programs, the flat language of this NCATE definition does not find its way into rubric assessments that are intended to determine if higher education institutional practices are acceptable. Unacknowledged in this NCATE goal is how the political economy of white supremacy, patriarchy, and class disparities directly impact "students and families from diverse populations."

Compounding these problems is NCATE's (2008b) definition of "global perspective" as "an understanding of the interdependency of nations and peoples and the political, economic, ecological, and social concepts and values that affect lives within and across national boundaries ... for the exploration of multiple perspectives on events and issues" (p. 87). Mainstream higher education multiculturalism with a NCATE human relations global perspective masks the interlocking elements of discrimination against marginalized populations, profit accruement on the backs of such groups, the prioritizing of military expenditures, and the decline of public funds for schools (Vavrus, 2002). Absent is any hint of the role that state-supported corporate globalization backed by the threat of military force and economic sanctions plays out in the twenty-first century to further dispossess millions of people throughout the world. Conducted under a hegemonic guise of protecting and expanding "free trade" and "democracy," corporate globalization negatively affects the availability of public goods and services. Inescapable are the negative effects of a decline in public resources for non-military expenditures that could be available for fundamental human needs, including public education opportunities (see, for example, Tabb, 2001).

Global Solidarity Alternative

Although generally deemed outside the higher education of teachers, a critical multicultural approach of global solidarity for emancipation of oppressed populations can offer higher education pragmatic insights into what it might actually mean to meet NCATE's (2008b) expectation that beginning teachers "demonstrate classroom behaviors that create caring and supportive learning environments" by being able to "communicate with students and families in ways that demonstrate sensitivity to cultural and gender differences [and] develop a classroom and school climate that values diversity" (pp. 20, 34). An emphasis on global solidarity for emancipation can help teacher education make important connections between globally oppressed peoples and domestic disenfranchised populations, the families and communities from which increasing numbers of school-age children and youth come. The seriousness for a recognition by higher education institutions about the importance of global solidarity cannot be overemphasized where, for example, in the United States alone "children living in poverty increased by 15% between 2000 and 2007" (Fass & Cauthen, 2008, ¶1) and 39% of all children live in either low-income or poor families (Douglas-Hall & Chau, 2008).

"[L]inguistic diversity"

NCATE (2008a) announced that it added "linguistic diversity to the rubrics" (¶7). NCATE's ahistorical approach to "linguistic diversity," however, fails to help higher education institutions to (a) incorporate a critique of the imperialistic determination of a nation-state's acceptable languages and (b) consider the origins of contemporary "English-only" movements in the United States by monocultural, anti-immigration groups (cf. Bartolomé; Kubota, this volume). Critical multicultural education, in contrast, posits the importance for teachers to see their work within a historical context of exclusionary practices of schooling that are naturalized and privileged in everyday discourse of the nation-state.

"[P]otential impact of discrimination"

To its diversity standard NCATE (2008a) inserted the statement "*Candidates are helped to understand the potential impact of discrimination based on race, class, gender, disability, sexual orientation, and language on students and their learning*" (emphasis in the original) (¶7). In a settler nation, however, such as the United States, that openly defined itself on a political economy of white male supremacy, discriminatory effects continue to be experienced—not just as a "*potential impact*," as NCATE phrases it—by various historically subordinated groups. It is an important step, though, for NCATE to have named commonly recognized categories of oppression. Nevertheless, NCATE refuses to go further to guide higher education to *explicitly* incorporate into their discourse the historical legacy of how these exclusionary practices and polices were aimed at specifically identified populations by those in economical and politically privileged positions, and how this is manifested in contemporary schools and society.

Culture Abstracted from Social Justice

Under NCATE (2008b) standards, colleges and universities are expected to default to teacher dispositions articulated by the 50-state leadership of the Council of Chief State School Officers (1992) nearly two decades ago in the Interstate New Teacher Assessment and Support Consortium (INTASC) standards. In these standards, INTASC (1992) employs a conservative, human relations multiculturalism—equivalent to liberal or benevolent multiculturalism—through abstracted references to "cultural sensitivity," "cultural norms," "cultural differences," and "human diversity" (pp. 14–15, 21–22). Framing diversity in these ways results in many teacher education programs embracing a culture-of-poverty ideology that avoids critiques of the *formation* of classes under a capitalist economy (Vavrus, 2008).

INTASC standards, disconnected from social justice, apparently continue to "represent a shared view among the states and within the profession of what constitutes competent beginning teaching" (Council of Chief State School Officers, 2008, ¶2). An analysis of INTASC and NCATE 2001 standards, taken together, concluded:

> Rather than a voice of multicultural authenticity, NCATE and INTASC multicultural indeterminacy is most likely a compromise among those nationally involved with managing professional teacher education. This condition reflects various political interpretations and positions on the actual existence, importance, and appropriateness in contesting potential racist exclusionary practices.
>
> (Vavrus, 2002, p. 55)

This conclusion continues to hold with NCATE's newest standards for higher education, despite NCATE's best intentions with its ambivalent social justice assertion (see NCATE, 2007).

White Privilege and Resistance to Critical Multiculturalism

In the late 1990s, the 21 higher education institutions in the U.S. state of Washington successfully lobbied the state legislature to drop a testing require-ment on pedagogy in lieu of a performance-based student teaching internship evaluation system that would be used uniformly across all institutions. Although by 2004 the final document did make significant strides to broaden expecta-tions for multicultural inclusiveness (see Office of the Superintendent, 2004), certain critical multicultural language was intentionally excluded by means of political pressure.

Resistance existed among various legislators and the state superintendent of public education. In 2002, conservative state legislators, along with the state's Business Roundtable, placed pressure upon the state superintendent of public education to withdraw an introductory conceptual framework to the student teaching internship evaluation instrument. Specific concerns centered on the inclusion in the introduction of a section titled "White Privilege and Color Blindness." This section originally included the statement "Teacher candidates represent an outdated dominant cultural model when their K-12 students are primarily engaged in traditional Eurocentric, white privileged learning materi-als and instructional activities." This critical multicultural discourse that cri-tiqued white privilege, color blindness, and related concepts was removed by the state (Vavrus, 2003).

Another source of resistance to a critical multicultural incorporation came from those teacher educators who viewed certain disciplines as color blind and outside the purview of multicultural education. This included faculty from the natural sciences and special education, the former a field disproportionately white that perceives itself color blind and outside of history and politics, while the latter is disproportionately filled with children of color and those from low-income families. Large universities faced opposition in efforts to orient legions of adjunct supervisors to new multicultural perspectives. A smaller number of teacher educators claimed that the inclusion of a critical multicultural perspective acknowledging a racialized, hierarchical society was "political" and, therefore, represented a "social agenda" that should be excluded from the assessment of teacher candidates in their full-time internships (Vavrus, 2003). Resistance continues to originate from higher education faculty who prefer a minimalist assessment instrument that can eliminate multicultural practices and leave undisturbed program status quo from external accreditation pressures (S. Walton, personal communication, March 31, 2009).

This case study of 21 colleges and universities working in collaboration with the state can help explain that *resistance to critical multicultural perspectives* stems from the following proposition: A significant number of people in higher education positions of institutional leadership, especially those who are white, consider themselves color blind and politically neutral and, therefore, see as irrelevant issues of race and racism. This hypothesis then leads to the following *ideological sources* that appear to underscore higher education resistance:

- Racism is a historical artifact that is only manifested through aberrant individual behaviors, rather than a regular experience for many children and youth of color.
- Schools and classroom are sites of fairness, not of institutional racism.
- Eurocentric curricula offer superior academic experiences.
- Academic achievement is independent of lived histories, even for those who experience forms of subordination through racism, classism, and sexism.
- Students of color and poor whites come to schools with knowledge deficits and lack the competence to succeed academically.
- The source of student academic failure rests with the family and community, not the learning environment of the school and a teacher's disposition toward social justice (Vavrus, 2003).

These ideological assumptions held by many educational leaders have also had the following *effects*: significant numbers of higher education faculty—including those in teacher education—avoid multiculturalism because the subject of race creates discomfort for them and because they lack a critical multicultural knowledge base. Hence, teachers who graduate from these higher education programs tend to defer to a color-blind belief system that is a common discourse in their public school workplaces (Vavrus, 2003). Likewise, Pollock (2008) observed through her work for the U.S. Department of Education's Office for Civil Rights, "Educators who resisted claims that their own everyday practices and interactions in schools and districts were harmful to students of color routinely dismissed students' and parents' experiences of unequal opportunity as too small to count as discrimination" (p. 138).

Promising Critical Multicultural Perspectives and Practices

Sleeter and Bernal (2004) note that critical multicultural education "tends to emphasize, more than the other fields, individual agency and institutional practices by highlighting what teachers can do" (p. 253). Sleeter and Bernal, however, confront the nexus of this theory–practice dilemma: "Since practice is often uninformed by complex understanding of oppression, culture, and power, one might ask if it is truly possible to use oppositional discourses in mainstream schools" (p. 254). In the context of the above-outlined U.S. accreditation-driven cases of National Council for the Accreditation of Teacher Education and the state of Washington, Sleeter and Bernal identify a significant challenge for critical multiculturalism to transform higher education practices.

As a pragmatic starting point, higher education teacher education programs should explicitly and legitimately incorporate studies on race, racism, and antiracism. Critical race theory, which provides a theoretical foundation for these concepts, is a perspective sorely missing in most education programs. Because critical race theory begins with the premise that "racism is normal, not aberrant" (Delgado, 1995, p. xiv), critical multiculturalism is well served by incorporating this perspective into pedagogical and institutional approaches. Critical pedagogy, then, can serve to link historical studies of white privilege and property rights with critical race theory that highlights legal foundations of exclusionary practices.

Critical pedagogy offers multicultural education a perspective on teaching and learning that can foreground such concepts as ideology, hegemony, resistance, power, knowledge construction, class, cultural politics, and emancipatory actions. Moreover, critical pedagogy can bring

> students to a place they have never been before in higher education: a terrain of discomfort where knowledge is too complex to simply give it out for use on multiple choice tests or convergent questions ... [T]he assumptions teacher candidates bring to the classroom about teaching are challenged, analyzed, and debated.
>
> (Kincheloe, 2005b, pp. 101–102)

This process, however, is marked by complaints from teachers who perceive the discourse of critical pedagogy as inaccessible and difficult to apply in practice (for example, Kehily, 2002).

History, Agency, and Teacher Identity Formation

To effectively overcome concerns of inaccessibility, critical multiculturalism must first be built on a historical foundation to counter master narratives that represent an oppressor's triumphant story of the nation-state. As related to practitioner objections to critical pedagogy, individual teacher education students exposed to critical history can perceive themselves as individuals outside this history. Students who encounter critical histories of white supremacy and sexism, for example, often deflect this information away from their identities in a manner that does not threaten stable status quo notions of themselves. Instead, what is needed is "the ability to historicize, at every moment, the present people and events we encounter individually and collectively" (Bracher, 2006, p. 121). What this suggests is a focus on the kinds of identities teacher candidates are being asked to form and what kind of agency is being sought from such constructed identities.

Each teacher's identity is fluid, situation specific, and historically contingent on power relations that constitute a society's cultural, political, and economic practices. Yet, too many programs take a cookie-cutter approach to stamping out teachers whose identities conform to constricted notions of "professionalism." A challenge for critical multiculturalism is how to help education students develop dispositions based in a critical consciousness so that they can come to see possibilities for resistance and transformative agency. Such an approach can act on Kincheloe's (2005a) observation that "[t]eacher education provides little insight into the forces that shape identity and consciousness" (p. 155).

Critical Autoethnographies and Teacher Identity Formation

The use of autobiographies is not new in teacher education. In multicultural education the primary purpose has been to deepen individual understandings of positionality (Vavrus, 2002; cf. Hanley, this volume). The outcome, however, is not always what critical multiculturalists anticipate. An unfocused autobiographical assignment on "diversity," for example, can result in color blindness along with racial inequalities being "rearticulated to maintain [white] privilege rather than disrupt it" (Chubbuck, 2004, p. 329).

Autoethnographies offer a more focused alternative to the autobiography. With an ethnographic approach, identity formation can be linked to social phenomena rather than imagined as historically autonomous from political forces. The autoethnography as "the personal text [serves] as critical intervention in social, political, and cultural life" (Jones, 2005, p. 763) and "reveals concretely realized patterns in one's own actions rather than the actions of others" (Roth, 2005, p. 4). When applied to a teacher's pedagogy, the process of excavating personal history in order to articulate a teacher's identity becomes "a way to put that identity on the line and risk needing to reform and recreate the self while also attempting to transform curricula" (Samaras, Hicks, & Garvey Berger, 2004, p. 915).

To create a *deep* critical pedagogy that supports critical multiculturalism and increases teacher accessibility necessitates "the purposeful incorporation into critical pedagogy social-psychological forces that interact with individual subjectivities in the formation of identities and subsequent behaviors" (Vavrus, 2006b, p. 92). This curricular strategy combines critical texts that education students interrogate through seminar dialog and related lectures and workshops with autoethnographic narratives. Students are provided specific writing prompts that tie multicultural content to individual lived experiences. This can be done for a variety of multicultural topics, such as issues of race, gender/ sexuality, and globalization/alienation. A final writing prompt, regardless of the multicultural topic, can ask teacher candidates to consider how this autoethnographic knowledge that they have revealed to themselves now affects formation of their respective teacher identity. This inevitably can be the most difficult prompt for education students to consider because they have come to realize that they are not outside the history that unfolds in front of them each day and that their identities shape the kind of learning environments and curricular experiences they will create in their primary and secondary public school classrooms. Through autoethnographies written under a critical pedagogy, education students regularly come to understand that they hold the agency to make critical multicultural commitments that can transform classroom practices and the life opportunities of their students (Vavrus, 2006a, 2006b, 2009).

Closing Comment

A critical multicultural curriculum is the one place in higher education where the dispossessed are no longer marginalized. When historically marginalized children and youth and their families and communities are placed in the center of higher education, a new urgency arises to transform public education so that *all* students can experience equity and hope. Substantial barriers remain to meet this goal, as evidenced from the discourse of master narratives and efforts to manage multicultural expressions. Pedagogical possibilities exist to help education students form identities that can confront the social inequities in our schools. Individual higher education faculty can lead the way, but it will take commitments across institutions for this to bear emancipatory fruit.

References

Bonilla-Silva, E. (2005). "Racism" and "new racism": The contours of racial dynamics in contemporary America. In Z. Leonardo (Ed.), *Critical pedagogy and race* (pp. 1–35). Malden, MA: Blackwell Publishing.

Bracher, M. (2006). *Radical pedagogy: Identity, generativity, and social transformation.* New York: Palgrave Macmillan.

Canen, A. (2005). Multicultural challenges in educational policies within a non-conservative scenario: The case of the emerging reforms in higher education in Brazil. *Policy Futures in Education, 3*(4), 327–339.

Chubbuck, S. M. (2004). Whiteness enacted, whiteness disrupted: The complexity of personal congruence. *American Educational Research Journal, 41*(2), 301–333.

Cochran-Smith, M., Davis D., & Fries, K. (2004). Multicultural teacher education: Research, practice, and policy. In J. A. Banks & C. A. M. Banks (Eds.), *Handbook of research on multicultural education* (2nd ed.) (pp. 931–975). San Francisco: Jossey-Bass.

Council of Chief State School Officers (2008, Sep. 12). *INTASC standards development.* Retrieved October 18, 2008, from http://www.ccsso.org/projects/interstate%5Fnew%5Fteacher%5 Fassessment%5Fand%5Fsupport%5Fconsortium/Projects/Standards%5FDevelopment/

Delgado, R. (1995). Introduction. In R. Delgado (Ed.), *Critical race theory: The cutting edge* (pp. xiii–xvi). Philadelphia: Temple University Press.

Douglas-Hall, A., & Chau, M. (2008, Oct.). *Basic facts about low-income children: Birth to age 18.* National Center for Children in Poverty, Mailman School of Public Health, Columbia University. Retrieved October 19, 2008, from http://www.nccp.org/publications/pub_845.html

Fass, S., & Cauthen, N. K. (2008, Oct.). *Who are America's poor children? The official story.* National Center for Children in Poverty, Mailman School of Public Health, Columbia University. Retrieved October 19, 2008, from http://www.nccp.org/publications/pub_843.html#1

Foster, J. B. (2007). The financialization of capitalism. *The Monthly Review, 58*(11), 1–12.

Freire, P. (1970). *Pedagogy of the oppressed* (M. B. Ramos, Trans.). New York: Seabury Press.

Gordon, T. T. (2007, Aug. 7). *Private financing grows to become global phenomenon in funding rising costs of higher education.* Institute for higher education policy. Retrieved April 9, 2009, from http://www.ihep.org/press-room/news_release-detail.cfm?id=57

Huggins, N. I. (1991). The deforming mirror of truth: Slavery and the master narrative of American history. *Radical History Review, 49,* 25–46.

INTASC (Interstate New Teacher Assessment and Support Consortium). (1992, Sep.). *Model standards for beginning teacher licensure and development: A resource for state dialogue.* Washington, DC: Council of Chief State School Officers.

Jones, S. H. (2005). Autoethnography: Making the personal political. In N. K. Denzin & Y. S. Lincoln (Eds.), *The Sage handbook of qualitative research* (3rd ed.) (pp. 763–791). Thousand Oaks, CA: Sage.

Kehily, M. J. (2002). *Sexuality, gender and schooling: Shifting agendas in social learning.* London: Routledge.

Kincheloe, J. (2005a). Critical ontology and auto/biography: Being a teacher, developing a reflective teacher persona. In W. Roth (Ed.), *Auto/biography and auto/ethnography: Praxis of research method* (pp. 155–174). Rotterdam, The Netherlands: Sense Publishers.

Kincheloe, J. (2005b). *Critical pedagogy primer.* New York: Peter Lang.

Mahalingam, R., & McCarthy, C. (2000). Introduction. In R. Mahalingam & C. McCarthy (Eds.), *Multicultural curriculum: New directions for social theory, practice, and policy* (pp. 1–11). New York: Routledge.

NCATE (National Council for the Accreditation of Teacher Education). (2001). *Professional standards for the accreditation of schools, colleges and departments of education.* Washington, DC: author.

NCATE. (2006, Apr. 5). *Quick facts.* Retrieved April 9, 2009, from http://www.ncate.org/public/factSheet.asp?ch=40

NCATE. (2007, Nov. 13). *NCATE issues call for action; Defines professional dispositions as used in teacher education.* Retrieved October 18, 2008, from http://www.ncate.org/public/102407.asp?ch=148.

NCATE. (2008a). *NCATE unit standards revision.* Retrieved July 30, 2008, from http://www.ncate.org/documents/standards/SummaryMajorChangesUnitStd.pdf

NCATE. (2008b). *Professional standards for the accreditation of teacher preparation institutions.* Washington, DC: author. Retrieved July 30, 2008, from http://www.ncate.org/public/standards.asp

NCATE. (2008c). *What is NCATE?* Retrieved April 9, 2009, from http://www.ncate.org/public/faqaboutNCATE.asp?ch=1

Office of the Superintendent of Public Instruction. (2004). *Pedagogy assessment of teacher candidates.* Olympia, WA: author. Retrieved December 14, 2004, from http://www.k12.wa.us/certification/profed/pubdocs/PerfBasedPedagogyAssessTchrCand6–2004SBE.pdf

Pollock, M. (2008). *Because of race: How Americans debate harm and opportunity in our schools.* Princeton, NJ: Princeton University Press.

Popkewitz, T. S. (1999). Introduction: Critical traditions, modernisms, and the "posts." In T. S. Popkewitz & L. Fendler (Eds.), *Critical theories in education: Changing terrains of knowledge and politics* (pp. 1–13). New York: Routledge.

Roth, W. (2005). Auto/biography and auto/ethnography: Finding the generalized other in the self. In W. Roth (Ed.), *Auto/biography and auto/ethnography: Praxis of research method* (pp. 3–16). Rotterdam, The Netherlands: Sense Publishers.

Samaras, A.P., Hicks, M. A., & Garvey Berger, J. (2004). Self-study through personal history. In J. J. Loughran, M. L. Hamilton, V. K. LaBoskey, & T. Russell (Eds.), *International handbook of self-study of teaching and teacher education practices: Part two* (pp. 905–942). Dordrecht, The Netherlands: Kluwer Academic Publishers.

Sleeter, C. E., & Bernal, D. D. (2004). Critical pedagogy, critical race theory, and antiracist education. In J. A. Banks & C. A. M. Banks (Eds.), *Handbook of research on multicultural education* (2nd ed.) (pp. 240–258). San Francisco: Jossey-Bass.

Tabb, W. K. (2001). *The amoral elephant: Globalization and the struggle for social justice in the twenty-first century.* New York: Monthly Review Press.

Tomasevski, K. (2003). *Education denied: Costs and remedies.* London: Zed Books.

Vavrus, M. (2002). *Transforming the multicultural education of teachers: Theory, research, and practice.* New York: Teachers College Press.

Vavrus, M. (2003, Apr.). *Incorporating a transformative multicultural perspective into a state's policy for teacher candidate pedagogy performance.* Paper presented at the Annual Meeting of the American Educational Research Association, Chicago (ERIC Document Reproduction Service No. ED 478389.)

Vavrus, M. (2006a, Mar.). *Resisting the effects of teacher alienation in an era of globalization.* Paper presented at the International Globalization, Diversity, and Education Conference, Washington State University, Pullman.

Vavrus, M. (2006b). Teacher identity formation in a multicultural world: Intersections of autobiographical research and critical pedagogy. In D. Tidwell & L. Fitzgerald (Eds.), *Self-study and diversity* (pp. 89–113). Rotterdam, The Netherlands: Sense Publishers.

Vavrus, M. (2008). Culturally responsive teaching. In T.L. Good, (Ed.), *21st century education: A reference handbook* (Vol. 2) (pp. 49–57). Thousand Oaks, CA: Sage Publishing.

Vavrus, M. (2009). Sexuality, schooling, and teacher identity formation: A critical pedagogy for teacher education. *Teaching and Teacher Education: An International Journal of Research and Studies, 25*(3), 383–390.

Wallerstein, I. (2004). *World-systems analysis: An introduction.* Durham, NC: Duke University Press.

Wroughton, L. (2008, Oct. 10). World Bank names 28 financially strained states. *Reuters Africa.* Retrieved October 11, 2008, from http://africa.reuters.com/top/news/usnJOE49901C.html

2

Empowering Preservice Teachers, Students, and Families Through Critical Multiculturalism

Interweaving Social Foundations of Education and Community Action Projects

VIRGINIA LEA

Introduction

Since its inception, public school in the United States has actively contributed to the reproduction of the society's socioeconomic and political hierarchy, with its deeply ingrained inequities. The primary goals of public school have been to socialize students through an organizational process Gramsci termed "hegemony" into becoming docile, patriotic citizens who would serve the nation-state, and to prepare young people to fit in to the corporate, global economy (Spring, 2008). Hegemony results in our agreeing to certain dominant ideas, values, and beliefs that have the consequence of reproducing asymmetrical power relationships. Indeed, we come to internalize these ideas, values, and beliefs to such an extent that we see them as "normal," or "common sense" (Boggs, 1976, p. 39). Hegemonic narratives convince those of us who benefit from dominant institutional and cultural arrangements *and* those of us who are oppressed by them that these arrangements are "natural."

Nevertheless, hegemony, in spite of its effectiveness in legitimizing inequalities, is not a watertight process. The normalcy of unequal and inequitable socioeconomic structures has to be constantly maintained. In response, significant numbers of people have recognized, re-cognized,[1] and struggled to transform inequitable socioeconomic and political systems. Educational goals, laws, policies, and practices have always been contested. For example, counter-hegemonic narratives were successful in ending de jure, if not de facto, segregation in schools with the landmark U.S. Supreme Court decision *Brown v Board of Education* in 1954. Counter-hegemony was also represented by alternative multicultural approaches to teaching and social activism that arose out of the 1960s and 1970s U.S. Civil Rights era in the Southern United States.

However, counter-hegemonic initiatives such as these can also become domesticated in their turn. This is what has happened with multicultural education. When schools began to tolerate, even accept, the admission of a few non-Eurocentric heroes and holidays (Nieto, 1994), and used this inclusion to claim equity, while doing little to transform the content and structure of public schooling, it became necessary to respond to this domestication of multicultural education. In the 1990s, critical multiculturalism developed as a theoretical framework with the goal of developing critical consciousness and equitable educational practice. It was and remains a welcome and necessary response to hegemonic narratives, as deeply ingrained in the educational system today as they were at its outset.

As a white person with partial Arab (Syrian) roots, from a middle-class background, the partner of an African American man, and the mother of multiethnic children, I own my interest in challenging race, class, gender, cultural, language, and other hegemonic forces that reproduce current societal inequities. However, while I am highly motivated to recognize, re-cognize, and take action to try to interrupt hegemony, I am aware of the situated, contradictory, and dynamic nature of my identity and the way I view the world. In my current role as a teacher educator, I, like many of my preservice teachers, interpret the world through lenses often distorted by the hegemonic narratives that I have come to embody through childhood and adult experiences. As I say to my preservice teachers, undoing hegemony requires vigilance throughout one's lifetime, and the assistance of a clearly defined theoretical framework. For me, this has been critical multiculturalism, and related theories.

In this chapter, I reflect on these theories in relation to one of my own small contributions to rendering visible and undoing hegemony—a new, required Social Foundations of Education course offered in the education minor, leading to a teaching certificate in the state of Pennsylvania, at the liberal arts college at which I teach. This course is taken by all of the disproportionately white, upper-middle-class undergraduate students in the program. The primary goal of the course is to help preservice teachers recognize and re-cognize the way hegemony continues to play out in schools, the wider society, and in themselves. The course also aims to aid preservice teachers in devising equitable, critical multicultural teaching and learning plans to interrupt hegemony in the educational lives of their students. First, however, I briefly explore some of the most egregious hegemonic discourses and acts of oppression that have given rise to the need to elucidate and enlighten all students with respect to the "hidden (hegemonic) curriculum" (Jackson, 1968) that constitutes much current educational practice in the United States.

Exploring Some Egregious Hegemonic Discourses and Acts of Oppression

In the United States, hegemonic public education goals have not changed since Thomas Jefferson proposed, in the 1779 Bill for the More General Diffusion of Knowledge, that all white, male children, a distinct minority of the population, should receive three years of free education. Women, black and indigenous people were basically excluded from Jefferson's plan. Children who did go to school would learn to read the Bible, the newspaper, and their taxes. In other words, the majority of those included in the civic body, citizens who would have been deemed "producers" in Plato's Republic (Spring, 2004), would receive enough enlightenment in the form of knowledge and skills to understand and consent to the principles of government dictated by their leaders.

Jefferson considered his educational system fair because the white male students would be assessed only on their achievements and abilities in the classroom, not on their socioeconomic characteristics. That the curriculum governing this educational competition, and access to school itself, might be biased, based on standards that favored those who owned and governed the means of production, was not at issue for Jefferson, any more than it is at issue for some who govern our educational process today. They, like many educators, are often duped through hegemony into seeing school arrangements like tracking and high-stakes testing as fair competition within a benign socioeconomic and cultural space, in spite of excellent research to the contrary (Wheelock, 1998; see also below).

Another example of hegemonic educational practice in the United States was initiated by Noah Webster, who believed that the birth of the new nation required the creation of a national consciousness that had at its heart narratives promoting the idea of a unified, universal, Eurocentric, American culture. Webster therefore advocated for a national history curriculum for schools, built on legends of the founding fathers (Spring, 2008). The national history curriculum that Webster envisaged has been taught to students in the United States over the last 200 years, albeit currently with slightly more inclusion of the injustices and inconsistencies that have interrupted U.S. society from attaining its rhetorical, egalitarian ideals. However, textbooks still ignore to a large extent the *consistent* inequities and contradictions at the heart of U.S. society (cf. Vavrus, this volume). Indeed, most people see the largely Eurocentric body of knowledge as representing the "normal" curriculum.

Many students have found and continue to find this typical, largely monocultural, anesthetized, dumbed-down version of history irrelevant, boring, or alienating (Gatto, 2002; Loewen, 1996). The social studies curriculum has rarely been connected with the real lives of students, especially students from low-income backgrounds and of color; it has rarely explained why the social hierarchy is constituted as it is; it has rarely explained the role of hegemony in there being fewer resources, fewer highly qualified teachers, and lower expectations of higher-order thinking and creativity in low-income schools (Anyon, 2005).

One of the main goals of the Social Foundations course described in the next section is to help preservice teachers understand that reifying dominant historical mythology can lead to the disempowerment of many of their students presented therein as inferior, stereotypical "also-rans," or not presented at all. Such historical mythology is revisionist, presenting the powerful as having "made history." It can also give people from affluent or privileged groups, who are disproportionately white, a false sense that their world genuinely serves the common good in fair and equitable ways.

This false sense of the generosity of their society often leads teachers to their own false generosity (Freire, 1993/1970), an example of which is the deficit

notion that students from low-income families, who are of color, who are indigenous or immigrant, whose first language is not English, or who speak a dialect
of English, have no cultural knowledge and practices of value, and are therefore
best served by being taught to replace their existing norms and values with those
of the white middle class. Such thinking makes it hard for the teachers from
these groups to recognize and re-cognize the impact that hegemony can have on
the lives of poor people, disproportionately of color. Moreover, the mismatch
between the 83.1% of the U.S. teaching population that is white, and the increasingly diverse, public school, student population (NCES, 2006), the fact that "the
average white teacher has no idea what it feels like to be a numerical or political minority in the classroom" (Ladson-Billings, 2001), and does not possess
diverse cultural competence, is a great problem: "The persuasiveness of whiteness makes the experience of most teachers the accepted norm" (Ladson-
Billings). While "race," ethnicity, and socioeconomic class are not theoretically
barriers to teaching all children in critical multicultural ways, white, middle- to
upper-middle-class teachers need considerable support in overcoming deficit
thinking so they can empower students from backgrounds other than their own
(cf. Bishop, this volume). At the same time, the serious institutional and cultural barriers to the recruitment of more teachers of color and from low-income
backgrounds should be removed.

In spite of growing re-segregation of public schools throughout the United
States, supported by federal apathy and/or complicity (Orfield & Lee, 2007),
"common sense" discourse has long acknowledged that public schools are the
primary vehicle for upward social mobility, and social and economic welfare in
the United States (Meier & Wood, 2004). However, during the 2000–2008 Bush
Administration, this discourse became difficult to sustain, with the entrench-
ing of a complex system of "state capitalism," in which the neo-liberal state has
become a sponsor of corporate and oligarchic wealth (Chomsky, in Cohen,
2008). As a result, public schools are being corporatized and privatized to continue to prepare children from low-income families to become corporate producers and service workers at or near the bottom of social class ladder in what
Naomi Klein (2008) calls "the new economy." I hear echoes of Jefferson's plan for
the more general diffusion of knowledge.

In the United States, the corporate government may be seen in the heavy-
handed, top-down, 2001 elementary and secondary education act, No Child Left
Behind (NCLB). NCLB has resulted in a largely monocultural, scripted schooling process governed by high-stakes testing (see also Locke, this volume), despite
numerous studies documenting its disastrous academic outcomes, particularly
for low-income students, disproportionately of color (Epstein, 2006; FairTest,
2008, 2009).

Critical multiculturalism is a lens that we can harness to resist the state capitalist juggernaut driving these developments. As a process, critical multiculturalism enables teachers and their students to identify the discourses that operate
to reproduce hegemonic practice, and develop strategies to address, and where
possible even transform, local injustices (Sleeter & Bernal, 2004).

The Pilot Social Foundations Course

The primary goal of the new Social Foundations of Education course, mentioned above is to help my disproportionately white, upper middle class, and female preservice teachers recognize and re-cognize the way hegemony continues to play out in schools, the wider society, and themselves, and to learn how to devise equitable, critical multicultural teaching and learning plans to interrupt hegemony in the educational lives of students. Readers who are teacher candidates might consider how to apply the ideas I use in my course, to their teaching of younger students.

The pilot course was framed, in part, in terms of critical literacy, which as Shor (1999) notes,

> challenges the status quo in an effort to discover alternative paths for self and social development. This kind of literacy – words rethinking worlds, self dissenting in society – connects the political and the personal, the public and the private, the global and the local, the economic and the pedagogical, for rethinking our lives and for promoting justice in place of inequity.

Indeed, critical literacy implies that we must first address how we embody hegemony, and in what ways we reproduce it in our interactions with others. Critical *multicultural* literacy helps us to focus on the *multiple* ways in which we inhabit hegemonic narratives of culture, race, ethnicity, socioeconomic class, gender, language, sexual orientation, and ability, and how these narratives inhabit us. It asks us to look for ways of contesting power and oppression as they play out in current society.

Critical multiculturalism is also based on the principle that human beings actively construct the meanings they hold about the world. While we live in a world in which obdurate hegemonic forces function to reproduce institutional structures and dominant cultural narratives that disproportionately serve the interests of the few, we possess the agency to engage in praxis by naming and at least challenging these forces *as they shape our own responses* in and outside of the classroom (Sleeter & Bernal, 2004)—consciously and reflectively applying critical multicultural theory to practice as that practice takes place (Darder, Baltodano, & Torres, 2003). Students who embrace a critical multicultural theoretical lens celebrate a new sense of their own agency. They are empowered to develop their own hybrid theoretical frameworks to guide the realization of their social justice-related, educational goals.

The pilot Social Foundations of Education curriculum has been designed to synergize tenets of previous social foundations courses with "Community Action Projects," to better meet the above goals. This complex course was structured as follows: (1) Addressing hegemony in self, school, and society; (2) Gathering cultural knowledge about a student; (3) Engaging in Community Action Projects; and (4) Teaching culturally relevant, critical literacy learning plans.

1. Addressing Hegemony in Self, School, and Society

During the first half of the semester, the preservice teachers engage in several experiences designed to help them recognize and re-cognize hegemony in themselves, in school and in the wider society. I have carefully structured these experiences so that the socially constructed nature of "normal" everyday practice is thrown into relief. The familiar is rendered unfamiliar.

One of the critical literacy challenges is helping preservice teachers address their own hegemonic assumptions, including deficit thinking, with respect to the students and families they are to encounter in the course, and in their future teaching practice:

> A deficit perspective … of students and families living in poverty … leaves little hope for students' academic success or for high expectations of them on the part of teachers and schools … Analyses of poverty, which educators need to become acquainted with, are grounded in an understanding of the larger structural issues that create and sustain poverty.
>
> (Nieto & Bode, 2008, p. 175)

Deficit thinking is a complex process. As an offshoot of hegemony, it is, in a sense, "normal." In order for people to consent to and engage in practices that subordinate others and reproduce the socioeconomic hierarchy, they must hold negative views of those at the lower ends of the socioeconomic hierarchy. Therefore, for those of us who strive for greater social and educational equity, finding ways to access our own deficit thinking is extremely important, as such discourses are necessary to the success of the powerful, reproductive, hegemonic process. This is true of children and youth as well as teachers and preservice teachers.

Consequently, becoming aware of one's own deficit thinking, and developing alternative ways of viewing the world, is a difficult process (cf. Bishop, this volume). Human beings hide their deficit thinking from themselves in order to be able to perceive themselves as fair and equitable in a society in which hegemonic rhetoric has promoted an egalitarian ideal.

> Attitudes towards concepts such as race or gender, for example, operate at two levels—at a conscious level our stated values direct our behavior deliberately, and at an unconscious level we respond in terms of immediate but quite complex automatic associations that tumble out before we have even had time to think. The adaptive unconscious is unintentional, effortless, and responsive to the here and now .... Conscious thought takes a longer view; it is controlled, slow and effortful.
>
> (Berlak, 2008, p. 51)

So, although there is no way in which a single course can undo deficit thinking, any course that purports to help students interrupt hegemony needs to assign considerable time to practices that bring hegemony to light. As they prepare to open themselves up to learning from low-income families, by unmasking any hegemonic, racist and classist, and other master-narratives that they have come to see as "normal" discourse, students in the Social Foundations course write and reflect on their educational autobiographies, goals and philosophies, engage in role plays, create masks (Lea, 2009; Lea & Griggs, 2005), engage in culture shock experiences, and watch some of the extraordinary documentary films available.

Mickey Mouse Monopoly: Disney, Childhood & Corporate Power is one such film (Chyng Sun, 2001). The video looks at the ways in which corporate power is promoted "under the guise of innocence and fun." It takes a close and critical look at the stories Disney tells about "race," gender, and class, and concludes that Disney is, in fact, engaging in a "cultural pedagogy" with a powerful "influence on our global culture" (Chyng Sun, 2001). Disney narratives, often stereotypical, enter the classroom curriculum vicariously in the hearts and minds of children, and yet the public has little or no influence over the form and the content of the narratives disseminated by this corporate giant. Disney is very protective of its products. For example, when Arab Americans struggled to delete anti-Arab stereotypes from the Disney film, Aladdin, they were less than fully successful. Amongst the statements that Disney retained in the film concerning Saudi Arabia was the following: "It's barbaric but hey, it's home!" (Giroux, 2001).

Social Foundations preservice teachers engage in *dialogue*, in small and large groups, around the themes and theory embedded in the film, and the impact of Disney on themselves (cf. McShay; Sharma, this volume). They are, at least, aware that dialogue requires an openness to being changed by the voices of others, as we discuss this process at the start of the semester when we negotiate classroom norms. As a result of dialogue, increasing numbers of them become conscious of the moments when their practice is inconsistent with their idealized view of themselves. In terms of "race," this often involves critiquing the hegemonic ideology of "color-blindness" (Bonilla-Silva, 2006) that allows them to evade recognizing and re-cognizing their deficit assumptions, embedded in some textbooks and media narratives, such as those propagated by Disney.

When students begin to see familiar and often-beloved cultural markers in a radically different light (Igoa, 1995), emotional and cognitive disruption follow. This process is called culture shock. It often accompanies preservice teachers' realization that classroom literature and media representations are not neutral. In the Social Foundations course, I ask preservice teachers to recognize and recognize culture shock by putting themselves in a "safe" culture shock situation, and monitoring their reactions. Their goal is to understand the disruptive impact this process has on many of their public school students when they enter dominant cultural classrooms. A few resist the new light thrown on old biases with strong emotion (see also Hanley, this volume); some express regret for their lack of awareness of the impact dominant narratives might have on the identities of students of color, girls, or low-income people. A third consistently express feeling enlightened. After visiting an African American Baptist church in the fall of 2008, as part of a culture shock assignment, one of my white, freshman students wrote a fairly typical response:

Through this experience (going to the Zion church with a black majority), I learned that culture shock is a process, which greatly affects the person to whom it happens, sometimes positively, and sometimes negatively. It is a scary and uncomfortable situation to be in, having customs and standards being challenged and varied. I believe culture shock can be made less severe if people are educated about it, along with the issues of race, gender, etc., at an earlier age – before they actually experience it. Therefore, although they would still go through culture shock, they would be prepared for it, and know that although it is uncomfortable, it can be learned from, and some positive can be taken from it … (It) opened my eyes to a different culture, and different way of worshipping the same God I believe in …

Addressing the ways in which race and class continue to play a significant role in reproducing the unequal and inequitable socioeconomic hierarchy occupies a large part of the course. Critical race theory is presented to the students to help them recognize racism, classism, and other forms of oppression, such as how power is sustained by constitutionally guaranteed property rights. I also use antiracist theory to emphasize uniting school and community, on problematizing whiteness and white privilege as hegemonic practice, and taking action to change the institutional and cultural arrangements that reproduce this privilege (Sleeter & Bernal, 2004).

2. Gathering Cultural Knowledge About a Student

During the first half of the semester, the preservice teachers also spend one hour a week getting to know a student from a low-income background, enrolled in a local after school program that serves mostly Latino students. To readers who are preservice teachers, I emphasize that it is virtually impossible to learn critical multicultural teaching in the abstract: you must invest time in getting to know children or youth who are from backgrounds different from your own, preferably outside school where you will learn more about the fullness of their lives than is usually possible in school. In my course, two preservice teachers get to know the same student, although they visit the after-school program center on different days. The preservice teachers pool the knowledge they glean about the student—knowledge upon which they will scaffold relevant, critical literacy learning plans to teach the student in the second half of the course.

The learning plans include, where relevant, appropriate second-language acquisition strategies. The course contextualizes the new English Language Learner (ELL) competencies mandated by the State of Pennsylvania but it also emphasizes the historical and ongoing hegemonic struggle between groups in the United States for and against Anglo linguistic and cultural dominance (cf. Bartolomé; Kubota, this volume).

3. Engaging in Community Action Projects

In applying a culturally responsive, critical multicultural lens to practice, the preservice teachers, supported by the facilitators,[2] get to know more about their students' wider cultural networks and identities during the second half of the semester, through engaging in community action projects with the students' families. This cultural knowledge is also used in the design of the culturally responsive, critical multicultural literacy learning activities, described above and below.

The Community Action Projects consist of "Oral History" (Featherston & Ishibashi, 2004), "Funds of Knowledge" (Moll, Amanti, Neff, & Gonzales, 1992), and "Educultural" projects (Lea & Sims, 2008). We invite some families to work with us. The families choose which project best suits them in *teaching* the pre-service teachers about their cultural knowledge. In the Oral History project, pre-service teachers listen to the stories and memories that the family is willing to share with them, with the conviction that these stories and memories have personal, cultural and historical importance. In the Funds of Knowledge project, through carefully structured questions that the families agree to answer or feel free not to answer, the preservice teachers investigate the families' histories, geographical knowledge, migrational patterns, cultural narratives, their everyday practices, and other knowledge that has formed the basis for their strength and resilience. In both projects, the preservice teachers create representations or codifications of the families' cultural knowledge existing in their past and present communities.

The families subsequently have the choice, in their own time, to become "community scholars"—to use these codifications, in the form of booklets, CDs, posters, artwork, and other products to teach classroom teachers to overcome their deficit assumptions about poor families (Featherston & Ishibashi, 2004), perhaps even those who taught their own children. Some school districts served by my college may offer resources for families who wish to enlighten teachers about their students' cultural backgrounds. Family-led seminars could help break down the deficit thinking of some of the teachers in their children's schools. The hope is that this process will also empower the families, and contribute in some measure towards positive change in their own lives.

The "Educultural" project represents an important addition to the new Social Foundations course. According to Lea and Sims (2008), "Educultural courses draw on hands-on experiences in music, the visual and performing arts, narrative, oral history, and critical dialogue. They deepen our critical consciousness … of deep-seated social and cultural assumptions and prejudices, and challenge and interrupt the social construction of whiteness, race, socioeconomic class, gender, and other social inequalities in our schools, classrooms, and ourselves" (p. 15). Educulturalism helps to clarify identity. The Educultural project might take many forms, including the making of a "cultural identity collage," in which the family cut and paste items that represent their cultural identities from magazines, journals, and newspapers adding, if wished, their own drawing and paintings. Through analysis of these codifications, the preservice teachers and even the families gain insights into the richness of their cultural identities, communities, and possibly their unconscious minds (Lea & Sims, 2008; cf. Hanley, this volume).

My primary goal was to structure a Social Foundations course that was marked by reciprocity, a tenet of social justice, in that all of the parties—preservice teachers, students, and their families—would in some way be empowered by the experience. It was therefore very important to address the concerns of the families who were invited to work with us. Before the course began, some of them were worried about how they might be perceived by the preservice teachers and, encouragingly, felt comfortable telling us about their concerns. In terms of power relations, their position was much more vulnerable that those of the white professor (myself) and the mostly white, middle- to upper-middle-class preservice teachers. Past experiences had suggested to the families that my preservice teachers and I might bring a deficit approach to this project (cf. Bishop, this volume). So, for reciprocity to work, the course had to conspicuously address the preservice teachers' potential deficit thinking about the families and students, as described above. I hoped that all aspects of the course would help the preservice teachers develop, amongst other critical multicultural educational goals, critical reflexivity on their "positionality"—how their identities and assumptions about their students and their families are related to how they have been and are socially situated.

It was also important that the families knew we were committed to ongoing dialogue, that they could withdraw from the project at any time, that they felt as empowered as possible to control their participation in the program, and that we were working hard to change the stereotypical roles and assumptions we might bring to intercultural contexts. It is important to note that I am aware that I hold my own less than conscious biases that could potentially disempower the very people I aim to empower.

4. Teaching Culturally Relevant, Critical Literacy Activities

As discussed above, much scripted, standardized curricula that colonize our current classrooms in the United States present discrete academic skills and knowledge in hegemonic, mythical, ahistorical, and abstract ways. Many students, not only low-income or poor students, disproportionately of color, are often alienated and/or find these curricula meaningless.

In response, I prepare preservice teachers for the difficult task of developing critical literacy learning plans that depend on teachers really knowing their students. Such plans are culturally responsive, relevant to their students' lived experience, and engage creativity and higher-order thinking skills (see also Locke, this volume). Inspired by the work of Paulo Freire (1993/1970) and others, preservice teachers are preparing to connect learning experiences not only with students' interests, everyday practices and future dreams, but also with the inequities and injustices that many students are aware exist in their communities. They aim to engage students in resolving the problems of their real lives by harnessing useful academic tools—social studies, art, physical education, and so on (Duncan-Andrade & Morrell, 2008; see also Flynn, Hanley, Fitzpatrick, this volume).

Critical multicultural education thus implies a commitment to students' formal academic achievement *and* social justice. Unlike the one-size-fits-all learning experiences promoted by corporate, standardized textbooks, critical multicultural learning plans are not abstracted from students' real lives, with the hegemonic outcome of obfuscating the origins of, and mechanisms that contribute to, inequality. They are a real attempt to interrupt the scripted world of the classroom, to motivate students to become empowered by developing a greater knowledge of formal academic skills and concepts, and to apply this knowledge to meet the critical multicultural educational goal of actively opposing injustice in their lives. This is how we can prepare students to become social change agents—by engaging them at an early age in developing their own voices and ideas for effecting equitable social change.

Conclusion

Public education in the United States, as elsewhere, has always been a political and contested process. It has, at one and the same time, reflected the heavy hand of hegemonic public policy and practice, and the critical analysis, energy, commitment, and optimism of critical activists for educational and social justice. Those of us who identify as critical multicultural educators evidence in our research and practice, on an ongoing basis, the power of hegemonic educational discourse to reproduce existing inequities. But we also attempt to find ways to interrupt the way hegemony works in and through school, society, and ourselves.

The Social Foundations course I have described is one attempt to engage preservice teachers in this effort, and at the same time to synergistically empower students and their families through a carefully structured, critical multicultural educational encounter with community partners. Guided by critical multiculturalism, critical literacy, and critical race and antiracist theory, preservice teachers are continually encouraged to try on for size different and hybrid ways of thinking, feeling, believing, and acting in the world that incorporate the families' solutions to local and global inequities and injustices. In doing so, they are more likely to re-conceptualize what "normal," "natural," and common sense means, and what is possible. They are more likely to recognize, re-cognize, and work to unravel everyday representations of hegemony policy and practice in education and the wider society.

Notes

1 Hegemony is maintained through language. Thus, it is my view that we will have to creatively restructure the language we use to allow for alternative conceptions of counterhegemonic practice or new ways to operate in the world. It is in this sense that I use the term "re-cognize" in this chapter. The verb is not in "standard" English dictionaries but should be read to connote "rethinking one's initial understanding."

2 Grant-supported student facilitators—chosen for their cultural competence, reflectivity, and empathy demonstrated in a previous Social Foundations course—support the work of the preservice teachers.

References

Anyon, J. (2005). *Radical possibilities: Public policy, urban education, and a new social movement.* New York: Routledge.

Berlak, A. (2008). Challenging the hegemony of whiteness by addressing the adaptive unconscious. In V. Lea & E. J. Sims (Eds.), *Undoing whiteness in the classroom: Critical educultural teaching approaches for social justice activism.* New York: Peter Lang.

Boggs, C. (1976). *Gramsci's Marxism.* London: Pluto Press.

Bonilla-Silva, E. (2006). *Racism without racists: Color-blind racism and the persistence of racial inequality in the United States.* Lanham, MA: Rowman & Littlefield.

Chyng Sun, C. (2001). *Mickey mouse monopoly: Disney, childhood and corporate power.* Northampton, MA: Media Education Foundation.

Cohen, B. (2008, Nov. 3). My interview with Noam Chomsky on the economy. *The Huffington Post.* Retrieved January 30, 2009: http://www.huffingtonpost.com/ben-cohen/my-interview-with-noam-ch_b_140323.html

Darder, A., Baltodano, M., & Torres, R. (2003). *The critical pedagogy reader.* New York: RoutledgeFalmer.

Duncan-Andrade, J. M. R., & Morrell, E. (2008). *The art of critical pedagogy: Possibilities for moving from theory to practice in urban schools.* New York: Peter Lang.

Epstein, K. K. (2006). *A different view of urban schools: Civil rights, critical race theory, and unexplored realities.* New York: Peter Lang.

FairTest (2008, July). Researchers document high-stakes testing damage, shortcomings. Retrieved January 11, 2009: http://www.fairtest.org/researchers-document-highstakes-testing-damage

Featherston, E., & Ishibashi, J. (2004). Oreos and bananas. In V. Lea & J. Helfand (Eds.), *Identifying race and transforming whiteness in the classroom.* New York: Peter Lang.

Freire, P. (1993/1970). *Pedagogy of the oppressed.* New York: Continuum.

Gatto, J. T. (2002). *Dumbing us down: The hidden curriculum of compulsory schooling.* Gabriola Island, BC, Canada: New Society Publishers.

Giroux, H. (2001). *The mouse that roared: Disney and the end of innocence.* Lanham, MA: Rowman & Littlefield.

Igoa, C. (1995). *The inner world of the immigrant child.* Mahwah, NY: Lawrence Erlbaum Associates.

Jackson, P. W. (1968). *Life in classrooms.* New York: Holt, Rinehart and Winston.

Klein, N. (2008). *The shock doctrine: The rise of disaster capitalism.* New York: Picador.

Ladson-Billings, G. (2001, Summer). Teaching and cultural competence: What does it take to be a successful teacher in a diverse classroom? *Rethinking Schools, 15*(4). Retrieved January 11, 2009: http://www.rethinkingschools.org/archive/15_04/Glb154.shtml

Lea, V. (2009). Unmasking whiteness in the teacher education college classroom: Critical and creative multicultural practice. In S. R. Steinberg (Ed.), *Diversity: A reader.* New York: Peter Lang.

Lea, V., & Griggs, T. (2005, Winter). Behind the mask and beneath the story: Enabling student-teachers to uncover the socially constructed nature of "normal" practice. *Teacher Education Quarterly, 32*(1), 93–114.

Lea, V., & Sims, E. J. (Eds.). (2008). *Undoing whiteness in the classroom: Critical educultural teaching approaches for social justice activism.* New York: Peter Lang.

Loewen, J. (1996). *Lies my teacher told me: Everything your high school history textbook got wrong.* New York: The New Press.

Meier, D., & Wood, G. (2004). *Many children left behind: How the No Child Left Behind Act is damaging our children and our schools.* Boston: Beacon Press.

Moll, L. C., Amanti, C., Neff, D., & Gonzales, N. (1992, Spring). Funds of knowledge for teachers: Using a qualitative approach to connect homes and classrooms. *Theory into Practice, 31*(2), 132–141.

NCES (2006). Characteristics of schools, districts, teachers, principals, and school libraries in the United States 2003–04: Schools and Staffing Survey. U.S. Department of Education.

Nieto, S. (1994). Affirmation, solidarity and critique: Moving beyond tolerance in multicultural education. *Multicultural Education, 1*(4), 9–12, 35–38.

Nieto, S., & Bode, P. (2008). *Affirming diversity: The sociopolitical context of multicultural education.* New York: Allyn & Bacon.

Orfield, G., & Lee, C. (2007, Aug.). Historic reversals, accelerating resegregation, and the need for new integration strategies. UCLA, LA: The Civil Rights Project/Proyecto Drechos Civiles.

Shor, I. (1999, Fall). What is critical literacy? *The Journal of Pedagogy, Pluralism, and Practice, 1*(4). Retrieved January 17, 2009: http://www.lesley.edu/journals/jppp/4/shor.html

Sleeter, C. E., & Bernal, D. D. (2004). Critical pedagogy, critical race theory, and antiracist education: Implications for multicultural education. In J. A. Banks & C. A. M. Banks (Eds.), *Handbook of research on multicultural education* (pp. 240–258). San Francisco: Jossey-Bass.

Spring, J. (2004). *The conflict of interests: The politics of American education.* New York: McGraw Hill.

Spring, J. (2008). *American education.* New York: McGraw Hill.

Wheelock, A. (1998). Keeping schools on track. *Rethinking Schools Online, 13*(2). Retrieved January 13, 2009: http://www.rethinkingschools.org/archive/13_02/tracksi.shtml

3
Daring to Infuse Ideology into Language-Teacher Education

LILIA I. BARTOLOMÉ

Introduction

The need to prepare qualified English-language teachers for the ever-increasing population of diverse linguistic minority students in English-speaking countries is well documented in the literature (Gándara & Maxwell-Jolly, 2000; Gonzalez & Darling-Hammond, 1997). Much of this literature calls for preparing English as a Second Language (ESL) and Sheltered English (SE) teachers, by teaching them language-acquisition theory, language-teaching methodologies and approaches, and a range of content/subject areas.

In view of the fact that ESL/SE teachers will most likely work with non-white, low-socioeconomic (SES) immigrants and other linguistic minority students from subordinated cultural groups, it is equally important that they understand that there are political and ideological dimensions to ESL/SE education that potentially may adversely impact their work. In particular, given the English-only, colonial, assimilationist tradition in the field of ESL (cf. Kubota, this volume), I argue that teacher education programs must include explicit study of the role of ideology in shaping the curriculum, and the often asymmetrical power relations that exist between the white, middle-class expectations inherent in the curriculum and students from groups that have been largely subordinated.

In this chapter, I describe the curricular efforts in one applied linguistics graduate department to prepare prospective and current ESL/SE teachers more effectively by infusing one key critical pedagogical principle—the explicit study of ideology and its role in teacher preparation—into the course of study. Before doing so, I first briefly define critical pedagogy and discuss the significance of studying ideology as part of any teacher preparation program.

Critical Pedagogy: Why Do ESL/SE Teachers Need to Study Ideology?

Critical pedagogy focuses on better understanding the links between ideology, power, culture, and language in educational contexts. Darder, Baltodano, and Torres (2003) explain that the study of ideology helps "teachers to evaluate critically their practice and to better recognize how the culture of the dominant class becomes embedded in the hidden curriculum that silence[s] students and structurally reproduce[s] the dominant cultural assumptions and practices that thwart democratic education" (p. 13). "Ideology" here refers to the framework of thought constructed and held by members of a society to justify or rationalize an existing social order (Darder et al., 2003; Eagleton, 1991; Heywood, 2003). Antonio Gramsci (1935/1971) defined dominant or hegemonic ideology as the power of the ideas of the ruling class to overshadow and eradicate competing views and to become, in effect, the commonsense or "natural" view of the world. Gramsci theorized that the role of schools and other institutions is to perpetuate dominant ideologies and to legitimize the existing order by manipulating the masses into thinking that embracing the dominant order is for their own good.

Because of this tendency to normalize and naturalize potentially discriminatory ideologies and render them "invisible" to the detriment of linguistic minority students, ESL/SE teachers have the moral obligation to acquire the necessary critical skills that will enable them to deconstruct these ideologies for what they are— classist and white supremacist orientations that they may sometimes unknowingly hold about low-SES immigrant and other subordinated students. These negative perceptions, if left unproblematized, will likely manifest themselves as discriminatory practices in the classrooms and schools that are supposedly meant to serve these students and the communities from which they come (Sleeter, 1993, 1994; Zeichner, 2003). Although there is no research that definitively links teachers' ideological stances with particular instructional practices, many scholars suggest that a teacher's ideological orientation is often reflected in his or her beliefs and attitudes and in the way he or she interacts with, treats, and teaches students in the classroom (Ahlquist, 1991; Marx & Pennington, 2003; Sleeter, 1993, 1994).

Teachers need to develop political and ideological clarity in order to increase their awareness of these assumptions, values, and views before they take action to ensure the language learning and academic success of their students. In fact, before teachers can raise their students' critical understanding of racial, gender, and class differences, the teachers themselves must first be able to engage in this type of critical analysis. A first step in developing political clarity is to understand that schools are ideological sites of struggle and, as such, are not politically neutral (cf. Lea, this volume). Given the impossibility of neutrality in education, one way to ensure that ESL/SE teachers develop political and ideological clarity is by having teacher preparation curricula explicitly explore how ideology functions to hide the asymmetries of power relations and the distribution of both cultural and economic capital.

Relevant to this discussion regarding the explicit study of ideology in applied linguistics is Pennycook's (2001) distinction between mainstream or "liberal" applied linguistics and "critical" applied linguistics. Pennycook argues that for too long, the tendency in language education has been to view language as a decontextualized phenomenon. Despite the claim that applied linguistics is concerned with studying language in context, Pennycook convincingly argues that "the conceptualization of context is frequently one that is limited to an overlocalized and undertheorized view of social relations" (p. 4). In fact, he maintains that a key function of critical applied linguistics is always to "concern itself with how the classroom, text, or conversation is *related to broader social cultural and political relations*" (p. 5, italics added). Without an understanding that the classroom is heavily influenced by social and political factors that are reflected in both material and pedagogical contexts, teachers often end up reproducing the very ideological elements that provoke cultural and linguistic resistance and/or subordination in students, who, by and large, feel excluded.

It is precisely via the study of societal macro-level and classroom micro-level connections across the course of study that ESL/SE teachers can begin to question and thus perceive the ideological, sociopolitical, and economic realities that inform their own and their students' lives. This type of teacher preparation would cultivate a form of conscientization (Freire, 1985; see also Gutstein; McShay, this volume), whereby a naïve understanding of the world is replaced with a more rigorous understanding of the reality within which these teachers operate. This broader comprehension of reality will hopefully give teachers tools to create their own pedagogical structures—structures that, on the one hand, will enhance the learning of English academic discourses and, on the other, create spaces for students' voices to emerge.

Many scholars maintain that there are insufficient opportunities for prospective teachers to be exposed to counter-hegemonic possibilities and the explicit study of ideology (Gonsalves, 2008; Haberman, 1991; Marx & Pennington, 2003). Gonsalves (2008) strongly argues for infusing teachers' entire course of study with a critique of hegemonic ideologies instead of offering "one-shot" multicultural education courses, as is typically the case (cf. Vavrus, this volume). He maintains that prospective teachers require time to work through their shocked reactions when first confronted by worldviews and practices that go against those they have been socialized to see as natural or commonsense. Gonsalves explains that middle-class, white prospective teachers, in particular, need repeated exposure to these ideas in order to work through their initial blind and angry resistance to counter-hegemonic ideologies (i.e., challenging their simplistic "blame the victim" explanations for African Americans' and Latinos' higher mortality rates, drop-out rates, etc., in the United States).

There is obviously an urgent need to go beyond the usual practice of "ghettoizing" and stigmatizing as "politically correct" the one sole course on multiculturalism that is ambivalently required in most U.S. teacher education programs. It is precisely the intent of the faculty members discussed in this chapter to avoid marginalizing such study and ensuring students' consistent and comprehensive analysis of ideology and unequal power relations among cultural groups by infusing numerous courses with these critical concepts.

Infusing Critical Perspectives into Applied Linguistics Graduate Studies

In this chapter, I describe three Applied Linguistics faculty members' attempts to infuse their courses with critical pedagogical concepts that make it apparent to graduate students that "education is involved in a complex nexus of social, cultural, and economic and political relationships that involve students, teachers, and theorists in different positions of power" (Macedo, 2006, p. 181).

Pedagogical spaces have been created in this graduate program in which students can develop greater ideological and political clarity, as well as coherent ethical postures that will inform and link to their technical acquisition of language-teaching knowledge and skills. In order to prepare these educators to neutralize or eradicate potentially discriminatory ideologies and practices where they work, and where they are often obligated to carry out state-mandated English-only instruction with students who do not yet speak or understand English, key courses have been infused with a language of critique that interrogates the antidemocratic imposition of "English only" in schools and explores strategies for subverting such undemocratic practices.

Two important critical pedagogical principles appear to inform the three courses discussed in this chapter: a critical understanding of how dominant ideologies work to produce and reproduce asymmetrical power relations along the lines of culture, ethnicity, gender, and language; and exposure to and development of effective counter-hegemonic discourses to name, interrogate, resist, and transform such oppressive ideologies and practices (Darder et al., 2003; Macedo, Dendrinos, & Gounari, 2003). Teachers are also exposed to literature dealing with resistance theory—particularly cultural and linguistic resistance—that may adversely impact student learning. The professors teach to these principles by sociohistorically contextualizing the particular subdiscipline studied (Multicultural Education, English as Second Language (ESL) pedagogy, Sociolinguistics). Furthermore, they consistently juxtapose both mainstream and critical literature as a strategy to simultaneously introduce *and* critically apprentice students into the specific subdiscipline. It is important to note that these professors do not attempt to cajole students into a particular ideological "party line." In fact, while the professors certainly exemplify individuals who are unambiguous regarding their own ideological and disciplinary orientations, a main goal in the courses is to challenge students to study counter-hegemonic concepts and perspectives seriously. Students are encouraged to develop their own positions as long as they are able to support them with relevant literature.

Given space constraints, in this chapter, I focus on three core courses and highlight evidence of the two pedagogical principles listed above. The findings are preliminary, and I intend to use them to engage our faculty in future dialog around self-critique and possible increased infusion of critical multicultural principles into the entire course of study.

The Three Applied Linguistics Courses

In order to identify when hegemonic and counter-hegemonic ideologies and practices are addressed in the graduate-level coursework, I conducted a preliminary analysis of three required course syllabi: Cross-Cultural Perspectives; Teaching ESL: Methods and Approaches; and Sociolinguistics. I also dialoged with the professors regarding my findings.

Cross-Cultural Perspectives is one of the first classes taken in the program, followed by Teaching ESL: Methods and Approaches, which students take in their second or third semester. Students take Sociolinguistics in their penultimate or final semester of study. The preliminary analysis suggests that students are exposed to hegemonic and counter-hegemonic ideological beliefs and practices throughout their course of study, while simultaneously developing expertise in the discipline of applied linguistics.

My discussion of each course includes (1) a general description of the course and relevant learning objectives; (2) an overview of textbooks and authors read in the course; and (3) a brief description of each professor's instructional approach and concrete examples of his or her teaching. Throughout my discussion, I highlight course concepts and issues that explicitly deal with both hegemonic and counter-hegemonic ideologies and practices. Finally, I discuss pedagogical commonalities across the three courses.

Cross-Cultural Perspectives

Cross-Cultural Perspectives "is designed to provide [the student] with a background in cultural politics, especially in multicultural theory and practice." Especially pertinent is the distinction the instructor makes between apolitical definitions of culture and "culture as it is affected by unequal power relations, institutional forms, antagonistic intergroup social relations, and resistance" (cf. May & Sleeter, this volume). The instructor highlights the fact that students will focus on structural and ideological analysis of oppression and inequality in the class, rather than on an individual level and that they will "identify and unravel the controversies over culture and multiculturalism . . . [and] address the ideological, pedagogical, and political patterns that play out in the United States [society and schools]."

Students examine specific forms of diversity, such as race/ethnicity, socioeconomic status, language, gender, and sexual orientation, and how these "cultural differences" are related to unequal power relations between members of these cultures and the dominant culture, as well as discriminatory beliefs, values, and practices that serve to rationalize these inequalities. Students study specifically how these inequalities often play out in classroom settings. Students are expected to become familiar with the interdisciplinary field of cultural studies and to apply this interdisciplinary lens to deconstructing mainstream "apolitical" or liberal multicultural education approaches and methods, while inventing their own.

Course Readings

The instructor uses one core textbook for this class, *Presence of Mind: Education and the Politics of Deception* by Pepi Leistyna (1999), and numerous mainstream and critical additional readings. The book covers a variety of key concepts, beginning with a detailed discussion of four common multicultural educational models (Sleeter & Grant, 1987), and highlights the fact that most of these approaches tend to simplify and essentialize ethnic culture and avoid discussing social and economic structural inequalities. Another chapter powerfully discusses white supremacist ideology—the social construction of whiteness and racial hierarchies in U.S. society.

The instructor also includes numerous articles by well-known authors—among them Ana Maria Villegas, John Ogbu, Gloria Anzaldua, bell hooks, Peggy McIntosh, Jean Anyon, Noam Chomsky, and Paulo Freire—who represent various disciplines, including education, cultural studies, and media studies. These readings include critiques of simplistic cultural incongruence models to explain linguistic minority academic underachievement, discuss the link between languages and identity, and make evident the invisibility of white privilege and the highly political nature of education.

Description of Instructional Approach

It is evident from the syllabus that the professor takes an unwavering and focused approach to studying how culture, ideology, and power manifest themselves across a variety of cross-cultural and linguistic contact situations. The instructor begins the semester by sociohistorically contextualizing the field of multicultural education. Time is spent reviewing the history of immigration and internal colonization and the consolidation of white supremacist ideologies in the United States.

Once a sociohistorical context has been established, the instructor examines the interrelationship among culture, ideology, and power by studying the historical experiences of various domestic minority groups through the prism of a colonial model. Specifically, the instructor utilizes a cultural studies framework to promote better understanding of multicultural education conventionally defined as focused on apolitical celebration of "differences." Cultural studies is a relatively young interdisciplinary field that explores the relationship between culture/cultural forms, the political economic base, and the resulting hegemonic ideologies (During, 2003; see also Sharma, this volume). Given this theoretical orientation for the course, it is apparent that the students are provided ample opportunities to link cultural diversity of many types (e.g., ethnic/racial, SES, linguistic, etc.) with their relationship to power. In doing so, students develop expertise in two multicultural education subdisciplines: mainstream multicultural education and critical multiculturalism, combined with cultural studies. Similar sociohistorical insertion and juxtaposing of ideologies and instructional practices occur in the ESL Methods and Approaches class discussed in the section that follows.

Teaching ESL: Methods and Approaches

The course, Teaching ESL: Methods and Approaches, which I have taught since 2001, introduces students to the history of ESL instruction and to current ESL/SE teaching approaches and methods. This historical perspective enables students to understand the legacy of imperialism and English language imposition inherent in their profession. Understanding the history of their professional community helps students to more explicitly perceive how an unacknowledged yet ever-present assimilationist and white supremacist tradition in ESL (and now, Sheltered English classrooms), often functions as an "invisible" foundation that can potentially taint their teaching unless they make concerted efforts to create more humane and respectful learning contexts that are conducive to linguistic minority students critically appropriating English rather than having it subtractively imposed. Thus, throughout the semester, students are challenged to consider historical, social, political, and cultural factors when selecting, modifying, and implementing instructional methods, especially in view of the current resurgence of English-only mandates in the United States, including in Massachusetts, where this program is taught.

Course Readings

I use three basic language methodology texts that offer students accessible descriptions of various current ESL/SE teaching approaches and methods such as the Natural Approach, and sheltered English instructional approaches (Echevarria & Graves, 2003; Larsen-Freeman, 2000; Richards & Rodgers, 2007). I also employ numerous articles that discuss Freirean participatory language and literacy approaches (see also Gutstein; McShay, this volume), skills-based teaching, whole language approaches, and other methodologies. The course readings reinforce concepts presented in class about a variety of ESL/SE methods and approaches, while concurrently critiquing concepts of decontextualized methods, or "magic recipes," and learning that no method, no matter how promising, can compensate for inadequate conditions of learning or overcome social and economic inequalities. Thus, while apprenticing students in the ESL discipline or "community of practice," which entails critically appropriating that discipline's professional discourse and knowledge base, students learn to become vigilant against the potential macro-level sociopolitical and ideological factors that can have an impact on their micro-level work, especially because of the colonial, assimilationist English-only tradition of the discipline of ESL/SE (cf. Kubota, this volume).

I also use a fourth textbook, *Designing Groupwork* by Elizabeth Cohen (1994), which offers an instructional approach that teachers can employ to purposefully prevent or undo the creation of unequal social student hierarchies in the classroom. Cohen explains that in society at large, status distinctions and expectations are made on the basis of limited English language proficiency, social class, ethnic group membership, and gender. These status distinctions are often replicated at the classroom level, unless teachers make a conscious effort to prevent their reproduction. Students respond enthusiastically to Cohen's accessible writing style and her concrete suggestions for engineering greater equality in the classroom, as well setting up enhanced interactive language-learning opportunities. Students also read various articles and book chapters by educators, such as Antonia Darder, Paulo Freire, Jim Gee, John Ogbu, Donaldo Macedo, and Tamara Lucas, which provide them additional opportunities to explore how various inequalities (racial/ethnic, linguistic diversity) are manifested in classroom settings, along with suggestions for more democratic and liberatory solutions or interventions.

Instructional Approach

I typically begin the semester by having students read about the colonial and assimilationist legacy in the field of ESL, and questioning if and how this legacy is reproduced in current sheltered English models of instruction. I also employ my article, "Beyond the Methods Fetish: Toward a Humanizing Pedagogy" (Bartolomé, 1994) and utilize it as an example for analyzing instructional methodologies for both their potential to offset unequal power relations between teachers and students and for critically and additively apprenticing linguistic minority students into academic discourses. In addition, we discuss strategies for honoring students' home cultures, and strategically using their first languages in school systems that prohibit the use of languages other than English. A good portion of the semester is spent juxtaposing state-of-the-art "best practice" literature with critical readings that challenge the students to consistently ask themselves, "ESL/SE instruction for whom and against whom?"

Sociolinguistics

In the syllabus, the instructor makes unmistakable the course's general approach to study language variation by highlighting the social, ideological/ political, and cultural significance of this variation, and, in particular, to consider the social and pedagogical results of linguistic minority language variation. For example, students examine Black English Vernacular (BEV) language structure using grammatical analysis, but they also go beyond descriptive linguistic analysis to study the social perceptions of mainstream society in general, and of teachers in particular, toward BEV and the people who speak it. The instructor's dual focus is to expose students both to the discipline of sociolinguistics and to the social and political ramifications of language variation, particularly in regard to public school students who speak socially designated stigmatized or low-status language varieties.

Course Readings

The course readings are made up of both critical and mainstream sociolinguistic literature. The mainstream sociolinguistic literature is exemplified in Ron Wardhaugh's (1998) textbook, *An Introduction to Sociolinguistics*. Wardhaugh's text has been reprinted numerous times and is a popular and much-used book in the field. It contains literature and research on sociolinguistic topics such as the history of discipline, pidgins and creoles, BEV, code-switching, language variation, speech acts, and discourse analysis.

The instructor also uses *The Hegemony of English* (Macedo et al., 2003), which exemplifies a more critical approach to sociolinguistics. The instructor uses the

Hegemony of English to compare, contrast, and expand on Wardhaugh's descriptive work, thus challenging students to take the additional step of problematizing language policies and the racist/classist ideologies that inform them. Particularly relevant for language teachers is the instructor's use of the two books (and other readings listed below) to elicit discussion regarding the link between colonial ideologies and current-day imposition of English-only language policies in U.S. society and public schools.

Additional readings of renowned sociolinguists include Joshua Fishman, William Labov, John Gumperz, and Basil Bernstein. Students are also exposed to classic sociolinguistic writings on BEV by such authors as John Dillard and Tommy Lott, as well as more recent writers Geneva Smitherman-Donaldson and Lisa Delpit. Very importantly, the instructor also includes articles outside mainstream sociolinguistics from fields as varied as cultural studies, women's studies, and critical pedagogy. The better-known authors from these critical disciplines include Gloria Anzaldua, Teun Van Dijk, Robert Phillipson, and Norman Fairclough. These authors' research focuses on the inextricable relationships between language, power, and identity. This pedagogical practice of juxtaposing ideologically and disciplinary diverse literature and perspectives reflects Pennycook's (2001) suggestion, discussed earlier, that the study of sociolinguistics be explicitly related to social, political, and ideological factors. One end result is that students come to the realization that language is not a mere vehicle for communication and that language policy is not an innocent and benign undertaking. Throughout the semester, students are challenged to consider how language practices and policies can either potentially empower or silence linguistic minority students.

Instructional Approach

As mentioned earlier, the instructor works to impart a conventional sociolinguistic disciplinary knowledge base, while also giving students an additional critical lens with which to identify the power and ideological dimensions related to linguistic variation. Students are consistently challenged to interrogate why mainstream studies in the field often remain trapped by empiricism, with little or no discussion regarding ideology, colonialism, power relations, and other key factors that shape and maintain language discrimination and oppression. They are provided numerous opportunities via the use of varied disciplinary and ideological perspectives to engage in the process of critically interrogating their study of sociolinguistic phenomena and to realistically imagine more democratic and just interventions.

Pedagogical Commonalities Across the Courses: Critical Apprenticeship and Sociohistorical Insertion

The three instructors utilized a variety of pedagogical strategies to assist their students in naming "invisible" dominant ideologies and realistically envisioning counter-hegemonic perspectives. Each instructor critically apprentices her/his students into the particular applied linguistics subdiscipline taught (Multicultural Education, ESL pedagogy, Sociolinguistics) by helping them master both mainstream and critical literature in the field. Students are expected to continually juxtapose hegemonic with counter-hegemonic views as well as cross-disciplinary perspectives of linguistic and cultural diversity. To reiterate a point made earlier in the chapter, students are not expected to blindly accept counter-hegemonic views; instead, the focus is to *challenge* students to *seriously* study counter-hegemonic educational perspectives and to compare and contrast them with more conventional views. The expectation is that students will arrive at their own philosophical/ideological conclusions and that they be able to support their positions using varied bodies of literature in the field.

A common starting point for critically apprenticing students consists of sociohistorically situating the subdiscipline of study as a strategy for helping students develop a more comprehensive and dialectical understanding of it. Taking a sociohistorical perspective forces students to contemplate the ideologies inherent in the social, political, and economic structures that, in turn, influence linguistic minority schooling. The development of a sociohistorical perspective enables students to critically and more thoroughly study current educational challenges. Paulo Freire (1985) claims that in order to solve an educational problem, it is necessary to first profoundly and historically understand it—that is, to comprehensively *construct* the problem. The second step is to analyze the problem critically—that is, to *deconstruct* it. The third and final step is to imagine alternative possibilities and to dream realistically about implementing more humane and democratic solutions—that is, to *reconstruct* the problem as an opportunity for change that can yield positive solutions.

Across the three course syllabi examined, it appears that, in addition to critical analyses, students are presented with numerous opportunities to realistically imagine potential short- and long-term solutions to current English-only practices and policies. For example, across the three courses, the instructors together with their students deconstruct English-only practices and policies in U.S. schools. Although each instructor's focus varies according to his or her specific course objectives, all three challenge the students to openly name and interrogate assimilationist and English-only ideology that is typically perceived as "natural" and "desirable." To varying degrees, the three instructors correctly sociohistorically situate the current English-only movement into U.S. history of internal colonization of domestic linguistic minority groups. Students discover that the sanctioned practice of linguistic suppression and cultural domestication has been the historical norm rather than the exception and is still present today in the form of English-only Sheltered English Instruction. They study the experiences of linguistic minorities of color and note that they have been noticeably different from those of European immigrants, in that the latter were assimilated with the aim of being integrated into the greater society, while the former were assimilated for domestication, since equal participation for them was never a serious aim (Wiley, 1999).

Using this line of thinking, current U.S. English-only instructional practices, policies, and laws are shown to mirror "monolingual language ideology" (Wiley,

1999). Students grapple with understanding the nation's assimilationist and English monolingual legacy, not only in terms of its application to earlier European immigrants but also, and most importantly for teachers working in inner-city schools, in terms of its application to indigenous and non-white linguistic minorities. Different pedagogical opportunities are created in the three classes for students to trace this particular ideology sociohistorically and to ask who benefits from and who is disadvantaged by such a belief system and its resulting practices.

For instance, in Teaching ESL: Methods and Approaches, the examination of past and current English-only models, as well as the prohibition on speaking languages other than English, occurs as part of studying the history of ESL instruction in the United States. Students come to understand that current state-mandated English-only policy and instruction are a continuation of past practices that they will have to struggle to purposefully subvert so as to honor their students' home cultures and languages while teaching English in an additive and respectful manner (see also Kubota; Locke, this volume).

With this more profound and comprehensive understanding of current English-only laws and practices, students and their professors consciously resist falling prey to hopeless cynicism and determinism. All three professors examine past and current resistance efforts to sustain students' hopeful beliefs that they can bring about positive changes in schools and communities. The expectation is that students will come away better understanding the complexity of issues and challenges in order to come up with equally complex short- and long-term interventions. The students come to understand the possibilities and limitations of their counter-hegemonic efforts as both teachers (functionaries of the state) and citizens. For example, in Teaching ESL: Methods and Approaches, past students have discussed and designed various practical interventions that range from consciously creating a plan for first language (L1) inclusion in their SE classrooms, by "pushing the boundaries" of what is allowed by the state. One group of students added a mandatory native language instructional category to the SIOP (Sheltered Instructional Observational Protocol) official lesson plan format required by their school districts. Others have come up with strategies for incorporating the use of L1 as a way to honor and build on students' existing knowledge bases and language skills (cf. Kubota, this volume). Students recognize that, as state employees, they are limited in terms of how far they can "push the envelope" at their place of employment. Nevertheless, they are equally conscious that they can overcome these restrictions by engaging in parent and community organizing efforts *outside* their own school districts.

I have witnessed students, who are currently teachers in local school districts, link forces with others in order to organize and work with each other's schools and communities so as to avoid being penalized by their own districts. They have worked with parents and community members in their colleagues' schools, and have advocated for first-language instruction and for repealing the repressive state English-only mandate in Massachusetts. In addition, some students have volunteered to provide free in-service preparation to interested teachers on topics that include "The benefits of native language instruction on ESL acquisition" and "Developing native language development opportunities at home."

As an instructor, it is inspirational to witness students' plans for strategically circumventing instructional practices that they deem harmful to their linguistic minority students. Without a doubt, assisting students in developing a sociohistorical understanding of current English-only policy and facilitating their mastery of mainstream and critical orientations in applied linguistics has produced generation after generation of critical, visionary, energetic, and committed educators.

In order to support graduate students (current and prospective teachers) in envisioning strategies for improving the academic success and English-language acquisition of linguistic minority students, it is necessary to first construct and deconstruct the dominant cultural ideologies that inform language practices and policies. This process enables graduate students to clearly comprehend the linguistic reality within which language minority students are situated. A lucid understanding of the asymmetrical power relations involved in language policies will hopefully enable educators to imagine more just and effective language-teaching practices and policies. In other words, the expectation is that educators will begin to understand the complex nature of bilingualism in the United States, especially as it relates to subordinated U.S. students populations, rather than to elite bilinguals such as affluent international students who come to the United States to perfect their English language skills.

Conclusion

The explicit and focused analysis of dominant ideologies frees students to profoundly understand current educational challenges in new and innovative ways, which are likely to stimulate solutions or interventions that more accurately reflect the reality lived by their students. This type of language-teacher education also requires that teachers reflect on their ethical postures with respect to their roles in either reproducing dominant values or producing values that humanize their pedagogies and, in so doing, protect the linguistic and cultural dignity of their students. The opportunity to compare and contrast ideologies around cultural and linguistic diversity demonstrates to students that so-called "problems" in education regarding student diversity are socially constructed and, as such, can also be socially deconstructed (cf. May & Sleeter, this volume).

Contrary to what conservative educators think, critical multicultural pedagogy does not impose a worldview on students to the extent that it exposes them to multiple and contradictory bodies of knowledge—a process through which students develop their own ideas and, hopefully, adopt ethical postures toward the world. In reality, critical multicultural pedagogy is a pedagogy of hope that challenges students to always imagine other and more liberatory possibilities— possibilities that humanize rather than dehumanize.

A critical stance challenges us to see through the dense fog of ideology so that we can take a stand on behalf of our students even when it is easier not to do so. As Paulo Freire (1997) reminds us, "One has to believe that if men and women created the ugly world that we are denouncing, then men and women can create a world that is less discriminating and more humane" (p. 315).

References

Ahlquist, R. (1991). Position and imposition: Power relations in multicultural foundations class. *Journal of Negro Education, 60,* 158–168.

Bartolomé, L. I. (1994). Beyond the methods fetish: Toward a humanizing pedagogy. *Harvard Educational Review, 64,* 173–194.

Cohen, E. (1994). *Designing group work: Strategies for the heterogeneous classroom.* New York: Teachers College Press.

Darder, A., Baltodano, M., & Torres, R. D. (2003). Critical pedagogy: An introduction. In A. Darder, M. Baltodano, & R. D. Torres (Eds.), *The critical pedagogy reader* (pp. 1–21). New York: RoutledgeFalmer.

During, S. (2003). *The cultural studies reader* (2nd ed.). New York: Routledge.

Eagleton, T. (1991). *Ideology: An introduction.* London: Verso.

Echevarria, J., & Graves, A. (2003). *Sheltered content instruction: Teaching English language learners with diverse abilities.* Boston: Allyn and Bacon.

Freire, P. (1985). *The politics of education: Culture, power, and liberation.* New York: Bergin & Garvey.

Freire, P. (1997). *Mentoring the mentor: A critical dialogue with Paulo Freire.* New York: Peter Lang.

Gándara, P., & Maxwell-Jolly, J. (2000). *Preparing teachers for diversity: A dilemma of quality and quantity.* Santa Cruz, CA: Center for the Future of Teaching and Learning.

Gonsalves, R. E. (2008). Hysterical blindness and the ideology of denial: Preservice teachers' resistance to multicultural education. In L. I. Bartolomé (Ed.), *Ideologies in education: Unmasking the trap of teacher neutrality* (pp. 3–28). New York: Peter Lang.

Gonzalez, J. M., & Darling-Hammond, L. (1997). *New concepts for new challenges: Professional development for teachers of immigrant youth.* McHenry, IL: Center for Applied Linguistics and Delta Systems.

Gramsci, A. (1971). *Selections from the prison notebooks* (Q. Hoare & G. Smith, Trans.). New York: International. (Original work published 1935.)

Haberman, M. (1991). Can culture awareness be taught in teacher education programs? *Teacher Education, 4,* 2–31.

Heywood, A. (2003). *Political ideologies: An introduction* (3rd ed.). New York: Palgrave Macmillan.

Larsen-Freeman, D. (2000). *Techniques and principles in language teaching* (2nd ed.). New York: Oxford University Press.

Leistyna, P. (1999). *Presence of mind: Education and the politics of deception.* Boulder, CO: Westview.

Macedo, D. (2006). *Literacies of power* (2nd ed.). Boulder, CO: Westview.

Macedo, D., Dendrinos, B., & Gounari, P. (2003). *The hegemony of English.* Boulder, CO: Paradigm.

Marx, S., & Pennington, J. (2003). Pedagogies of critical race theory: Experimentations with white preservice teachers. *International Journal of Qualitative Studies in Education, 16,* 91–110.

Pennycook, A. (2001). *Critical applied linguistics: A critical introduction.* Mahwah, NJ: Lawrence Erlbaum.

Richards, J. C., & Rodgers, T. S. (2007). *Approaches and methods in language teaching* (2nd ed.). New York: Cambridge University Press.

Sleeter, C. (1993). How white teachers construct race. In C. McCarthy & W. Crichlow (Eds.), *Race identity and representation in education* (pp. 157–171). New York: Routledge.

Sleeter, C. (1994). A multicultural educator views white racism. *Multicultural Education, 39,* 5–8.

Sleeter, C. E., & Grant, C. A. (1987). An analysis of multicultural education in the United States. *Harvard Educational Review, 57,* 421–444.

Wardhaugh, R. (1998). *An introduction to sociolinguistics* (3rd ed.). Malden, MA: Blackwell.

Wiley, T. J. (1999). Comparative historical analysis of U.S. language policy and language planning: Extending the foundations. In T. Huebner & K. Davies (Eds.), *Sociopolitical perspectives on language policy and planning in the U.S.* (pp. 17–38). Philadelphia: Benjamins.

Zeichner, K. M. (2003). The adequacies and inadequacies of three current strategies to recruit, prepare, and retain the best teachers for all students. *Teachers College Record, 105,* 490–519.

4

Discursive Positioning and Educational Reform

RUSSELL BISHOP

This chapter explores the positioning, often in deficit terms, of indigenous Māori students in New Zealand education. While the focus of the chapter is thus on Māori students, wider lessons can be drawn from this discussion about the often-pejorative treatment of indigenous students in other national contexts, as well as other minoritized students more generally. The chapter also explores, via *kaupapa Māori* (Māori philosophy), how such deficit treatment can be contested, an approach consonant with critical multiculturalism.

The Gap Between Equitable Aspirations and Ongoing Educational Inequalities

Despite aspirations to the contrary, statistical data continues to show the persistence of social, economic, and political disparities between the descendents of the European colonizers and the indigenous Māori people in New Zealand. Māori have higher levels of unemployment, are more likely to be employed in low-paying employment, have much higher levels of incarceration, illness, and poverty than the rest of the New Zealand population and are generally underrepresented in the positive social and economic indicators of the society. These disparities are also reflected at all levels of the education system.

Mainstream policies and reforms have resulted in little if any shift in these disparities for the large proportion (over 90%) of Māori students who attend mainstream schools since they were first statistically identified over 40 years ago (Hunn, 1960). This is because they continue largely to emphasize deficiencies for Māori students—for example, of homes in terms of literacy resources (Nash, 1993). These outcomes stand in sharp contrast to the aforementioned aspirational goals to improve the educational experiences of indigenous Māori students, and it is suggested that while these negative outcomes are most clearly exhibited in high schools, the foundations for these problems commence in the elementary or primary school years. Indeed, there are indications (Crooks, Hamilton, & Caygill, 2000), that while there are achievement differentials evident on children entering primary school, it is by years 4 and 5 that these achievement differentials begin to stand out starkly.

The ongoing nature of these problems suggests two major implications for Māori education and, as we identified in Shields, Bishop, and Mazawi (2005), for other minoritized peoples as well. The first is that the status quo in New Zealand education has become one where educational disparities are ethnically based, and despite many protestations to the contrary, this has been the case for over 40 years. The second is that despite the best intentions of teachers, teacher educators, and policy agencies, currently we do not seem to have an adequate theory of practice that allows teachers to systematically address these disparities. The question therefore arises: how will teachers (and teacher educators) be able to produce equitable outcomes for children of different ethnic, racial, cultural, class, and language groups in the face of these long-term and seemingly immutable disparities?

Timperley, Wilson, Barrar, and Fung (2007) identify the first part of a solution from their detailed synthesis of best evidence regarding what constitutes effective professional development and learning for teachers. They identified that effective and sustainable educational practices appear to be dependent on whether teachers acquire an in-depth understanding of the underlying theoretical principles associated with their practice, what Smylie (1995) terms their "theories of action," so that they can use their learning flexibly in their classrooms when new situations and challenges arise. Alton-Lee (2006) adds the second part to the solution when she identifies that "teachers require an explanatory theory of how different ways of managing the classroom and creating activities are related to student outcomes" (p. 618). With these suggestions in mind, I now turn to a consideration of what constitutes an effective theoretical framework for teachers and teacher educators.

The Need for an Explanatory/Theoretical Framework

What influences student achievement is a useful starting place for an examination of what constitutes appropriate theory for practice. Hattie's (2003a) meta-analyses on the influences on student achievement have led him to conclude that "almost all things we do in the name of education have a positive effect on achievement" (p. 4). However not all effects are equal.

With this caution in mind, in two recent studies (Bishop, Berryman, Tiakiwai, & Richardson, 2003; Bishop, Berryman, Cavanagh, & Teddy, 2007), we considered the relative importance of influences on Māori student achievement such as families, home and community, classroom relationships and pedagogy, teachers, schools and school systems, students themselves, and many contributing and confounding factors on learning and achievement including socioeconomic contexts and systemic and structural conditions. In both of these studies, we spoke with and listened to Māori students talk about their schooling experiences in secondary schools, and the meanings these experiences of schooling in mainstream settings had for them and for other young Māori people. Both groups of students, in 2003 and again in 2007, identified that the development of caring and learning relationships between the teacher and the students was the crucial factor in their being able to effectively engage in education. Importantly, in both cases, students (and their families) understood themselves to be powerless to make changes to bring about such relationships where they did not already exist and that it was the teachers who had the power to bring about the necessary changes.

The recent large meta-analyses by Hattie (1999, 2003a, 2003b) and Alton-Lee (2003) support the understandings of these young Māori people and their families by telling us that the most important systemic influence on children's educational achievement is the teacher. This is not to deny that other broad factors are also influential—such as, prior learning and experience, socioeconomic background, the structures and history of the school, and the socially constructed impoverishment of Māori created by the processes of colonization. It is just that teacher effectiveness stands out as the most easily alterable from within the school system. Further, as Hattie suggests, this is the most useful site for the provision of professional learning opportunities for teachers when seeking to change the learning culture in schools and to reduce the persistent disparities in educational achievement. This position is supported by numerous international scholars, including Sidorkin, (2002), Fullan (2003), Hargreaves and Fink (2005), and Elmore (2007) among others, who advocate that changing classroom practices and modifying school structures are the most likely strategies to improve student performance.

Using Smith's (1997) terms, it is clear that these somewhat "culturalist" approaches stand in contrast to the more "structuralist" notions of Nash (1993), Chapple, Jefferies, and Walker (1997), and Thrupp, (2001, 2007), among others, who advocate in the New Zealand context a social stratification (low social class, low socioeconomic status, and resource/cultural deprivation) argument that being poor or poorly resourced inevitably leads to poor educational achievement. Much research in this area looks at the associations between variables such as socioeconomic status, ethnicity and other family attributes, and resulting achievement, in ways that suggest that such variables predetermine, or at least strongly influence, achievement outcomes. Anyon (1997, cited in Thrupp, 2001) speaks for this group when she states that:

> Unfortunately educational "small victories" such as restructuring of a school or the introduction of a new pedagogical technique, no matter how satisfying to the individuals involved, without the long-range strategy to eradicate underlying causes of poverty and racial isolation, cannot add up to large victories in our inner cities with effects that are sustainable over time.
>
> (p. 20)

Culturalists tend to point to pedagogic reform and changes to school culture as being necessary. For example in Australia, from an extensive analysis of research projects, Rowe (2003) identified that "quality teachers and teaching, supported by strategic teacher professional development" (p. 21) was the most important factor in determining schooling outcomes for students. He went on to identify that the socioeconomic background of students, the characteristics of the whole school or system, the gender of the teacher, and other factors had very little

effect. However, such an analysis tends to ignore the lived reality of Māori people, what Ballard (2007) identified as the "racialised social context" of current
New Zealand society, and promotes a pedagogy that is supposed to suit all students, irrespective of their cultural and ethnic origins—a color-blind approach,
in effect.

On the other hand, the more structuralist positions rightly identify the impact
of society-wide power imbalances on children who do not achieve well in school
as being on those who come from cultural groups which are not respected, and
are minoritized and impoverished by the majority. However, they also tend to
promote the argument that teachers do not have agency in their practice in that
there appears little that teachers can achieve in the face of overwhelming structural impediments such as "school mix" and structural poverty. While useful,
both sets of arguments thus pose problems for educational practitioners in their
search for reform models.

However, what is more problematic is that neither group of theorists has an
adequate means of identifying how society-wide power differentials are played
out in classrooms on a day-to-day basis and the part teachers, school leaders, and
policymakers may play in the perpetuation of power imbalances and educational disparities. Māori students and their families are only too aware of how
these power imbalances are played out (Bishop & Berryman, 2006). New
Zealand educators such as Alton-Lee (2003) and Timperley et al. (2007), along
with Smith (1997), as well as international educators, such as Freire (1997),
McLaren (2003), Kincheloe and Steinberg (1997), and Valencia (1997), also
emphasize that the product of long-term power imbalances needs to be examined by educators at all levels in terms of their own cultural assumptions and a
consideration of how they might be participants in the systematic marginalization of students in their classrooms, their schools, and the wider system.

Smith (1997) warned that neither culturalist nor structuralist analyses can satisfactorily account for indigenous Māori language, knowledge, and cultural aspirations as major components of existing and developing educational
interventions for Māori. To Smith (1997), what is needed is a model that locates
culture at the center of educational reform in the face of deeper structural limitations, in the same manner as that practiced by the Māori language educational
initiatives of *Kohanga Reo* and *Kura Kaupapa Māori*. To Smith (1997) these institutions have developed "our forms of resistance and transformative praxis which
engage both culturalist and structuralist concerns" (p. 222). Such a model is congruent with the broader principles of critical multiculturalism. It addresses the
concerns and limitations of both culturist and structuralist positions, and also
provides a way for educators at all levels of the education system to critically
reflect upon the part they might play in the wider power plays that mediate
Māori educational participation, as well as that of other minoritized groups.

Harker (2007) demonstrates such positioning when reconsidering large data
sets from previous studies of student achievement outcomes in New Zealand high
schools, which attempted to chart the relative effects of school, socioeconomic
class, and ethnic differences. He concludes that:

It is clear from the data presented here that any uni-causal explanation based on socio-economic circumstances is inadequate to explain ethnic differences. ... The most likely explanation would seem to lie in the interaction between school environments and the values, attitudes, motivations that underpin the school "culture" and the culture of the home and community environments and the values, attitudes and motivations on which they are based.

(p. 17)

Harker goes on to suggest that:

While it is important (even necessary) for the family and community culture of the students to be understood and supported by schools, it is also important (even necessary) for the culture of the school to be understood and supported by families and communities.

(p. 17)

Harker suggests that arguments about whether "schools make the difference," or "is it down to the family" are really not all that useful. It is more a function of the interactions between these two sets of players that offers us explanations of variation in achievement and, more importantly, provides us with solutions to problems of educational disparities.

Such a relational theory is put forward in Bishop (2007) and Bishop et al. (2007), where Māori aspirations for self-determination are placed at the center of the theoretical frame. Self-determination, in Durie's (1995) terms, "captures a sense of Māori ownership and active control over the future" (p. 16). Nevertheless, despite self-determination meaning the right to determine one's own destiny, there is a clear understanding among Māori people that this autonomy is relative, not absolute; that it is self-determination *in relation to others*. It is not a call for separatism or non-interference, or for non-Māori to stand back and leave Māori alone, in effect to relinquish all responsibility for the ongoing relationship between the peoples of New Zealand. Rather this *kaupapa Māori* (Māori philosophy) position is a call for all those involved in education in New Zealand to reposition themselves in relation to these emerging aspirations of Māori people for an autonomous voice and successful participation in the mainstream of society *on their own terms* (Bishop, 1994; Durie, 1998; Smith, 1997).

Young (2004) explains that indigenous peoples' aspirations for self-determination are relational, acknowledge interdependence, and "are better understood as a quest for an institutional context of non-domination" (p. 187). That is, being self-determining is possible if the relations in which peoples and individuals stand are non-dominating. To ensure non-domination, "their relations must be regulated both by institutions in which they all participate and by ongoing negotiations among them" (Young, 2004, p. 177). Therefore, the implications for educational institutions and classrooms from this position are that they should be structured and conducted in such a way so as to seek to mediate these potential tensions by actively minimizing domination, coordinating actions, resolving conflicts, and negotiating relationships. In Young's terms, this is an education where power is shared between self-determining individuals within non-dominating relations of interdependence. In association with these aspirations, other supportive conditions need to exist: where culture counts; learning is interactive, dialogic, and spirals; and participants are connected and committed to one another through the establishment of a common vision for what constitutes excellence in educational outcomes. In this way, the pattern is similar to that identified by Gay (2000) and Villegas and Lucas (2002), via their concept of Culturally Responsive Teaching, and Sidorkin (2002) and Cummins (1995), via their concept of a Pedagogy of Relations. The merging of these concepts is a useful means of describing the pattern, identified from the set of Māori cultural metaphors examined in Bishop (2007), as a Culturally Responsive Pedagogy of Relations.

Discursive (Re)positioning in the Classroom

To illustrate how useful it is to theorize from a relational discourse, compared to just from a culturalist or a structuralist discourse, we can examine the problem presented to us by many teachers in our 2001 and 2005/6 interviews (Bishop et al., 2003, 2007) about why they, with the best intentions in the world, were frustrated in their attempts to reach indigenous Māori learners. (Readers from outside New Zealand can apply this analysis to discourses and racialized communities in their own contexts.) From a relational positioning, Bruner (1996) offers a solution by identifying that when teaching occurs, progress is decided upon and practices modified as "a direct reflection of the beliefs and assumptions the teacher holds about the learner" (p. 47). This means that "our interactions with others are deeply affected by our everyday intuitive theorizing about how other minds work" (p. 45). In other words, our actions as teachers, parents, or whoever we are at that particular time, are driven by the mental images or understandings that we have of other people. Thus despite our being well-meaning, if students with whom we are interacting as teachers are led to believe that we think they are deficient, they will respond negatively. We were told time and again by many of the interview participants in 2001 (Bishop & Berryman, 2006), and again in 2007 (Bishop et al., 2007), that negative, deficit thinking on the part of teachers was fundamental to the development of negative relations and interactions between students and their teachers. In 2001, the students, their *whānau* (families), the principals, and the teachers gave us numerous examples of such thinking, the resultant problematic and resistant behaviors and the frustrating consequences for both students and teachers. The teachers spoke of their frustration and anger; the students spoke about negative relations being an assault on their very identity as Māori people.

Such understandings have major implications for teachers hoping to be agentic in their classrooms and for educational reformers. Elbaz (1981, 1983) explains that understanding the relationship between teachers' theories of practice about learners and learning is fundamental to teachers being agentic. The principles teachers hold dear and the practices they employ are developed from the images they hold of others. To Foucault (1972), the images that teachers create when describing their experiences are expressed in the metaphors that are part of the language of the discourses around education. That is, teachers draw from a variety of discourses to make sense of the experiences they have when relating to and interacting with Māori students.

Therefore, rather than it being anything inherent or even biological within the students or teachers, it was the *discourses* that teachers drew upon to explain their experiences that kept them frustrated and isolated. It was not their attitudes or personalities. It was what Foucault termed their "positioning within discourse." That is, by drawing on particular discourses to explain and make sense of our experiences, we are positioning ourselves within these discourses and acting accordingly in our classrooms. The discourses already exist, they have been developing throughout our history, are often in conflict with each other through power differentials, and importantly for our desire to be agentic, in terms of their practical importance, some discourses hold solutions to problems, others don't.

The crucial implication from this analysis is that discursive positions that teachers take are key to their being able to make a difference (or not) for Māori students (and, by extension, other indigenous and/or minoritized students). Therefore, to promote new quality teaching classroom practices, such as culturalist theorists promote, teachers need to be provided with learning opportunities where they can critically evaluate where they discursively position themselves when constructing their own images, principles, and practices in relation to Māori students in their own classrooms. Such an activity is necessary so that they can reflect upon the part they might play in the wider power plays that mediate Māori participation in the benefits that education has to offer. It is clear that unless teachers engage in such considerations of how dominance manifests itself in the lives of Māori students (and their families), how the dominant culture maintains control over the various aspects of education, and the part they themselves might play in perpetuating this pattern of domination, albeit unwittingly, they will not understand how they, and the way they, relate to and interact with Māori students may well affect learning. Further, an appreciation of relational dynamics without an attendant analysis of power balances, as in many liberal multicultural approaches, can promote professional development that emphasizes ways of "relating to" and "connecting with" students of other cultures without there being a means whereby teachers can understand, internalize, and work towards changing the power imbalances of which they are a part. Insisting on this combination is a key feature of a relational approach and also, of course, of critical multiculturalism more broadly. In particular, teachers need an opportunity to challenge those power imbalances that are manifested as cultural deficit theorizing in the classroom, which, in turn, support the retention of traditional classroom interaction patterns and that perpetuate marginalization.

To this end, Valencia (1997) traced the origins of deficit thinking, including various manifestations such as intelligence testing, constructs of "at-riskness" and "blaming the victim" (see also McLaren, 2003). More recently, in Shields et al. (2005), we detailed how educators and policymakers continue to construct negatively the lived experiences of minoritized children, through our examination of the experiences of American Navajo, Israeli Bedouin, and New Zealand Māori children's schooling. In general, we detailed the common practice of attributing school failure to individuals because of their affiliation with a minoritized group within society by a process termed "pathologizing," which according to Shields et al. (2005) is:

> a process where perceived structural-functional, cultural, or epistemological deviation from an assumed normal state is ascribed to another group as a product of power relationships, whereby the less powerful group is deemed to be abnormal in some way. Pathologizing is a mode of colonization used to govern, regulate, manage, marginalize, or minoritize primarily through hegemonic discourses.
>
> (p. 120)

Pathologizing the lived experiences of children is most often seen in deficit thinking and practices, which is a form of power that, as Foucault (1972) explains, works on and through individuals as they take up positions offered to them in discourse and as they become objects of discourse. This is because discourses provide each of us with a self-narrative that we use to talk and think about our positioning within society. We construct meaning out of our experiences in an interactive social process that locates us within sense-making frameworks that are discourses, or languages in action.

Struggles over the representation of what constitutes appropriate knowledges (struggles that are common to colonized peoples) are struggles over whose meaning or sense will prevail. Meaning does not lie in images as such, nor does it rest entirely with those who interpret what they see. "[R]ather it emerges in the dialogue between those who do the interpreting and the images they perceive" (Ryan, 1976, p. 5) and who has the power to determine the knowledge which is most legitimate. Thus, those who are positioned within the dominant discourse have recourse to a means of framing the ways which "subordinate groups live and respond to their own cultural system and lived experiences" (McLaren, 2003, p. 77), rather than referring to the sense-making of those "othered." This represents a challenge for educational reformers, teacher educators, and teachers alike in that, as Bruner (1996) identified, it is not just a matter of intervening in part of the system; what is necessary is that we challenge whole discourses and move ourselves beyond our current positionings to alternative discourses that offer educators an opportunity to act as change agents.

As we identified in 2001, when we commenced our project, called Te Kotahitanga, in New Zealand high schools, the majority of teachers we spoke to were positioned in discourses that limited their agency and efficacy. In particular, the discourses were those that suggest the supposed deficiencies posed by students, families, schools, the education system, and society create situations and problems that are far beyond the power of teachers to address in the classroom. Therefore, the learning opportunities offered to teachers in the professional development program needed to provide them with an opportunity to undertake what Davies and Harre (1997) called *discursive repositioning*, which means they need to be offered an opportunity to draw explanations and subsequent practices from alternative discourses that offer them solutions instead of reinforcing problems and barriers. This approach is supported by Marzano, Zaffron, Zraik, Robbins, and Yoon (2005), who have identified that most educational innovations do not address the "existing framework of perceptions and beliefs, or paradigm, as part of the change process—an ontological approach," but rather assume "that innovation is assimilated into existing beliefs and perceptions" (p. 162). They go on to suggest that reforms that are more likely to succeed are those that are fundamentally ontological in nature, providing participants with an "experience of their paradigms as constructed realities, and an experience of consciousness other than the 'I' embedded in their paradigms" (p. 162). Or as Sleeter (2005) suggests,

> [i]t is true that low expectations for students of color and students from poverty communities, buttressed by taken-for-granted acceptance of the deficit ideology, has been a rampant and persistent problem for a long time … therefore, empowering teachers without addressing the deficit ideology may well aggravate the problem.
>
> (p. 2)

According to Burr (1995, p. 146), we are all able to reposition ourselves from one discourse to another because, while we are partly the product of discourse, we have agency that allows us to change the way we see and make sense of the world by drawing from other discourses. We are free agents and we have agency; what is crucial to understand is that some of the discourses we draw from limit our power to activate our agency.

Conclusion

The *kaupapa Māori* analysis adopted in this chapter is broadly similar to May's (1999) definition of "critical multiculturalism," in that this concept suggests that

> a critical multiculturalism needs both to recognize and incorporate the differing cultural knowledges that children bring with them to school, *while at the same time* address and contest the differential cultural capital attributed to them as a result of wider hegemonic power relations.
>
> (p. 32; emphasis in original)

In other words, the effects of power imbalances as played out in the lives of indigenous Māori children on a daily basis in their classrooms needs to be recognized and addressed. This then will allow Māori children the opportunity, currently mainly open to majority (white) children, to make choices for themselves from a secure cultural framework. This analysis draws on culturalist (the need for micro-level teaching reform), structuralist (the need to address macro-level power imbalances), and relational discourses to address micro-level power imbalances at all levels of education. It suggests that the key to educational reform for Māori and other minoritized peoples is the discursive (re)positioning of teachers within a relational discourse.

Acknowledgment

I wish to thank the members of the Te Kotahitanga research and development team, the schools, students, and school communities who have participated in and supported the development of this project.

References

Alton-Lee, A. (2003). *Quality teaching for diverse students in schooling: Best evidence synthesis.* Wellington, New Zealand: Ministry of Education.

Alton-Lee, A. (2006). How teaching influences learning: Implications for educational researchers, teachers, teacher educators and policy makers. *Teaching and Teacher Education, 22*(5), 612–626.

Ballard, K. (2007) *Educational and imagination: Strategies for social justice.* The Herbison Lecture presented to the NZARE, University of Canterbury, Christchurch, New Zealand.

Bishop, R. (1994). Initiating empowering research. *New Zealand Journal of Educational Studies, 29*(1), 1–14.

Bishop, R. (2007). Lessons from Te Kotahitanga for teacher education. In L. F. Detretchin & C. J. Craig (Eds.), *International research on the impact of accountability systems* (pp. 225–239). Lanham, MD: Rowman & Littlefield Education.

Bishop, R., & Berryman, M. (2006). *Culture speaks: Cultural relationships and classroom learning.* Wellington, New Zealand: Huia Publishers.

Bishop, R., Berryman, M., Tiakiwai, S., & Richardson, C. (2003). *Te Kotahitanga: The experiences of year 9 and 10 Māori students in mainstream classrooms.* Wellington, New Zealand: Ministry of Education.

Bishop, R., Berryman, M., Cavanagh, T., & Teddy, L. (2007). *Te Kotahitanga phase 3 Whanaungatanga: Establishing a culturally responsive pedagogy of relations in mainstream secondary classrooms.* Wellington, New Zealand: Ministry of Education.

Bruner, J. (1996). *The culture of education.* Cambridge, MA: Harvard University Press.

Burr, V. (1995). *An introduction to social constructionism.* London: Routledge.

Chapple, S., Jeffries, R., & Walker, R. (1997). *Māori participation and performance in education. A literature review and research programme.* Report for the Ministry of Education, Wellington, New Zealand.

Crooks, T., Hamilton, K., & Caygill, R. (2000). New Zealand's national education monitoring project: Māori student achievement, 1995–2000 [electronic version]. Retrieved May 9, 2007 from http://nemp.otago.ac.nz/i_probe.htm

Cummins, J. (1995). Power and pedagogy in the education of culturally diverse students. In J. Fredericskon & A. F. Ada (Eds.), *Reclaiming our voices: Bilingual education, critical pedagogy, and praxis* (pp. 139–162). Ontario, CA: California Association for Bilingual Education.

Davies, B., & Harre, R. (1997). Positioning the discursive production of selves. *Journal of the Theory of Social Behaviour, 20,* 43–65. Reprinted in M. Wetherall, S. Taylor, & S. Yates (Eds.). (2001). *Discourse theory and practice: A reader* (pp. 261–271). London: Sage.

Durie, M. (1995). Tino Rangatiratanga: Self determination. *He Pukenga Korero, 1*(1), 44–53.

Durie, M. (1998). *Te Mana, Te Kawanatanga: The politics of Māori self-determination.* Auckland, New Zealand: Oxford University Press.

Elbaz, F. (1981). The teachers "practical knowledge": Report of a case study. *Curriculum Inquiry, 11,* 43–71.

Elbaz, F. (1983). *Teacher thinking: A study of practical knowledge.* New York: Nichols.

Elmore, R. F. (2007). Professional networks and school improvement. *The School Administrator, 64*(4), 20–24.

Foucault, M. (1972). *The archaeology of knowledge.* New York: Pantheon.

Freire, P. (1997). *Pedagogy of the heart.* New York: Continuum.

Fullan, M. (2003). *The moral imperative of school leadership.* Thousand Oaks, CA: Corwin Press.

Gay, G. (2000). *Culturally responsive teaching: Theory, research and practice.* Columbia University, New York; London: Teachers College Press.

Hargreaves, A., & Fink, D. (2005). *Sustainable leadership.* San Francisco: Jossey Bass.

Harker, R. (2007). *Ethnicity and school achievement in New Zealand: Some data to supplement the Biddulph et al. (2003) best evidence synthesis: Secondary analysis of the progress at school and Smithfield datasets for the iterative best evidence synthesis programme.* Wellington, New Zealand: Ministry of Education.

Hattie, J. (1999). *Influences on student learning.* Inaugural Lecture, University of Auckland, Auckland, New Zealand: www.staff.auckland.ac.nz/j.hattie

Hattie, J. (2003a). *Teachers make a difference: What is the research evidence?* Paper presented at the Australian council for educational research annual conference.

Hattie, J. (2003b). *New Zealand education snapshot: With specific reference to the yrs 1–13.* Paper presented at the Knowledge Wave 2003 The Leadership Forum, Auckland, New Zealand.

Hunn, J.K. (1960). *Report on the Department of Māori Affairs.* Wellington, New Zealand: Government Print.

Kincheloe, J., & Steinberg, S. (1997). *Changing multiculturalism.* Buckingham, England: Open University Press.

Marzano, R., Zaffron, S., Zraik, L., Robbins, S., & Yoon, L. (2005). A new paradigm for educational change. *Education, 116*(2), 162–173.

May, S. (1999). Critical multiculturalism and cultural difference: Avoiding essentialism. In S. May (Ed.), *Critical multiculturalism: Rethinking multicultural and antiracist education* (pp. 11–41). London, RoutledgeFalmer.

McLaren, P. (2003). *Life in schools: An introduction to critical pedagogy in the foundations of education* (4th ed.). Boston: Pearson Education.

Nash, R. (1993). *Succeeding generations: Family resources and access to education in New Zealand.* Auckland, New Zealand: Oxford University Press.

Rowe, K. (2003). *The importance of teacher quality as a key determinant of students' experiences and outcomes of schooling.* Sydney, Australia: ACER.

Ryan, W. (1999). *Race and ethnicity in multi-ethnic schools: A critical case study.* Clevedon, England: Multilingual Matters.

Shields, C.M., Bishop, R., & Mazawi, A. E. (2005). *Pathologizing practices: The impact of deficit thinking on education.* New York: Peter Lang.

Sidorkin, A. M. (2002). *Learning relations: Impure education, deschooled schools, and dialogue with evil.* New York: Peter Lang.

Sleeter, C. (2005). *Un-standardizing curriculum: Multicultural teaching in the standards-based classroom.* New York: Teachers College Press.

Smith, G. H. (1997). *Kaupapa Māori as transformative praxis.* Unpublished doctoral thesis, University of Auckland, Auckland, New Zealand.

Smylie, M. (1995). Teacher learning in the workplace: Implications for school reform. In T. Guskey & M. Huberman (Eds.), *Professional development in education: New paradigms and practices.* New York: Teachers College Press.

Thrupp, M. (2001). Sociological and political concerns about school effectiveness research: Time for a new research agenda. *School Effectiveness and School Improvement, 12*(1): 7–40.

Thrupp, M. (2007). *Education's "inconvenient truth": Persistent middle class advantage.* Inaugural professorial lecture, School of Education, University of Waikato, Hamilton, New Zealand, March 2.

Timperley, H., Wilson, A., Barrar, H., & Fung, I. (2007). *Teacher professional learning and development: Best evidence synthesis iteration.* Wellington, New Zealand: Ministry of Education.

Valencia, R. R. (Ed.). (1997). *The evolution of deficit thinking.* London: Falmer.

Villegas, A. M., & Lucas, T. (2002). *Educating culturally responsive teachers: A coherent approach.* Albany, NY: State University of New York Press.

Young, I. M. (2004). Two concepts of self-determination. In S. May, T. Modood, & J. Squires (Eds.), *Ethnicity, nationalism and minority rights* (pp. 176–198). Cambridge, UK: Cambridge University Press.

5

Critical Multicultural Practices in Early Childhood Education

JEANETTE RHEDDING-JONES

All the children are sitting in the circle with their teacher. Of the eighteen children here, only one child speaks only the national language, Norwegian. The teacher does not know any of the languages the rest of the class knows and all of what she says to the children is in Norwegian. This is the language they must learn well, so that they can get through their schooling. What seems to be missing is the idea that perhaps being able to speak more than one language is an advantage. This school is often called a multicultural school, because of the many cultures the children have as their backgrounds, and that might be visible through their bodies or their clothing.

If we take up a critical multicultural stance here, we see that maybe we could be taking the multicultural further. What could be done so that the richness of this community's languages is not lost in this classroom? How could this teacher change her curriculum program with these children so that her own monocultural experiences are not what determines everything that happens here? Who could be invited in to work and play with these children? Could there be any funding for culturally diverse people to work in this school even if they are not educated as teachers? How could more languages get to be heard and written?

This chapter starts by pointing to some "usual" monocultural practices often found in early childhood education. It does so to then say what a critical multiculturalism implies. As the next events from practice show, a teacher faces much variation within and across ethnic groups and their cultural practices. How can teachers be prepared for the kinds of associated "cultural challenges," exemplified by what follows? How can the children deal with cultural difference here?

There are four young children at this school from the same family, one boy and three girls. The girls are always "sick or not well" when their class is going on excursions outside school. This school takes the children out two or three times a month, to the fire station, or into the woods in the snow, or to ride on the trains to the city as part of their "multicultural" program. The three sisters always tell the same story the day after the excursions they have missed. The other children do not believe them, and neither do their teachers. But the parents always say their daughters are sick and keep them home on these days. Everyone notices that the little brother of the three girls is never unhealthy or sick. He gets to go on every excursion there is.

Here, it is clear that not all parents agree with what the dominant culture thinks of as safe and acceptable. How could this school's program be more inclusive of the sorts of cultural differences this family represents? What sorts of discussions could the parents have with the teachers? Whose values should dominate, or how could both teachers and parents change their ideas and plans a little? Would it be possible for parents to go on these excursions too? How much do these teachers know about cultural differences determining what is acceptable for girls to do?

Many teachers are aware of such challenges, and are trying to not assimilate or colonize minorities any more than they "have to." Instead, they are hoping for new forms of transformation as the basis of what happens in their classrooms. Children from culturally different backgrounds all have to cope well in the dominant society. They have to become highly skilled in the national standard language, and they need to know how to get on in a contemporary world that is not just made up of the majority culture around them. In a global sense, what is the majority in one place becomes the minority somewhere else. How can children grow up able to thrive in a changing world made up of many languages, many cultures and many differences? What can teachers do to resist a monocultural education for the children they work with, and to resist a devaluing of the values of their school's community of families? This chapter is an attempt to help teachers find some answers to questions like these.

The next event presented takes place in a preschool. Here there is a program of pedagogy combined with a program of care. In what follows the children are not described. What is described, however, is the relationship of the preschool staff to the parents. If we are looking for the critical multicultural here we might miss it, until the reflections that come after the description.

It is the first meeting for the parents. The preschool teacher is talking to them. She explains that when a child's birthday is celebrated she will give that child a birthday crown and let him or her sit on a pretend throne. Then she tells the small group of parents who have managed to get to this evening meeting, without their children, about what plans the preschool has for the next few months. "Any questions?" she asks briefly, apparently thinking that there might be some details that need clarifying. There are a few questions asked and answered. Later the parents are divided into small groups to discuss and write down what they see as important for their children in the everyday curriculum. None of the parents with minority backgrounds is here though. They have all stayed home. Maybe they knew the level of language would be beyond them. Maybe they had no one to mind their children while they went to the meeting. Maybe they thought it was more important to be with their children that evening than to be with the adults they did not know. Maybe they could not read the language that invited them.

Learning how to be with adults and children of many ethnic and cultural backgrounds is not easy. In some ways, the problem is that your own self gets decentered. You have to put aside your own usual ways of being, and make a space for what you might never have thought about before. The next event, again from a preschool context, took place ten years ago. Could this still happen today?

The preschool assistants and teachers are getting the lunches ready for the smallest children. The children are aged between two and three. Not all of them are talking a lot yet, and some will be speaking more than one language when they do. I don't know if any of them heard and understood what the adults said here. "You can't give her that. It's bacon." "No it's not, it's only bacon spread." [What they are talking about is in a tube, and it comes out as a flavored cheese spread. Here it is usual to eat this bacon cheese spread squirted onto a slice of bread.]

The problem for the teachers concerns Islam. One of them knows that Muslim children do not eat pork. The question is: Is this pork or isn't it? Maybe the bacon flavoring is artificial. What should happen in a situation of uncertainty like this? What happens when no-one caring for the children realizes what the cultural complexities are? How is a child positioned when there is no one around her who follows the same rules and ethics as her family? It is easy to say we are working in multicultural locations, and do the "multicultural" in tokenistic ways. This chapter is an attempt to go beyond this, and to show what can happen, and is happening, to implement critical multicultural practices and thinking in early childhood education.

Critical Multiculturalism in Early Childhood Education

Since the mid 1990s, much has been written internationally about critical multiculturalism (see, e.g., May, 1999; Sleeter & Delgado Bernal, 2004). This writing is intended to change practices, but it also functions to construct a research field for practice. What follows are examples from various national contexts that reflect, or are congruent with, critical multicultural practices in early childhood education, irrespective of whether they denote themselves specifically as being critically multicultural.

In early childhood education in the USA, Lourdes Diaz Soto (1997) published *Language, Culture and Power: Bilingual families and the struggle for quality education*. With American colleague Beth Blue Swadener, she then worked to decolonize early childhood theory, research, and praxis in cross-cultural contexts (Soto & Swadener, 2005). Also working as an early childhood reconceptualist in the USA, Gaile Cannella (2000, p. 218) put critical and feminist perspectives together to point to "the celebration of diversity … [and] the multiple voices of those who are younger."

Publishing from the United Kingdom, Iram Siraj-Blatchford and Priscilla Clarke (2000) co-authored a book about "supporting identity, diversity and language in the early years." Cultural differences in childrearing are presented, and a section on "ensuring the curriculum supports diversity" (pp. 85–88) details practices related to the "home corner," "puzzles and manipulative equipment," music, books, a bilingual library, and keeping sessions with children short.

In New Zealand, the early childhood education curriculum frameworks document (Te Whāriki, 1996) was a radical move towards bilingualism and biculturalism. Here Māori/Indigenous and Pākeh/European perspectives were combined to produce a reconceptualized guide for preschool practice and policy. Relatedly, the work of Margaret Carr (2001) around *Assessment in Early Childhood Settings: Learning stories* focused on theorizing development and learning as reflected in assessment practice. This acknowledged the fact that "any valued endpoint is a cultural construction not a developmental inevitability" (p.14). More recently, Jenny Ritchie (2008) presents learning initiatives that honor Māori subjectivity in preschooling. For Ritchie, and her collaborator Cheryl Rau, this involves Indigenous knowledge, values, language(s), and spirituality (see also Bishop, this volume).

In Australia, Barbara Comber (2003, p. 360) has focused on ethnic and cultural backgrounds in early childhood education, and what might count as critical literacy when these are taken into account. Kerry Robinson and Christine Jones Díaz, also from Australia, wrote about "critical multiculturalism, whiteness and early childhood education" (2006, pp. 63–81) in which they discussed the limits to multicultural pluralism, and pointed to early childhood practices and to adopting a reflexive stance. From Norway, an expatriate Australian (Rhedding-Jones, 2002, p. 90) has specifically explored the implications of critical multiculturalism for early childhood education. From Australia and the United States respectively, Sue Grieshaber and Gaile Cannella (2001) edited a book about diversity and possibilities in "embracing identities" in early childhood education.

From Belgium, Michel Vandenbroeck (2004) points to European constructions of multicultural societies and presents critiques of "the multicultural discourse in the early childhood field" (p. 32). Viewing education politically, he writes as a Foucault scholar, as does Veronica Pacini-Ketchabaw (2007), critiquing and reconceptualizing multicultural early childhood education in Canada.

A More Critical Multicultural Practice in One National Context

This growing international trend of addressing the implications of critical multiculturalism in early childhood education is perhaps most apparent in Oslo, Norway, where a group of early childhood educators have been working together in recent years to take up critical issues, critical theories and critical practices for cultural diversities (see Andersen, 2006; Angell-Jacobsen & Becher, 2007; Becher,

2004, 2006; Bustos, 2009; Fajersson, Karlsson, Becher, & Otterstad, 2009; Otterstad, 2005, 2008; Rhedding-Jones, 2001). What follows details some Norwegian practices in early childhood settings with young children that have developed as a result of this work. To make practice visible, I present events from particular sites. These are Norwegian *barnehager* (preschools and day care centers with children aged from one to six). The notes about these events were first written in Norwegian by a preschool teacher.

> "Where's the skin color?" a four-year-old girl asks herself loudly while sitting at the table where drawing activities usually are done. Remembering from her own childhood that the skin-color pencil was a peach-like color representing white skin, the preschool teacher challenges the girl by asking "What skin color are you looking for? Brown or white?"

The writer of this note says that thinking about particular moments of practice can be starting points for critical reflection. In professional work, such moments are remembered and discussed, so that new ways of acting and speaking can resist marginalizing discourses. This teacher now knows that whiteness is a critical issue to do with race. Here the critical practice is to say what will cause this child to think deeply. That everyone has a "race," not only Blacks and "Asians," is a critical multicultural positioning. Relatedly, Camilla Andersen's reflections (Andersen in Gjervan, Andersen, & Bleka, 2006, pp. 44–46) show ways of working against marginalization with children and families. Andersen suggests not just focusing on what every individual child is doing, but rather on what happens because of power relations between people, as multiple knowledges operating in the field. Here is another event for critical consideration, with pointers to a changing practice.

> The children's lunchboxes are already placed on the table, one in front of each chair. It is almost half past ten and the children are asked to get ready for their early lunch. Five-year-old Hassan arrives during the meal and a space is made beside his friend Ali. "I am always late," he mutters, knowing the structure of the day. Ali agrees, "Yes you are." A critical practice here would connect the preschool's ideas about time and the daily routines to those of Hassan's family. Although it is usual for the children to arrive before 10 in the morning, Hassan's family finds it impossible to get him there so early. Maybe time doesn't matter. Maybe the teachers need to adjust their ideas to what this family wants or thinks is normal. Maybe the preschool could be more flexible with its routines. Maybe the teacher could make careful explanations to the family about what is expected, getting a translator if necessary.

The next practice exemplified is monolingual instruction. In the normalized monolingual instruction practices of early education, children risk not knowing how diverse the world is and what skills are required to communicate transnationally.

Circle time finishes and the teacher says the children with red socks can go and wash their hands. She continues calling out new pieces of clothing and new colors until all of the children have left the area they were sitting in. Almost all of the children understand this game, or rather what is said, except Chen and Maya who are quite new here. They have not yet learned the majority language spoken. They are helped by the teacher and pointed to when they must stand and go to the bathroom.

Chen and Maya will learn the majority language eventually, because they must. No teacher can know all the languages the children in her care are speaking at home, but if there was someone in the classroom who knew the languages Chen and Maya speak, then this uncomfortable moment for them might not happen. The ability to shift from one language to another, at particular moments, is what happens with awareness and bilingual ability. Yet in early schooling and preschooling it is usually only one language that is heard. Making use of the adults and children in the community who speak both Vietnamese and Norwegian in Chen's case, and Hindi and Norwegian in Maya's case, would position these two children as having an ability the monolingual children and their teacher do not have.

A common practice regarding language is that only one language is thought to matter. Here Mona-Lisa Angell-Jacobsen, a preschool practitioner, argues that Norwegian preschools are not working much with critical multiculturalism, especially regarding languages. There is very little published about this in Norwegian texts set as undergraduate coursework. From her research data (Angell-Jacobsen, 2008) she traces a discourse of multiculturalism that she suggests can be read as "traditional" multiculturalism—the equivalent of "liberal multiculturalism" in the U.S. context. Additionally, she sees attempts to move towards a more critical discourse of multiculturalism. The traditional discourse is expressed through having "Asian," pink and brown dolls, and a "wall of flags" where all the national backgrounds of the people in the preschool are represented. Attempts to move to a more critical discourse of multiculturalism can be read in a preschool's local plan for the year (årsplan). Here documents say that linguistic, cultural, and religious diversity "enriches and strengthens the feeling of community" (2008, p. 64). This can be seen as the preschool teachers' resistance to a discourse of multiculturalism where cultural diversity is solely about minority groups. Yet when it comes to "mapping children's linguistic skills," it is mainly the minority children whose linguistic skills are being mapped. Moreover, the language being mapped is the majority language, and the norm the bilingual children's language skills are being measured against is that of so-called "average" monolingual majority children (p. 90). This is a key point and a normative practice in early childhood education worldwide.

In Oslo's early childhood education much is being done to question cultural differences, and to develop the theorizing and the doing of research that resists culturally essentialist categories. This has its effects on what happens as pedagogical practices with children as these researchers are teaching the teachers, and also working in the schools and preschools. Aslaug Andreassen Becher uses her own primary school teaching practice, and her ethnographic notes from an inner city school with six-year-olds, to put forward particular cases illustrating critical issues (Becher, 2004). Following the critique of essentialism, she discusses the cultural challenges involved in theory and in practical work with young children. Here is an event she describes.

> One teacher told me about her experiences of teaching a controversial subject: Christianity, Religion and Human Ethics. Muslim parents at the school had been active in their resistance against the legislation that followed the presentation of the 1997 Norwegian curriculum for schools, which included this. This curriculum no longer allowed children to take an alternative subject. Following the new legislation, children had to be present during the lesson unless parents came and took their child out of the class. This created situations where children were instructed at home by their parents not to attend the class. The solution for some of the children was to simply put their hands over their ears to shelter themselves from the Christian influence.

A critical question here is: What is involved for a child in a situation where the school and parents demand totally opposite behaviors in important and sensitive matters about different cultural norms and values? For practitioners, what is needed here might be more than they can manage. What is needed is government legislation to change the curriculum, and that is in fact what happened in Norway. To get a national policy document changed there needs to be a public outcry and this is where teachers can raise their voices and be outspoken where there is injustice and lack of equity. The teachers are the people in daily contact with the children, not the politicians, government advisors, and bureaucrats. In situations like this, teachers can write to newspapers, and publish articles in the popular press and in teachers' journals, to convince the public, and hence the politicians, to change the policies.

There is now an established network between the praxis of teachers in preschools and Oslo University College. Dealing with multicultural matters in critical ways, this network is formalized and funded (http://arenahio.oppdaterings fabrikken.no/index.php). It functions as an umbrella of collaborations and meeting points in different spaces and places. Aims include discussing and initiating interdisciplinary research projects and changing the practices with families and children. As leader of the network, Ann Merete Otterstad (2005) discusses how equal opportunities based on shared values and knowledge can challenge egalitarian ideology in building up children's subjectivities, as children are citizens of the national state. Her critical question is: What and who will represent national heritage in the future? Currently (2009) about 37% of all children in schools in the capital city of Oslo reflect other heritages than mainstream Norwegian. Otterstad's analysis points to the ideology of "sameness" critiqued by Norwegian researcher Marianne Gullestad (2006). This ideology constructs the widespread Scandinavian practice of gate keeping, which functions to exclude cultural minorities. Professionals who travel around Norway as part of their job for the National Centre for Multicultural Training (*Nasjonalt senter for flerkulturell opplæring*) report that preschool teachers welcome critical perspectives on the multicultural. Further, a national collaboration between eight Norwegian universities and university colleges works to achieve a "critical multicultural" goal of the Norwegian Ministry of Education. This involves increasing the number of bilingual preschool teachers in early childhood settings.

What is apparent in all of this is the recognition of unequal power relations, and this is what is missing in non-critical multicultural discourses, where those in power are not seeing how they operate and who they are. In a normalized or liberal multiculturalism, the pedagogies and practices are those desired by the dominant culture, and minorities simply have to do as everyone else does. Thus alternative knowledges and subjectivities are subjugated, through hegemonies and misrepresentations.

The next section briefly presents some implications of working with a group of people often overlooked in multicultural discourse. Western skepticism towards religion has meant that families of Muslims are simply seen as embodying their earlier nations, rather than as a group with shared beliefs and ways of being within their new nation. What are some implications here for early childhood education and its practices of critical multiculturalism? In the next section, I write more personally, from my positioning as an Australian non-Muslim with permanent residency in Norway.

Working With One Key Minority Group: Muslims in the West

Four years ago and following an invitation, I met Muslims in an Oslo preschool. Getting to know Muslims and having them get to know me has almost totally changed what it is that I do and want to do now as a critical multicultural practitioner. I had been writing critically about "the multicultural" from my positioning as an immigrant speaking my painfully learned Norwegian language, and from not knowing all the cultural referents of Norwegian (Rhedding-Jones, 2004, 2005, 2007a, 2007b). Then I became critical of my own critiques and decided to engage in doings. For one day each week I went to this Muslim preschool, and to others where there are many Muslims. I became a sort of grandmotherly assistant who listened when people wanted to talk, and played when children wanted someone to slide down in the snow with them, or fold tiny paper birds in the patterns of Islamic art. I've joined in with Muslim celebrations of *Eid* at the end of *Ramadan*, in the preschool with the children, and in a *halal* restaurant with men and women, in the evening. We women have danced together, shared sadness and happiness. There is a power difference though: it's about money, status, education, my age and their relative youth, my lack of Arabic, Somali, Urdu and Bosnian, and their lack of English.

I am not saying that what I have been doing with Muslims is research, although we have three years of working and playing together with the children in the preschool, and my paid job includes "research and development." I say this is a development project, where practitioners and I now write stories together (Rhedding-Jones et al., 2009), and Muslims make videos and take digital photos for their own use, in the preschool and elsewhere. Sometimes, I have been given these videos and photos to show people who do not know about Islamic practice with young children. The children are not in these documents. Instead the teachers and assistants have photographed the preschool building, the playrooms and the playground, and the Norwegian woods they go into with the children. The talk on the videos is in many languages, about pedagogy and care with young children, as the Muslim practitioners explain their practice. You could call this professional learning. If so, then it is just as much my learning as anyone else's. As a critical multicultural practice (the Muslim practitioners and the children's families came to Norway from Somalia, Kurdistan, Bosnia, Turkey, Syria, Tunisia, Morocco, and Iraq), this is an amazing location, community, and process of engagement. It is amazing because the multicultural practices go against the mainstream. Yet they are within it at the same time. Here Muslims are the majority. In fact almost everyone is a Muslim. But we are in Norway, following the national curriculum, and speaking Norwegian.

What is this saying about critical multicultural practice? Many national and linguistic cultures come together via the shared religion of Islam in Norway. Yes it is multicultural, and various people from different locations are represented, but how is it critical? It seems to me that the critical here is about what happens to the people from dominant groups: we simply have to transform our own practice, maintain our difference yet at the same time support the differences to practice wanted by Muslims. Here is an apparent hybridity, where normalized national discourses and practices blend with the Muslim practices that also operate in Muslim preschools in England, Germany, Malaysia, and Indonesia (Rhedding-Jones, 2010). The critical non-Muslims in Oslo include parents who want their children growing up knowing about cultures, languages, and compassion, and who send their children to private Muslim preschools with Muslim practitioners. These parents are critical of monocultural, monolingual practice. Other critical non-Muslims in Oslo are those practitioners who work as minorities in Islamic settings, as welcomed friends and colleagues. These professionals are critical of the practices of nationally constructed pedagogy and care, and of normalized "multiculturalism," and want these to change. Such people are making a critical difference to the lives of children. These children know about and enact cultural and linguistic diversity, and they respect Islam, whether their parents practice it or not.

As not all the families and practitioners in the Muslim preschool are Muslim, there is a high degree of tolerance for difference, and an honoring of the differences. There are also many languages in constant use, every day, and no one person knows all of them. So always you are positioned as someone who only knows part of what is being said. That is a very comfortable positioning, as there is much laughter, much eye contact, and much understanding of what it is like to be not 100% sure of what is happening. I have learned about Islam in the process of all this. But knowing about washing practices in bathrooms, and how not to shake a man's hand if you are a woman, and how Muslims caringly inquire after the health of your family, is only a part of the bigger picture of what has happened within me. Because this chapter has worked around descriptions of events I'll end it with one more.

The location is Madison, Wisconsin, USA. I am at an early childhood education conference and this evening we are privileged to be listening to a room full of teachers telling us about their challenging new practices. The teachers will be sitting together in twos, each pair at a small round table. We can join them and look at their photos and chat, then move on to another table. About 100 people will be in the room, with about 20 round tables. We first meet in a big reception place where drinks and small savories are served. Because I'm working with Muslims in Norway I walk towards the only woman in the reception room who is wearing *hijab*. I tell her about the project in Oslo and how we are starting to write together. She is surprised. She would love to be in a group writing stories of practice together. No one has asked her what Muslims might want for their children as early childhood education in the West. She is just trying to do what everyone else thinks ought to be done. Are there preschools where Islamic practices are possible? Can teachers have a place to pray? Can the children learn the stories of the prophets and to count in Arabic? She is eating and drinking nothing at this reception and she is standing against the wall. When she gets home that evening, she tells me, at around nine o'clock she will be able to start to cook the family meal and break her fast. Later I go to her round table. There is nothing Muslim about what she is doing with the children except her own self and what she brings to her practice. She is calm and articulate, speaks four languages but only uses English at work. Her university degrees are in bioengineering and now early childhood education.

If I try to pull the threads of this chapter together and say how this brief focus on Muslims informs a critical multicultural approach to early childhood education, I would say the following:

1   A critical multiculturalism implies looking at our own practices and what we do.
2   A normalized or liberal multicultural practice is insufficient because there are differences not yet imagined and we have to be able to adapt ourselves to whatever these are.
3   If we look at small moments of practice, and reconsider what happened in them, we can make some changes to what happens in future.
4   Each national context for critical multicultural practice needs to evolve because of who is there and the various cultures that are represented.

Acknowledgment

Camilla Eline Andersen and Aslaug Andreassen Becher wrote about some of the events presented in this chapter.

References

Andersen, C. E. (2006). Troubling ethnicity and cultural diversity in Norwegian preschool discourses. *Australian Research in Early Childhood Education, 13*(1), 38–50.

Angell-Jacobsen, M.-L. (2008). *Anerkjennelse av kulturelt mangfold i barnehager: Rekonseptualiseringer av "anerkjennelse" ved hjelp av (auto)etnografi og rhizoanalyser.* [Recognizing cultural diversity in preschools: Reconceptualizations of "recognition" through (auto)ethnography and rhizo analyses.] Master of Education thesis in Multicultural and International Education. Oslo, Norway: Oslo University College. Published as *HiO-masteroppgave 2008 nr 7.*

Angell-Jacobsen, M.-L., & Becher, A. A. (2007). Paradoxer i strategier for sosial utjevning: Økt kartleggingspress lest i i lys av teorier om postkolonialisme og privilegier. [Paradoxes in strategies for social equity: Reading testing agendas in the light of postcolonialism and privilege.] *Norsk tidskrift for migrasjons forskning* [*Norwegian Journal of Immigration Research*], *8,* 49–62.

Becher, A. A. (2004). Research considerations regarding cultural differences. *Contemporary Issues in Early Childhood, 5*(1), 81–94.

Becher, A. A. (2006). *Flerstemmig mangfold: Samarbeid med minoritetsforeldre.* [*Multilingual diversity: Collaborations with ethnic minority parents.*] Bergen, Norway: Fagbokforlaget.

Bustos, M. M. F (2009). Hvor kommer du egentlig fra? Problematiseringer av språklige konstrUnited Kingdomsjoner av virkeligheter. [Where do you actually come from? Problematising language constructions and reality.] In K. E. Fajersson, E. Karlsson, A. A. Becher, & A. M. Otterstad (Eds.), *Grip sjansene! Profesjonskompetanse, barn og kulturelt mangfold.* [*Take the chance: Professional competence, children and cultural difference*] (pp. 43–52). Oslo, Norway: Cappelen Akademiske Forlag.

Cannella, G. S. (2000). Critical and feminist reconstructions of early childhood education: Continuing conversations. In Colloquia. *Contemporary Issues in Early Childhood, 1*(2), 215–221.

Carr, M. (2001). *Assessment in early childhood settings: Learning stories.* London: Thousand Oaks; New Delhi: Sage.

Comber, M. (2003). Critical literacy: What does it look like in the early years? In N. Hall, J. Larson, & J. Marsh (Eds.), *Handbook of early childhood literacy* (pp. 355–368). London: Thousand Oaks; New Delhi: Sage.

Fajersson, K. E., Karlsson, E., Becher, A. A., & Otterstad, A. M. (Eds.). (2009). *Grip sjansene! Profesjonskompetanse, barn og kulturelt mangfold.* [*Take the chance: Professional competence, children and cultural difference.*] Oslo, Norway: Cappelen Akademiske Forlag.

Gjervan, M., Andersen, C. E., & Bleka, M. (2006). *Se Mangfold! Perspektiver på flerkulturelt arbeid i barnehager.* [*Celebrate diversity! Perspectives for multicultural praxis in early childhood education.*] Oslo, Norway: Cappelen Akademiske Forlag.

Grieshaber, S., & Cannella, G. S. (Eds.). (2001). *Embracing identities in early childhood education: Diversity and possibilities.* New York: Teachers College Press.

Gullestad, M. (2006). *Plausible prejudice: Everyday experiences and social images of nation, culture and race.* Oslo, Norway: Universitetsforlaget.

May, S. (Ed.). (1999). *Critical multiculturalism: Rethinking multicultural and antiracist education.* London: Falmer Press.

Otterstad, A. M. (2005). Different "reading" of the multicultural within early childhood (con)texts. *Barn* (*Children:* a refereed journal in Norway), *3,* 75–90.

Otterstad, A. M. (Ed.). (2008). *Profesjonsutøvelse og kulturelt mangfold—fra utsikt til innsikt?* [*Performing professionalism and cultural diversity.*] Oslo, Norway: Universitetsforlaget.

Pacini-Ketchabaw, V. (2007). Child care and multiculturalism: A site of governance marked by flexibility and openness. *Contemporary Issues in Early Childhood Education, 8*(3), 222–232.

Rhedding-Jones, J. (2001). Shifting ethnicities: "Native informants" and other theories from/for early childhood education. *Contemporary Issues in Early Childhood Education, 2*(2), 135–156.

Rhedding-Jones, J. (2002). An undoing of documents and other texts: Towards a critical multiculturalism in early childhood education. *Contemporary Issues in Early Childhood Education, 3*(1), 90–116.

Rhedding-Jones, J. (2004). Classroom research or w(h)ither development: Gender, complexity and diversity in the UK, the USA and Australia. *British Educational Research Journal, 30*(1), 187–193.

Rhedding-Jones, J. (2005). Questioning diversity: Rethinking early childhood practices. In N. Yelland (Ed.), *Critical issues in early childhood education* (pp. 131–145). New York and Berkshire, England: Routledge.

Rhedding-Jones, J. (2007a). Monocultural constructs: A transnational reflects on early childhood institutions. *Transnational Curriculum Inquiry, 4*(2), 38–54. http://nitinat.library.ubc.ca/ojs/index.php/tci

Rhedding-Jones, J. (2007b). Reading "diversity": Implications for early childhood professionals. *Early Childhood Matters, 108,* 47–49.

Rhedding-Jones, J. (2010, forthcoming). *Muslims in early childhood education: Discourses and epistemologies.* Amsterdam and New York: Springer.

Rhedding-Jones, J., Nordli, H., Abdellaoui, N., Dhoski, S., Karaman, S., & Tanveer, J. (2009, forthcoming) *Beretninger fra en muslimsk barnehage.* [*Tales from a Muslim preschool in Norway.*] Bergen, Norway: Fagbokforlaget.

Ritchie, J. (2008). Honouring Māori subjectivities within early childhood education in Aotearoa. *Contemporary Issues in Early Childhood, 9*(3), 202–210.

Robinson, K., & Jones Díaz, C. (2006). "It's more than black dolls and brown paint": Critical multiculturalism, whiteness and early childhood education. In K. Robinson & C. Jones Diaz, *Diversity and difference in early childhood education* (pp. 63–81). Buckingham, England and New York: Open University Press.

Siraj-Blatchford, I., & Clarke, P. (2000). *Supporting identity, diversity and language in the early years.* Buckingham, England and Philadelphia: Open University Press.

Sleeter, C., & Delgado Bernal, D. D. (2004). Critical pedagogy, critical race theory, and anti-racist education: Implications for multicultural education. In J. A. Banks & C. A. Banks (Eds.), *Handbook of Research on Multicultural Education* (2nd ed.) (pp. 240–260). San Francisco: Jossey Bass.

Soto, L. D. (1997). *Language, culture and power: Bilingual families and the struggle for quality education.* Albany, NY: State University Press.

Soto, L. D., & Swadener, B. B. (Eds.). (2005). *Power and voice in research with children.* New York: Peter Lang.

Te Whāriki (1996). *He Whāriki Mātauranga mōngā Mokopuna o Aotearoa early childhood curriculum.* Wellington, New Zealand: Ministry of Education.

Vandenbroeck, M. (2004). Diverse aspects of diversity: A European perspective. *International Journal of Equity and Innovation in Early Childhood, 1*(2), 27–44.

II

Critical Multiculturalism
in Language and Language Arts

6

Critical Multiculturalism and Subject English

TERRY LOCKE

Critical multiculturalism has been challenged on a number of fronts in recent years. Both proponents and detractors have focused on its apparent inability to transform itself into something useful to classroom teachers, that is, to articulate a range of practices consistent with its ideals. The second challenge comes from the widespread uptake at policy level of outcomes- or standards-based testing and qualifications regimes, which have narrowed the multicultural debate to a concern with achievement gaps and ways of closing them.

In this chapter, I begin with a brief description of critical multiculturalism. I then identify key requirements of an English/literacy course that are consistent with this understanding. While acknowledging that subject English varies across different Anglophonic settings, I use a map of its different paradigms to explore how each of these might help or hinder the instantiation of a critical multicultural discourse in classroom programs. Referencing recent New Zealand (and other) research, I suggest some actual classroom strategies that appear consistent with a critical multicultural approach. In doing so, I address the first of the challenges above and acknowledge the constraints of the second.

Critical Multiculturalism

May (2003) identifies four characteristics of critical multiculturalism:

1 Acknowledging the role of ethnicity and culture in identity formation *without* essentializing them;
2 Recognizing unequal power relations as a part of life and that "individual and collective choices are circumscribed by the ethnic categories available at any given time and place" (p. 209);
3 Recognizing the ways in which certain cultural knowledges can become marginalized in society;
4 Recognizing the social situatedness and provisionality of one's "speaking position" (p. 211).

To concretize these four characteristics, let me draw on the writings of three high-school English teachers working in classrooms in South Auckland, New Zealand, characterized by large degrees of cultural and linguistic difference.

These teachers participated as teacher-researchers in a two-year project on "Teaching literature in the multicultural classroom," which was concerned to identify effective ways of enhancing responses to and composition of literary texts in "multicultural" classrooms. In the initial stages of the project, baseline data were collected from teacher-researchers using such instruments as reflective profiles, Wiki-based forums and focus groups. What emerged quickly was a shared sense that identity formation is a complex business, drawing on a range of discourses (only some ethnicity-based). One teacher wrote the following in a Wiki forum:

> I guess to me a multicultural classroom is one that is rich in a variety of cultural backgrounds and identities and that within these there is also lot of cross-pollination. A student in a multicultural classroom can bring with them a different ethnic background but they may also have strong regional affiliations or subcultural identities that cross over ethnicity. All of these things may influence their way of thinking and behaviour towards learning. They may come from a similar cultural background but belong to a specific ethnic group that has its own specific beliefs or behaviors e.g. Samoan vs. Tongan, NZ-born vs. Island-born, or new immigrants like refugees and bring with them traumatic experiences. They may identify with certain clothing like hip hop or Goth or religious requirements like the burqa. Accents may vary between different cultural groups but they may also identify with regional accents like those of South Auckland. There may also be a culture of food identities e.g. they may be PI and see corned beef as being a food of choice but they may also be PI and be Seventh Day Adventists and be vegetarian. The multicultural mix may also be socio-economic i.e. many families from a Decile 1 area may be on some form of assistance which cuts across ethnic back grounds so they share the cultural struggle of trying to make ends meet and the impression others have towards their suburb. So I suppose I see a multicultural class as being one that is really diverse in many aspects, from what they bring with them from their family and socio-economic background to what they may identify with among themselves.
>
> (Wiki posting)

May's second characteristic can be reformulated in critical discourse analytical terms. If language shapes reality via discourse, and if certain discourses are more powerful than others, then one's personal power is severely circumscribed by the discourses one subscribes to. One of the teachers expressed this idea thus:

> The media represents South Auckland and [the suburb of] Otara in particular ways and I want students to be able to be aware of that and question it and reject it if necessary. Representations can be very powerful, they can influence how we see the world, they can promote ideas. I want

students to be able to look at advertisements for a 'White Sunday Loan' and be able to question it. It may help their families in some way.

(Reflective profile)

This sentiment recognizes the ways "loan sharks" target poor, Pacific Island families in South Auckland by manipulating a perceived tendency to spend extravagantly for White Sunday, a special day focused on children.

Third, critical multiculturalism recognizes the ways certain cultural knowledges can become marginalized and misrepresented by more privileged discourses. This recognition is evident in the words of the teacher in the previous paragraph. Like other teachers in this project, he was aware of his *own* privilege as a white teacher (albeit raised in Otara and with a Pacific Island wife). Likewise, he shared an attitude that acknowledged his students as experts in particular kinds of linguistic and cultural knowledge.

May's fourth characteristic relates to the situatedness and provisionality of identity. Human subjects are not single and enduring, but inscribed by a variety of discourses (often contradictory) in complex and not necessarily stable ways. One of the participating teachers expressed this when she wrote: "I mean, is anyone purely from one cultural heritage? I myself am half British and half Greek Cypriot, and have lived in NZ for 35 years" (Wiki posting).

Some Critical Multicultural Parameters for Subject English

What might an ideology such as critical multiculturalism want from an English/literacy curriculum? I suggest there are five requirements:

1 A recognition of the complex ways in which textual practices have a role in the identity formation of individuals and groups;
2 An active recognition of cultural difference and cultural preference in relation to the selection of program materials, in the classroom interactive styles fostered, and in the design of learning activities;
3 The fostering of textual practices which draw attention to the relationship between texts and issues of power, inequality, injustice, marginalization, and misrepresentation in the wider society;
4 Teaching practices that reflect a deep respect for linguistic and cultural resources as advantages rather than deficits and which welcome all linguistic heritages into the English classroom, viewing knowledge of these heritages as enhancing the linguistic understanding of all students;
5 Using assessment strategies which, as much as is possible, build on the teaching practices adopted at classroom level (i.e., are ecologically valid) and which avoid one-size-fits-all tests which erase cultural and linguistic difference.

How does such a prescription fit with current paradigms of subject English?

To address this question, I offer a map of the subject, setting out the broad range of paradigms likely to be found across a range of Anglophonic settings (Locke, 2007):

- *Cultural heritage:* There is a traditional body of knowledge (including a canon of precious texts and specialist literary and grammatical knowledge) which should be valued and inculcated as a means of "rounding out" learners so that they become fully participating and discriminating members of a society or culture (e.g., Brooks & Warren, 1976).
- *Personal growth:* Sometimes called "progressive" English, this model argues that it is valuable to engage with literary (canonical *and* popular) and other texts because this facilitates the personal, individual growth of learners, for whom the acquisition of certain cognitive, cultural, and linguistic competencies will play a central role in their ongoing task of making sense of their world (e.g., Rosenblatt, 1989).
- *Rhetorical or textual competence:* At its worst, this version promotes decontextualized skills acquisition. At its best, however, the model puts a value on the mastery of the forms and conventions of a range of textual practices or genres, including the literary. Pedagogically, it links with the Australian "genre" school (e.g., Cope & Kalantzis, 1993a) and with rhetorical framings of the subject (e.g., Bakhtin, 1986).
- *Critical practice:* A "critical literacy" model encourages language-users to see themselves as engaged in textual acts which are part of a wider set of discursive practices that actively produce and sustain patterns of dominance and subordination in the wider society and offer members of society prescribed ways of being particular sorts of people (see Morgan, 1997).

A *Cultural Heritage Model of English*

The cultural heritage model of English inevitably raises issues about the place of the canon, a set of texts deemed worthy of esteem, emulation, and study. The idea of a canon becomes problematic when one asks the question, "Deemed by whom?" If the answer is a powerful social elite—white, male, and monolingual—then the canon becomes something both oppressive and irrelevant to women and minority groups of all kinds. Viewed this way, the canon is antithetical to the requirements identified earlier.

Another possible answer is: curriculum or program developers and publishers. Most English teachers are confronted with some version of the canon during their degree studies. However, by the time they begin practicing as teachers, these canons will be mediated via textbooks (especially in textbook-oriented settings such as the United States), the text selections to be found in departmental resource rooms and by curriculum documents, where these prescribe reading lists. What often operates through the agency of these prescribed canons is a kind of benevolent or liberal multiculturalism verging on the tokenistic.

However, there is another approach to the canon which *is* consistent with critical multiculturalism. It is possible to conceive of literature—not just as a body of esteemed texts, but as a social phenomenon characterized by processes of production, consumption, and distribution. In such an approach, the notion of canonicity can be recognized, but also problematized. A dynamic and critical view of the canon regards it as socially constructed, contestable, unstable, and multiple. Different cultural groups esteem different texts (including texts orally transmitted) for different reasons. Such a reorientation means that a cultural heritage model of English becomes potentially empowering for students. It is evident, for example, in the research of Korina Jocson (2006), aimed at exposing African American students to the heritage being built up through the "(re)emergence of spoken word poetry across US cities" (p. 233).

In the New Zealand study mentioned earlier, teachers positioned themselves as contesting and reshaping the canon in their own contexts in recognition of the kinds of difference staring them in the face each morning. One teacher, noting that she taught little that would be considered part of the "traditional canon," commented:

> I guess merit is a pretty fluid term—has someone "told us" a text is of merit … OR is it enough that we think the text is of value/merit because it reflects the social and cultural concerns of the students, is relevant and will interest the students?
>
> (Wiki posting)

These teachers were also reconstituting the canons represented by their departmental resource rooms. All referred to the criterion of *relevance.* One teacher talked about drawing

> on their cultural backgrounds, especially New Zealand born Pacific experiences. I talk with the students and take note of their interests (rugby league, gang culture, experiences of Pacific youth in New Zealand, church/Christianity, family) then try to find texts that can link in with that.
>
> (Reflective profile)

Another focused on Maori writers, especially in the junior high school. All would have concurred with the broad principles encapsulated in the following statement:

> I source as many texts as possible by NZ, Maori and Pacific authors/directors/artists, use articles from weekend and local newspapers for wide reading and NZ film and art for viewing. I also keep in mind that it is important to supplement this with other world view texts to so I can expand their knowledge so select other texts but these would have that have themes/characters they can relate to.
>
> (Reflective profile)

Implicit in this critical reorientation of the cultural heritage model is a determination to collapse the barrier between classroom and community, for example, by selecting bilingual texts, texts in translation, and first-language texts of relevance to the local community. Another way is to accord recognition to literacy practices taking place in the home in ways that can be viewed as complementing the work done in the English classroom (Conteh & Kawashima, 2008). Clearly this reoriented model favors additive approaches to bilingualism and practices aimed at first-language maintenance. A recent study by Sneddon (2008) has shown how bilingual children of elementary-school age in Britain who have become dominant in English are learning to be literate in the language of the home using dual language books provided by the school. The study highlighted the positive impact on children's confidence, on their personal identity as bilinguals in a multicultural British society, on their English literacy achievement, and on parental involvement.

A Personal Growth Model of English

Developers of a "genre"-based theory of English/literacy in the early 1990s, drawing on Halliday's (1994) functional system grammar, criticized the personal growth or progressive paradigm of English on a number of counts pertinent to this discussion. Cope and Kalantzis (1993b), for example, saw this paradigm as culturally bound, favoring social elites, and productive of social inequality (p. 6). At best, they argued, the paradigm might allow for a benevolent or liberal form of multicultural education but was incapable of supporting the critical multicultural requirements identified previously.

For two reasons, however, I argue that this paradigm has something to offer critical multiculturalism in the context of an English classroom. First, the individual focus of progressive English does not *necessarily* preclude the social. Indeed, a careful reading of a reader-response theorist such as Rosenblatt (1978) shows that part of what readers bring to their transactions with texts is their cultural capital, for example, the connotations their cultural groups assign to particular images. Subject English theorists such as Sumara (2002) have deliberately incorporated a cultural studies lens into their versions of the personal growth model. Underpinning Sumara's view of textual engagement is a theory of learning "that conceptualizes human identity as co-evolving with the production of knowledge." This view supports the first critical multicultural requirement identified above. "Identity," he asserts, "is not some essential quality of the individual human subject. Identity emerges from relationships, including relationships people have with books and other communicative technologies based on language" (p. 9). In this model, the concept of "personal voice" is less individualized and more in line with a Bakhtinian view of an agentive, social self inhabiting a web or chain of textualized interactions (Bakhtin, 1986).

Second, a reoriented personal growth model has something to offer critical multiculturalism because it reminds us that literacy is not just a *social* practice, but also a *cognitive, technologized* one. Critical multiculturalism is not about feeding students with an unremitting diet of texts from their own cultures.

Related to the argument for relevance in textual selection is recognition of hybridization in identity formation and also the ways texts from a range of cultural settings can serve children's developmental needs in culturally and linguistically diverse classrooms. In other words, there are reasons other than the cultural for the selection of texts for study. In a recent British three-year case study, Obied (2007) tracked the development of two refugee children's emerging literacy and "cross cultural responses" to poetry (p. 40). The developing bilingualism was found to draw on the students' auditory imaginations and the enjoyment of language play in sounds, images, and motifs, using poems from a range of contexts. This shift in emphasis from word-centered meaning to image-centered meaning is also reflected in Datta's (2000) work in Britain with 10- and 11-year-old bilingual students, which also utilized diverse texts. In short, a personal growth orientation can be consistent with and supportive of a critical multicultural frame for English.

A Textual or Rhetorical Competence Model of English

In one version, a textual or rhetorical competence model of English is highly skills-focused and compellingly attractive to governments concerned to enhance their competitive advantage by "upskilling" those sections of their populations deemed to be illiterate in certain respects. This version tends to view cultural minorities in terms of a deficit model of education, viewing the home background as a hindrance. There are two problems here that are particularly pertinent to critical multiculturalism.

The first problem with a decontextualized skills-based model of English—and outcomes-based education in general—is its character of spurious neutrality. As Peters and Marshall (1996) have pointed out,

> a skill is like a technique; it is a performance, an action, a doing. Like a technique, like technology more generally, 'skills' are often seen as neutral or as value-free. "Skills" are, therefore, considered to be generic, separable from their learning contexts, transferable or transportable from one context to another.
>
> (p. 34)

What is suppressed here is a recognition of the agenda this version of literacy is serving, for example, a commodification of education with a primary emphasis "upon competitive individuals acquiring skills and competencies required by the market and the economy" (Ball, Kenny, & Gardiner, 1990, p. 77).

The second problem with decontextualization is the evacuation of content that characterizes many outcomes-based regimes. In the absence of a syllabus, and even where there is a national curriculum, outcomes-based testing regimes rapidly assume the status of quasi-curriculums. Inevitably, teachers teach to the test. Because assessment is the driver, curriculums tend to be "constructed" by the way outcomes are worded. These wordings are often fatuous, illogical, and flawed (Locke, 2008). Of pertinence to critical multiculturalism, these testing regimes—in the guise of a rhetoric of flexibility, transferability, and transparency—are actually a one-size-fits-all approach to assessment. In relation to multicultural education, their discourse is assimilationist, since cultural difference is elided and erased.

However, a second version of the textual competence model, developed by various genre theorists, is far more socially aware. For a start, this version drew its metalanguage from systemic functional grammar, a top-down grammar which viewed texts as explicable only in relationship to contexts of situation and culture. As Kress (1993) put it, genre theorists emphasized "cultural and social dimensions which enter into the formation and constitution of language and of texts" (p. 23). Early on, however, Kress was asking questions about multiculturalism and the nature of sustainable economic, social, and cultural futures on a global scale and began distancing himself from the "Genre School." Kress identified four points of a language curriculum he saw as serving the needs of a multicultural society:

1 "Equal importance to considerations of oral language";
2 An emphasis on "the whole set of connections of culture, society and language, codings of value systems, structuring and realizations of systems of power, and to the possibilities of making meanings in language as such, and in the languages of a specific plurilingual society in particular";
3 A willingness to analyse and critique the status of various languages in terms of "existing particular configurations of power";
4 A willingness to debate the relation "between a language curriculum, society, and societal change" (p. 29).

In Kress's view, the Genre School's version of the textual competence model was insufficiently critically literate and culturally inclusive, despite its desire to further the upward mobility of disadvantaged groups. While the Genre School theorists identified and systematically taught what they saw as the relevant and empowering genres associated with schooling, they did not question the status of these genres. In that respect, their version of English was integrationist.

That being said, a view of English based in rhetorical competence is not necessarily integrationist. A rhetorical view of English also focuses on the situatedness of language acts, and can draw upon approaches to genre that are more dynamic and less formulaic that that pursued by the Australian Genre School and more in keeping with Kress's prescription above. One of the teachers in the New Zealand project adopted this approach in a unit of work with a multicultural Year 9 (ages 13–14) English class. The students studied the movie *Shrek* and compared representations of "prince" and "princess" in this movie with stereotypes they had identified on the basis of their own cultural knowledge. Through this comparison, they were able to see ways in which the movie challenged and subverted these stereotypes. They then researched a range of fairytales in their own and other cultures, investigating ways in which plot and other narrative elements were patterned on a regular basis. From this, they produced their *own* fairytales, creating characters and plots that in some way deviated from the norms of practice they had established.

A Critical Literacy Model of English

I have left consideration of a critical literacy model of English until last in order to challenge those who would view other English paradigms as antithetical to critical multiculturalism and assert unreservedly that critical literacy and critical multiculturalism are discursive bedfellows. While I broadly agree with this, I argue that there are shortcomings in the ways critical literacy can be practiced. Based as it is in a sociocultural or poststructuralist view of literacy, it has difficulty in accommodating biologically or evolutionary based views of an autobiographical self as "a nontransient collection of unique facts and ways of being which characterize a person" (Damasio, 2000, p. 17). I also argue that, for similar reasons, it is limited in its attempts to address the aesthetic (Misson & Morgan, 2006). Versions of critical literacy drawing on the work of Foucault can appear to position human subjects as powerless, in the grip of discourses they are barely aware of, and as relatively lacking in agency. Other versions derive their metalanguage too exclusively from systemic functional grammar. Another potential problem with critical literacy is that while it espouses pupil empowerment as a goal, in practice it may be the ideological axes of the teacher that are heard grinding away in classrooms. A critical literacy teacher can still be authoritarian rather than authoritative.

Notwithstanding these caveats, all high-school English teachers in the New Zealand project identified critical literacy as a paradigm of English that enabled them to address the literacy needs of their culturally diverse classrooms. Typically, one teacher wrote:

> I am sympathetic to the critical literacy view that literature is ideological, maintains social structures, and empowers certain groups, and that there needs to be new discourses to have a more just society. I agree with the view that we should be encouraging students to be resistant readers and be empowered language users.
>
> (Reflective profile)

One teacher designed a Year 13 (ages 17–18) course for a relatively "underachieving," multicultural class with the following objectives:

- Students understand that social (cultural) and historical (time periods) contexts impact on texts.
- Students can identify the ways in which texts construct (represent) different viewpoints on medical experimentation.
- Students are aware that language is not a neutral medium and that the way language is used affects the way in which something is seen, for example, scientific or technological intervention into human life.
- Students can apply the above awareness in the production of their own texts by being critically aware of their language choices.

Her theme was "Technology—playing God or just playing?," focusing on medical intervention to prolong human life. Texts included: *Frankenstein* (a film version and extracts from the Mary Shelley novel), *The Island* (film), "Te Manawa" (a short story by Briar Grace-Smith, 2006), scientific journal and magazine articles on xenotransplantation, and the novel *Pig Heart Boy* (Blackman, 1997). A sense of the kind of discourse operating in her classroom in relation to the critical reading of texts is communicated by the following question prompt for "Te Manawa," the story of a Maori woman who has had a heart transplant from a Samoan donor:

> On p. 24 we get a description of a scene where "the woman's" brother Tem offers a boar's heart to a doctor for possible use as an organ for transplant. Why does he do this? On the basis of careful reading, what can you deduce about: a. the doctor's attitude to Tem? b. the doctor's attitude to using a pig's heart in a human patient? What do you make of the doctor's statement: "I'm talking science here." In what way does this tell us something about how the author of the story is encouraging us to think about this sort of doctor?

In accordance with her teaching goals, students are being lead into a consideration, through close attention to stylistic and linguistic features, of the ways in which texts position readers to take up certain readings and not others.

Conclusion

I have argued that a range of paradigms of subject English have something to offer a critically multicultural agenda. All of us are ideologically driven, but that doesn't make us ideologues. None of the teachers in the New Zealand study discussed here based their teaching in a particular ideology of the subject. On the contrary, their range of practices might be described as eclectic and very much determined by the interests and backgrounds of the students they taught. All, in varying degrees, engaged in practices consonant with the critical multicultural requirements identified earlier.

All, however, were constrained by the high-stakes testing regimes that currently dominate the New Zealand educational landscape, as elsewhere, where even diagnostic testing is beginning to be valorized as "high-stakes," as schools strive to provide evidence of value-addedness, regardless of the validity of the measures on offer. The fifth critical multicultural requirement identified earlier was: "Using assessment strategies which, as much as is possible, build on the teaching practices adopted at classroom level (i.e. are ecologically valid) and which avoid one-size-fits-all tests which erase cultural and linguistic difference." Such a requirement is not easy in educational settings dominated by outcomes fetishism, as is the case in many Anglophone contexts. However, teachers might consider two broad strategies.

The first is to get smart. This can mean separating formative assessment practices from flawed summative assessment practices and devising ecologically valid tests (Whitehead, 2007) that mirror the teaching and learning practices of the culturally and linguistic diverse classroom. Sometimes, this means instituting a classroom or school-based assessment regime which makes sense, in parallel with an official one which doesn't. The second is to get political. As I have argued elsewhere, a classical view of teacher professionalism will take us only so far (Locke, 2004). What teachers need to develop is a kind of critical savvy as professionals. In their own quiet ways, the teachers in this project were critically savvy. They could hardly have been otherwise, given the care they were exercising in respect of their students, and the deep understanding they had of what many of their culturally and linguistically diverse students were up against. Up to a point, they were also activists. The project itself was a form of activism, an opportunity for oases of meaningful and critical conversations in a desert of workload intensification. For all that, they were constrained by prevailing assessment and curriculum practice, work intensification and resourcing issues, in what they could do in terms of affecting the academic and social destinies of their students. Sadly, too many people in the educational sector, in positions much more powerful than the ones these teachers occupied, subscribed to discourses antithetical to the interests of students like theirs. This is what a critical multicultural approach must continue to challenge.

References

Bakhtin, M. (1986). The problem with speech genres. In C. Emerson & M. Holquist (Eds.), *Speech genres and other late essays: M. M. Bakhtin* (V. McGee, Trans.) (pp. 60–102). Austin, TX: University of Texas Press.

Ball, S., Kenny, A., & Gardiner, D. (1990). Literacy, politics and the teaching of English. In I. Goodson & P. Medway (Eds.), *Bringing English to order: The history and politics of a school subject* (pp. 47–86). London: Falmer Press.

Blackman, M. (1997). *Pig-heart boy*. London: Doubleday.

Brooks, C., & Warren, R. P. (1976). *Understanding poetry* (4th ed.). New York: Holt, Rinehart and Winston.

Conteh, J., & Kawashima, Y. (2008). Diversity in family involvement in children's learning in English primary schools: Culture, language and identity. *English Teaching: Practice and Critique, 7*(2), 113–125.

Cope, B., & Kalantzis, M. (1993a). *The powers of literacy: A genre approach to teaching writing.* Pittsburgh, PA: University of Pittsburgh Press.

Cope, B., & Kalantzis, M. (1993b). Introduction: How a genre approach to literacy can transform the way writing is taught. In B. Cope & M. Kalantzis (Eds.), *The powers of literacy: A genre approach to teaching writing* (pp. 1–21). Pittsburgh, PA: University of Pittsburgh Press.

Damasio, A. (2000). *The feeling of what happens: Body, emotion and the making of consciousness.* London: Vintage.

Datta, M. (Ed.). (2000). *Bilinguality and literacy: Principles and practices.* London/New York: Continuum.

Grace-Smith, B. (2006). Te Manawa. In *The six pack: Winning writing from New Zealand Book Month* (pp. 17–34). Auckland: New Zealand Book Month/Whitireia Publishing.

Halliday, M. (1994). *An introduction to functional grammar* (2nd ed.). London: Edward Arnold.

Jocson, K. (2006). "Bob Dylan and Hip Hop": Intersecting literacy practices in youth poetry committees. *Written Communication, 23*(3), 231–259.

Kress, G. (1993). Genre as social process. In B. Cope & M. Kalantzis (Eds.), *The powers of literacy: A genre approach to teaching writing* (pp. 22–37). Pittsburgh, PA: University of Pittsburgh Press.

Locke, T. (2004). Reshaping classical professionalism in the aftermath of neo-liberal reform. *Literacy Learning: the Middle Years, 12*(1)/*English in Australia, 139*, 113–122.

Locke, T. (2007). *Resisting qualifications reforms in New Zealand: The English Study Design as constructive dissent.* Rotterdam/Taipei: Sense Publishers.

Locke, T. (2008). English in a surveillance regime: Tightening the noose in New Zealand. *Changing English: Studies in Culture & Education, 15*(3), 293–310.

May, S. (2003). Critical multiculturalism. In M. Peters, C. Lankshear, M. Olssen, & J. Kincheloe (Eds.), *Critical theory and the human condition: Founders and praxis* (pp. 199–212). New York: Peter Lang.

Misson, R., & Morgan, W. (2006). *Critical literacy and the aesthetic: Transforming the English classroom.* Urbana, IL: NCTE.

Morgan, W. (1997). *Critical literacy in the classroom: The art of the possible.* London: Routledge.

Obied, V. (2007). "Why did I do nothing?" Poetry and the experiences of bilingual pupils in a mainstream inner-city secondary school. *English in Education, 41*(3), 37–52.

Peters, M., & Marshall, J. (1996). The politics of curriculum: Busnocratic rationality and enterprise culture. *DELTA: Policy and Practice in Education, 48,* 33–46.

Rosenblatt, L. (1978). *The reader, the text, the poem: The transactional theory of the literary work.* Carbondale, IL: Southern Illinois University Press.

Sneddon, R. (2008). Young bilingual children learning to read with dual language books. *English Teaching: Practice and Critique, 7*(2), 71–84.

Sumara, D. (2002). *Why reading literature in school still matters: Imagination, interpretation, insight.* Mahwah, NJ: Lawrence Erlbaum Associates.

Whitehead, D. (2007). Literacy assessment practices: Moving from standardised to ecologically valid assessment in secondary schools. *Language and Education, 21*(5), 1–20.

7

Critical Multicultural Education and Second/Foreign Language Teaching

RYUKO KUBOTA

Introduction

Second or foreign language education is located in a pedagogical space where linguistic, racial, cultural, and class differences meet. Learning a new language, and the culture associated with it, exposes students to diversity and provides them with a new cultural perspective. Language teaching is thus often viewed as inherently compatible with multiculturalism. Nonetheless, a common approach to diversity in second language education often reflects the liberal form of multiculturalism, which promotes a superficial form of pluralism, reinforces color- or difference-blindness, and exoticizes and essentializes the culture of the Other, while obscuring issues of power and privilege (Kubota, 2004).

Appearing to support linguistic and cultural diversity, such second language education ironically promotes monolingualism, monoculturalism, normatism, and elitism. It supports monolingualism in the sense that teaching English as a second language (ESL) to immigrant students often assimilates them into the monolingual English-speaking community without maintaining their native language heritage. It promotes monoculturalism in that the cultural instruction tends to focus on the dominant group in terms of race, ethnicity, social class, and religious identity. It also endorses normatism because the language to be learned is usually the standard form of language of the middle class as opposed to nonnative and nonstandard varieties including dialects (Train, 2007). Furthermore, foreign language learning is an elitist activity, as it is often made available only in wealthy school districts. Thus, the common approach to second language education with a multicultural outlook ironically parallels the ideology that eradicates diversity.

In the last two decades or so, critical scholars and practitioners in second language education have critiqued the dominant ideology and advocated critical pedagogies for social transformation (e.g., Norton & Toohey, 2004). While such critiques have mostly focused on unequal linguistic and cultural relations of power, recent scholarship has increasingly paid attention to racialization and racism in relation to language teaching and learning (e.g., Curtis & Romney,

2006; Kubota & Lin, 2006, 2009). A less frequently discussed topic is the intersection between social class and second/foreign language education. Critical engagement in issues of racialization, racism, and class in second language education is clearly part of the larger mission of critical multicultural education. This chapter reviews some recent literature in second language education, illustrates how scholars and practitioners engage in issues of racialization, racism, and their intersection with class, and offers some suggestions for critically engaged practice.

Second language education encompasses several subfields, including ESL and EFL (English as a foreign language, taught outside of Anglophone countries), foreign language instruction, bilingual education (for minority and/or majority students), and heritage language education. Since much of the discussion on racialization and racism is found in ESL/EFL literature, this chapter mainly considers these subfields.

English Teachers of Color and Critical Race Theory

Recently, several publications in the field of teaching English to speakers of other languages (TESOL) specifically focused on race and second language education. They illuminate how racialization and racism construct and affect instructional practices and experiences of teachers and students. One popular theoretical framework used is critical race theory (CRT). CRT uses counterstorytelling to uncover everyday experiences of racial oppression and injustice reflected in social practices and structures and has become a common theoretical and methodological framework for inquiry in second language education. The power of personal narratives is demonstrated in the stories told by ESL teachers of color (Curtis & Romney, 2006).

The field of TESOL encompasses quite diverse contexts, from teaching immigrant and international students in Anglophone countries to teaching in former British and American colonies where English has an institutionalized status, and to other non-Anglophone countries where English is taught as a foreign language. While many teachers of ESL/EFL are White native speakers of English, others are teachers of color from diverse ethnic origins and identify themselves as either native or nonnative speakers of English. Many of these teachers of color, especially in ESL contexts, share painful childhood experiences of being ridiculed because of the racial difference perceived by others. As professionals, many of them have experienced students' biased attitudes toward them, or employment discrimination. In the classroom, some students displayed disrespectful behavior and an unwillingness to accept these teachers as qualified or competent.

In terms of employment, Mahboob (2006), who grew up in both Pakistan and United Arab Emirates and received English-medium education throughout his life, recounts his experience of not being hired as an ESL teacher at a U.S. university where he was a graduate student of TESOL. The ESL program director told him that the students wanted to study with Americans and that his English accent would be a problem. However, the fact that the program hired Europeans, one of whom was not even a native speaker of English, convinced Mahboob that his accent was used only as a pretext—it was his racialized background that barred him from obtaining employment. Similar experiences of racial discrimination in employment, sometimes camouflaged by accent, are shared by many qualified English teachers of color in the contexts of Japan, Hong Kong, and other countries.

ESL/EFL teachers' narratives uncovered the prevalent belief that White people are the only legitimate speakers of English and are thus the ideal teachers of English. This belief often underlies employers' hiring decisions and students' desire to learn from native speakers of English. A native speaker of English is often viewed as synonymous with a White person, demonstrating the intertwined and inseparable nature of race and accent.

Race, Class, and Language

As the above-mentioned experience of Mahboob (2006) clearly indicates, the superiority of the native speaker of English indexes not only linguistic privilege but also the dominance of Whiteness. The flip side of the coin is the construction of people of color as nonnative or illegitimate speakers of English. A match-guise experiment set in a university-level lecture (Rubin, 1992) demonstrated that listeners' visual perception of the speaker's racial background affected how well they comprehended the lecture and how much accent they perceived. This explains why U.S.-born native-English-speaking Asian Americans constantly receive questions and comments such as: "Where did you learn your English?" and "Your English is very good" (Fujimoto, 2006, p. 45). The linguistic label *native speaker of English* indeed refers to a racial category.

Hill (2001) discusses the connection between language and race in the context of *language panics* or the (standard) English-only discourse. Examples of these can be observed in the 1996 Oakland School Board's resolution in California to utilize Ebonics (African American Vernacular English) in instruction and the 1998 Proposition 227 in California, which promoted English-only instruction in schools and ended the bilingual education that had served many Spanish-speaking Latino students. Both cases attracted a large amount of media attention and are part of a larger discourse of moral panics in the United States, such as teenage pregnancy, school drop out, youth crime, and illegal immigration, which all implicitly refer to African Americans or Latinos exclusively as the problem groups. This follows that language panics are not primarily about language but about race. Hill (2001) argues that the racial discourse hidden in these language panics is demonstrated by the sheer intensity of the debates, the total neglect of research evidence on language learning and language policy, and racist content that supports the system of exclusion. Given that the average socioeconomic status of African Americans and Latinos is lower than that of Whites, the (standard) English-only policies also privilege the middle class.

Speakers of English are further racialized by additional linguistic categories such as World Englishes. Motha (2006) demonstrates how a school district in the United States uses the linguistic category of *World English speakers* to index students of color who are native speakers of English from African, Caribbean, and South Asian countries. Despite their first language background (i.e., English), they are enrolled in the ESL program, which signifies the view of these students' linguistic, cultural, and racial background as a deficit. Here again, a linguistic category signifies racial alienation that assigns the meanings of inferiority, deviation, and deficit.

Just as Whiteness is the invisible norm that marks non-Whiteness, proficiency of (standard) English is the inaudible norm making speakers of other languages or non-standard varieties of English marked. And yet, nonstandard varieties of English spoken by Whites of European descent are not usually so controversial. What is operating here is not just linguicism[1] (Phillipson, 1992), but also racism. The irony is that even if African Americans and Latinos become monolingual speakers of standard English, discrimination might still continue because of their perceived racial background.

This parallels Luke's (1996) argument that the acquisition of genres of power in school (socially and educationally valued textual forms) that are taught explicitly for the purpose of empowerment does not automatically make all students equal members of the dominant society. This is because literacy skills do not inherently or universally endow every student with an equal amount of power; rather, institutional norms and expectations within certain contexts determine the distribution of power. Thus, as long as institutional racism exists, being able to speak the standard form of the dominant language alone does not guarantee equal access to power. And it is not only race but also other social categories, such as gender, class, sexual identity, and physical ableness, that all affect how much the ability to speak the standard language is recognized as legitimate cultural capital (Bourdieu, 1991) and that enables one to access social power in a specific field.

As discussed so far, language is interlocked with race, class, and other social categories. Just as racial difference is often substituted by *cultural difference* in the contemporary color-blind discourse (see below), it is sometimes indexed by *linguistic difference* as well. The standard form of language is usually associated with the dominant racial and socioeconomic group, whereas, in reality, it is spoken by people from diverse backgrounds. The common assumption that links language with a particular ethnicity has been problematized, as seen in research on world Englishes that explores diverse features of English used globally. Even in the context of advocating minority language rights, May (2005) questions the rigid language-identity nexus that is often used as a rationale for preservation of minority languages. May argues that this one-on-one link between language and ethnic identity ignores individual choice and cultural/linguistic hybridity. Going beyond the essentialist understanding of language to affirm the diversity of not only the forms but also the users of language constitutes an important aspect of critical multiculturalism in second language education.

Students' Experiences of Racialization and Racism

While racialized experiences of ESL/EFL teachers of color in the classroom and in employment indicate the serious need to address issues of social justice, students' experiences also demonstrate how racialization and racism affect their experiences both in and outside of the classroom. Some recent studies have used interviews and ethnographic observations to uncover students' experiences of oppression and resistance.

Students' Experiences of Racial Oppression

ESL students of color in U.S. schools often feel alienated because of their peers' unwelcoming attitudes or their teachers' insensitivity. Quach, Jo, and Urrieta (2009) demonstrate a typical example of how racism and assimilation pressure shape immigrant students' identities. The Asian immigrant students in their study felt isolated, different, and alone growing up in the U.S. South, which has been predominated by Black and White populations. Many of them had the experience of being called "chink" and "gook," made to hear karate shouts, or shown gestures of slanted eyes—a perpetual racist act that Shelley Wong (2006) experienced in the 1950s when she was growing up as a Chinese American (see also Motha, 2006). They felt great pressure to assimilate, to the extent that they avoided learning their home language. Some assimilated themselves to Whiteness by socializing only with White peers and simultaneously looking down on African American peers, while others who found their ethnic peers in college identified themselves as Asian and strived to maintain their Asian heritage.

Influence of Teachers on Students' Racialized Identity Formation

In the process of students' identity formation, some teachers transmit racist ideas and practices. Comments made in passing or attitudes that they display are not usually overt expressions of racism but reflect color-blind or new racism that are "subtle, institutional, and apparently nonracial," couched in remarks on cultural and linguistic difference (Bonilla-Silva, 2003, p. 3). Teachers often talk about racially and linguistically minority students as a group that is "lacking" certain dispositions, skills, and backgrounds, such as motivation, critical thinking, and family support. Although White teachers make their best effort to assist these students, their subtle condescending, patronizing, and non-accommodating attitudes, stereotyping racial minority groups, viewing students as having deficits, and being unable to relate to minority students all index hidden color-blind subtle racism.

May (1999) and Bonilla-Silva (2003), among others, argue that contemporary color-blind racism is characterized by the substitution of racial difference with cultural difference—a more neutral and acceptable term than the other. I would add, based on the previous discussion of the language/race nexus, that linguistic difference has also replaced racial difference in color-blind racism. Thus, cultural and linguistic stereotypes carry undertones of racial stereotypes, which further reflect a historical legacy of colonial discourse. The ways in which cultural/linguistic/racial stereotypes affect teaching and learning is demonstrated in an ethnographic study in an intensive university-level ESL program for international students in Australia (Ellwood, 2009). Ellwood describes how a teacher's preconceived idea that European students are more vocal and capable of critical thinking than Japanese students made her not notice Japanese students' participation and willingness to take part in class discussion. Here, the teacher's binary stereotypes about the two groups of students influenced her differential treatment of them and the ultimate (non)participation of the students in the classroom.

Racialization and Racism in Peer Relations

Racialization that students experience is also produced through peer relations. As mentioned earlier, the childhood memories of racial minorities demonstrate the emotional devastation caused by their peers' racist remarks positioning them as the racial *Other*. Peer racial Othering also occurs among ESL students themselves. For example, O'Neill (2000) reports conflicts among linguistic minority students. High-school students who came to the United States from Asia in elementary school recalled their experience of being called names by Latino boys. Having a racially and linguistically inferior status does not necessarily exclude these minority students from becoming perpetrators of racism.

Likewise, foreign language learners, who appear to be sensitive to racial/cultural/linguistic diversity, might exhibit racist attitudes toward immigrants. For instance, high-school students in the United States who have been learning Spanish as a foreign language since elementary school might still express xenophobic attitudes toward Latino immigrants in the local community (Kubota, 2001). This indicates a lack of attention to issues of race in foreign language teaching. The disconnect between foreign language learning and sociopolitical issues is reflected in the tendency of university students of foreign languages, especially beginning-level learners, to believe that learning a language does not invite them to reflect on issues of race, gender, class, and social justice (Kubota, Austin, & Saito-Abbott, 2003). Many of these students equate learning a foreign language with developing language skills only. Discussing complex issues entirely in the target language is undoubtedly difficult in beginning-level language instruction, so if such discussion is to take place, it has to be done in a language that students are competent in. Nonetheless, avoiding these issues would only perpetuate the status quo.

Students' Development of Racial Identities

While teachers and peers often position students in particular racial categories, students identify themselves with certain racialized groups. Whereas racialization by teachers and peers can be called *racial identification*, which refers to the crude classification of people into simplified racial groups, some students seek *racial identity*, which indexes an ongoing fluid negotiation of racial group membership (Pollock, 2004). Formation of racial identity is influenced by racial identification and racism; yet this process is not uniform. In a White-dominant society, individual students negotiate Whiteness—while some try to assimilate themselves into Whiteness (e.g., Quach et al., 2009), others maintain their ethnic identities through the use of their mother tongue at home and frequent visits to their native countries.

For instance, Ibrahim (2009) shows how African immigrant and refugee students in a Francophone high school in Canada invest themselves to *become Black* through adopting Rap and Hip-Hop culture and learn Black English as a second language. Bashir-Ali (2006) shows how Maria, a student from Mexico in a U.S. high school, chose to identify herself as African American through learning African American Vernacular English and socializing with African Americans. In this predominantly Black school, African American culture and language constitute the *cool* social norm, positioning African American students at a superior position to the status of ESL students, despite the fact that the instructional norm is standard White American English. The stigma attached to Mexican identity and the animosity between the majority African American students and the minority Mexican students made Maria take on an African American identity. Second language learners might seek to develop a marginalized cultural and linguistic identity, which is viewed as oppositional and cool. Identifying oneself with such a marginal norm that exists in opposition to the White middle-class norm can be viewed as a form of resistance.

These studies indicate that one's linguistic and cultural identity is fluid, unstable, and *performed* rather than predetermined, fixed, or aligned with the racialized image constructed by the dominant discourse. Judith Butler's (1999) notion of the performativity of gender identity can be applied to racial and linguistic identity formation. In this perspective, identity is viewed as a discursively constrained set of repeated acts to seek the idealized identity. Racial and linguistic identities are not pre-given based on perceived phenotypes or the language-ethnicity nexus—they are constructed by a set of repeated performed acts, although they are not arbitrary products of free will. Rather, they are discursively constrained by what is socially sanctioned and what is not. And yet, performativity allows the disenfranchised to perform subversive acts and appropriate the dominant identities, enabling the construction of fluid identities and meanings. Butler (1999) argues that "gender is always a doing, though not a doing by a subject who might be said to preexist the deed" (p. 33). Similarly, race and language are a doing; they are not based on pre-existing human categories or linguistic regulations (cf. Pennycook, 2004).

Critical Engagement in Racialization and Racism in Second Language Education

As reviewed above, recent studies in second language education have uncovered the painful effects of racism on the experiences of second language teachers and students of color within and outside of the classroom. Racial minority students' experiences of oppression are partly caused by racial/cultural/linguistic stereotypes that teachers uncritically support. While students are often racialized by others in schools, they also form their own identity in order to affiliate themselves with what they consider to be a *cool* racial group, which is constructed by a yet larger discourse about racialized social structures and attendant hierarchies. This indicates the need for an anti-essentialist approach to understanding racial identity. Moreover, the fact that students' second language learning experience or their linguistic minority status does not necessarily reduce racial/cultural/

linguistic prejudice indicates a need for explicit antiracist critically engaged pedagogies.

Based on these observations, I propose the following directions for second language education: (1) non-essentialist understanding of race, culture, and language; (2) explicit engagement in antiracist pedagogies; (3) critical scrutiny of teaching materials and curriculum; and (4) transforming practice at the administrative/institutional level.

Non-essentialist Understanding of Race, Culture, and Language

Many of us have been conditioned by the modernist/colonialist understanding that there is a one-on-one relationship between a group of people identified with a certain phenotype and a racialized category, as seen in commonly used racial/ethnic labels such as Asian, Black, Latino, and Middle Eastern. While the scientific community's consensus is that *race* does not exist as a biological category, it is a very real socially constructed marker used for classifying people. Because *race* is often masked by *culture* and *language*, the same fixed one-dimensional relationship is found in how a certain culture and language is defined. For instance, a rigid one-on-one relationship is created between Chinese culture and Chinese people or between Japanese language and Japanese people. However, the diverse, dynamic, diasporic, and hybrid nature of human societies indicates that such simplistic racial/cultural/linguistic categorizations of people are untenable. It is thus important for teachers to acknowledge the complexity and fluidity of racial, cultural, and linguistic categories, and liberate themselves from a fixed worldview conditioned by stereotypes. People are far more complex than we often imagine them to be.

However, this does not follow that differences should be ignored. Denying the fact that students belong to or want to belong to a certain racial/cultural/ linguistic group would lead to a color/difference-blind worldview. It is important to be aware that different groups are positioned relative to each other in a power hierarchy and do not stand on an equal playing field. Relying on a color/ difference-blind approach of equal treatment for everyone would merely perpetuate the existing relations of power. Instead, teachers should problematize inequalities and engage in situated ethics for establishing equity among groups.

It is also important to acknowledge the strategic uses of racial/cultural/ linguistic difference and their political significance. For instance, the concept of difference can be appropriated as strategic essentialism (Spivak, 1993), which enables a group of people who have historically been oppressed to reclaim their racial/cultural/linguistic difference as a unique identity. It is a form of resistance and its emphasis on distinct identities does not result from the imposition by the dominant group but rather symbolizes a political struggle of the marginalized to disrupt the status quo. Nonetheless, again, essentialism is a problematic aspect of such identity politics—it excludes and silences divergent voices that exist within the group (Collins, 1998). Thus, what is necessary is a constant critical reflection on the purpose and consequence of endorsing group differences through interrogating relations to power that inhere in those claims.

Explicit Engagement in Antiracist Pedagogies

Antiracist pedagogies take racism as an entry point and build "students' capacities to analyze and act on the ways all forms of discrimination/privilege (e.g., hetero/sexism, classism, Islamophobia) interlock in everyday interactions" (Taylor, 2006, pp. 524–525). Being aware of the politics of difference in various social categories, as well as the existence of overt and covert forms of racism, sexism, and classism, enables teachers to address issues of social injustices in many ways.

One way is to engage students in discussions at teachable moments when certain topics appear in learning materials (e.g., texts, visual images, audio information, vocabulary, expressions, grammar) or in students' daily experiences with their family, peers, and community (cf. Gutstein; Sharma, this volume). For instance, a racist comment heard in class can become an entry point to discuss questions such as: Do you all agree with the comment? Where does such a view come from? How would we feel if a derogatory comment was made about us? Can we create a society without prejudice? For what purpose do we strive to create such a society? In the discussion, a safe and open space should be created in order to engage students in a genuine dialogue about taken-for-granted assumptions (cf. Fitzpatrick, this volume). This can be done by having students construct their own ground rules, such as respecting diverse opinions, listening attentively, not dominating, and making sure to critique ideas rather than individuals (Kailin, 2002).

Another way is to develop explicit intervention activities. For instance, Hammond (2006) developed a simulation activity for university EFL students in Japan based on the "blue eyes/brown eyes" exercise that Jane Elliot conducted in 1968 with third-grade students in the United States—students were divided into favored and non-favored groups and had a firsthand experience of discriminating and being discriminated against. The purpose of the activity is to raise students' awareness of the effects of racism. Although this is a powerful experience, Hammond found it challenging to direct students' attention to covert or subtle forms of racism that are hidden in everyday interactions, such as complimenting on someone's skills or physical features that evoke racialized images, or encouraging them to directly confront racism without diverting to analogies with other forms of discrimination.

Another example is an ESL antiracism camp conducted in Canada for high-school students of ESL (Taylor, 2006). The camp sought personal, institutional, and societal transformation through developing students' ability to analyze and act on the ways in which racism and other forms of discrimination influence everyday experiences. Taylor (2006) documents significant changes in some students' awareness—a shift from an understanding of racism merely at the individual level to the recognition of institutional racism, and White ESL students' acknowledgement of their own White privilege (cf. Bartolomé, this volume).

Although these interventions are not a panacea for challenging various forms of social injustice, they provide a potentially powerful means to directly involve teachers and students in critical reflections.

Critical Scrutiny of Teaching Materials and Curriculum

While students are expected to develop antiracist awareness and attitudes, they are constantly exposed to racially biased textbooks and other materials. Taylor-Mendes (2009) asked EFL students and teachers in Brazil about their impressions of the visual images represented in the English textbooks that they were familiar with. The main impressions were that the United States is a country of White wealthy elites, Blacks are represented as poor and powerless, and racial divisions are geographically assigned, with no consideration of diversity and diaspora. While some participants took these images as a matter of fact, others voiced criticisms. In the context of foreign language education, similar trends have been found. Herman (2007) examined the countries, themes, and topics that appear in high-school Spanish textbooks commonly used in the United States. She found that the general images projected in these textbooks is that "everyone in the Spanish-speaking world is light-skinned and middle-class or upper middle-class" (p. 132) and that indigenous people are portrayed only as "part of happy festivals" (p. 137), rather than as constituting an integral aspect of Latin American culture and politics. Multicultural books for bilingual young children are no better—they treat superficial themes such as ethnic food, clothes, and shelter (Michael-Luna, 2009). Even a well-meaning text that deals with racism, drawing on Martin Luther King, Jr., forces students to take on either a White or Black identity—simplistic dual racial categories, which excludes the identities of Latino bilingual students (Michael-Luna, 2008). On the contrary, as Michael-Luna (2009) shows in the context of a first-grade bilingual class for students predominantly from Mexican origin, introducing counternarratives of Mexican leaders can create a powerful opportunity for students to develop positive ethnic identity through comparing the social impact of Mexican and American leaders (e.g., Cesar Chavez vs. Martin Luther King, Jr.).

As these studies suggest, teachers need to raise students' critical awareness of racial, gender, and class representations in textbooks and other materials and engage them in discussions of the discursive construction and sociopolitical consequences of these images. As Herman (2007) proposes, second language teachers can find alternative resources that provide students with multiple perspectives, such as those that focus on the lived experiences of real people from diverse backgrounds in terms of race, ethnicity, language, class, and gender. Furthermore, the entire curriculum should integrate minority/indigenous/marginalized voices and their histories for deeper cultural understandings and critical analyses of power embedded in the White-centric knowledge (Luke, 2009; cf. Bishop; Stewart, this volume).

Transforming Practice at the Administrative/Institutional Level

The majority of the teaching force in the United States is White. While there might be a higher percentage of non-White teachers in bilingual education, ESL and foreign language teachers are predominantly White. Furthermore, the majority of ESL teachers are monolingual English-speakers. In order to truly embrace racial, cultural, and linguistic pluralism and to make the campus a societal role model for students, schools, universities, and other educational institutions should make an effort to hire more non-White teachers from diverse cultural and linguistic backgrounds. Excluding nonnative speakers of English from the teaching force, as seen in a recent initiative in the state of Massachusetts, causes a detrimental effect on fostering antiracist awareness among students (Austin, 2009).

In teaching ESL/EFL, there is a prevailing discourse that supports the superiority of the native speaker—a label that masks White dominance. Although professional activities in the community of teachers tend to focus on the academic dimension (e.g., curriculum development, instructional improvement, and research), they also need to engage in activism in order to address social injustices and to transform the status quo.

Conclusion

Addressing racialization, racism, and other sociopolitical issues in the classroom is not easy because it could bring about uncomfortable feelings and defensive reactions (cf. Bartolomé; Hanley, this volume). Furthermore, addressing these issues might not always create the same symbolic meaning for students, because teachers and students in a specific context occupy different positions in a racial hierarchy of power. For instance, as Motha (2006) shows, when a White teacher strongly encourages non-White marginalized students to complain about the lack of their representation in a school newspaper, such supportive encouragement carries a significance of privilege, as it comes from an authoritative position of a White person who does not have to be afraid of losing her privilege by engaging in such subversive acts (Lin, Kubota, Motha, Wang, & Wong, 2006). Thus, many questions pertaining to racial/cultural/linguistic inequalities and essentialism often do not have a simple answer that applies to all individuals or all contexts, running counter to the current test-driven climate in education.

However, not addressing these issues merely perpetuates the painful feelings experienced by marginalized groups, the social structures that privilege the hegemonic group, and the knowledge tinted with the dominant group's worldview. To explicitly address these issues, we need to accept the unsettled pedagogical space of *unintelligibility* of not having a definite answer to questions (Ellwood, 2009). Although teachers are typically perceived as the knower, in this unsettled pedagogical space, they are learners of the marginalized yet fluid identities that the students bring, as well as the dynamic intersections of race, culture, and language. Thus, learning antiracist critical multicultural education is an ongoing process. This process requires teachers and students to reflect on their understanding of Self and Other, to negotiate conflicting meanings, acts, and identities, and to engage in teaching and learning for social justice with situated ethics.

Note

1 Linguicism is defined as "ideologies, structures, and practices which are used to legitimate, effectuate, and reproduce an unequal division of power and resources (both material and immaterial) between groups which are defined on the basis of language" (Phillipson, 1992, p. 47)

References

Austin, T. (2009). Linguicism and race in the United States: Impact on teacher education from past to present. In R. Kubota & A. Lin (Eds.), *Race, culture, and identity in second language education: Exploring critically engaged practice* (pp. 252–270). New York: Routledge.

Bashir-Ali, K. (2006). Language learning and the definition of one's social, cultural, and racial identity. *TESOL Quarterly, 40*, 628–639.

Bonilla-Silva, E. (2003). *Racism without racists: Color-blind racism and the persistence of racial inequality in the United States.* Lanham, MD: Rowman & Littlefield.

Bourdieu, P. (1991). *Language and symbolic power.* Cambridge, MA: Harvard University Press.

Butler, J. (1999). *Gender trouble: Feminism and the subversion of identity* (tenth anniversary edition). London: Routledge.

Collins, P. H. (1998). *Fighting words: Black women and the search for justice.* Minneapolis: University of Minnesota Press.

Curtis, A., & Romney, M. (Eds.) (2006). *Color, race, and English language teaching: Shades of meaning.* Mahwah, NJ: Lawrence Erlbaum Associates.

Ellwood, C. (2009). Uninhabitable identifications: Unpacking the production of racial difference in a TESOL classroom. In R. Kubota & A. Lin (Eds.), *Race, culture, and identity in second language education: Exploring critically engaged practice* (pp. 101–117). New York: Routledge.

Fujimoto, D. (2006). Stories through perceptual frames. In A. Curtis & M. Romney (Eds.), *Color, race, and English language teaching: Shades of meaning* (pp. 37–48). Mahwah, NJ: Lawrence Erlbaum Associates.

Hammond, K. (2006). More than a game: A critical discourse analysis of a racial inequality exercise in Japan. *TESOL Quarterly, 40*, 545–571.

Herman, D. M. (2007). It's a small world after all: From stereotypes to invented worlds in secondary school Spanish textbooks. *Critical Inquiry in Language Studies, 4*, 117–150.

Hill, J. H. (2001). The racializing function of language panics. In R. D. González & I. Melis (Eds.), *Language ideologies: Critical perspectives on the official English movement, Volume 2, History, theory, and policy* (pp. 245–267). Mahwah, NJ: Lawrence Erlbaum Associates.

Ibrahim, A. (2009). Operating under erasure: Race/Language/Identity. In R. Kubota & A. Lin (Eds.), *Race, culture, and identity in second language education: Exploring critically engaged practice* (pp. 176–194). New York: Routledge.

Kailin, J. (2002). *Antiracist education: From theory to practice.* Lanham, MD: Rowman & Littlefield.

Kubota, R. (2001). Teaching World Englishes to native speakers of English: A pilot project in a high school class. *World Englishes, 20*, 47–64.

Kubota, R. (2004). Critical multiculturalism and second language education. In B. Norton & K. Toohey (Eds.), *Critical pedagogies and language learning* (pp. 30–52). Cambridge, England: Cambridge University Press.

Kubota, R., Austin, T., & Saito-Abbott, Y. (2003). Diversity and inclusion of sociopolitical issues in foreign language classrooms: An exploratory survey. *Foreign Language Annals, 36*, 12–24.

Kubota, R., & Lin, A. (Eds.). (2006). Race and TESOL (special topic issue). *TESOL Quarterly, 40*(3).

Kubota, R., & Lin, A. (Eds.). (2009). *Race, culture, and identity in second language education: Exploring critically engaged practice.* New York: Routledge.

Lin, A., Kubota, R., Motha, S., Wang, W., & Wong, S. (2006). Theorizing experiences of Asian women faculty in second- and foreign-language teacher education. In G. Li & G. Beckett (Eds.), *"Strangers" of the academy Asian women scholars in higher education* (pp. 56–82). Sterling, VA: Stylus.

Luke, A. (1996). Genre of power? Literacy education and the production of capital. In R. Hasan & G. Williams (Eds.), *Literacy in society* (pp. 308–338). New York: Addison Wesley Longman.

Luke, A. (2009). Race and language as capital in school: A sociological template for language education reform. In R. Kubota & A. Lin (Eds.), *Race, culture, and identity in second language education: Exploring critically engaged practice* (pp. 286–308). New York: Routledge.

Mahboob, A. (2006). Confessions of an *Enraced* TESOL professional. In A. Curtis & M. Romney (Eds.), *Color, race, and English language teaching: Shades of meaning* (pp. 173–188). Mahwah, NJ: Lawrence Erlbaum Associates.

May, S. (1999). Critical multiculturalism and cultural difference: Avoiding essentialism. In S. May (Ed.), *Critical multiculturalism: Rethinking multicultural and antiracist education* (pp. 11–41). London: Falmer Press.

May, S. (2005). Language rights: Moving the debate forward. *Journal of Sociolinguistics, 9,* 319–347.

Michael-Luna, S. (2008). *Todos somos blancos/*We are all white: Constructing racial identities through texts. *Journal of Language, Identity, and Education, 7,* 272–293.

Michael-Luna, S. (2009). Narratives in the wild: Unpacking Critical Race Theory methodology for early childhood bilingual education. In R. Kubota & A. Lin (Eds.), *Race, culture, and identity in second language education: Exploring critically engaged practice* (pp. 234–251). New York: Routledge.

Motha, S. (2006). Racializing ESOL teacher identities in U.S. K-12 public schools. *TESOL Quarterly, 40,* 495–518.

Norton, B., & Toohey, K. (Eds.) (2004). *Critical pedagogies and language learning.* Cambridge: Cambridge University Press.

O'Neill, N. S. (2000). Multicultural, multiracial high school students' feelings toward Hispanic cultures. *Foreign Language Annals, 33*(1), 71–81.

Pennycook, A. (2004). Performativity and language studies. *Critical Inquiry in Language Studies, 1,* 1–19.

Phillipson, R. (1992). *Linguistic imperialism.* Oxford: Oxford University Press.

Pollock, M. (2004). *Colormute: Race talk dilemmas in an American school.* Princeton, NJ: Princeton University Press.

Quach, L. H., Jo, Y-J. O., & Urrieta, L. Jr. (2009). Understanding the racialized identities of Asian students in predominantly White schools. In R. Kubota & A. Lin (Eds.), *Race, culture, and identity in second language education: Exploring critically engaged practice* (pp. 118–137). New York: Routledge.

Rubin, D. A. (1992). Nonlanguage factors affecting undergraduates' judgments of nonnative English-speaking teaching assistants. *Research in Higher Education, 33,* 511–531.

Spivak, G. (1993). *Outside in the teaching machine.* New York: Routledge.

Taylor, L. (2006). Wrestling with race: Implications of integrative antiracism education for immigrant ESL youth. *TESOL Quarterly, 40,* 519–544.

Taylor-Mendes, C. (2009). Construction of racial stereotypes in English as a foreign language (EFL) textbooks: Images as discourse. In R. Kubota & A. Lin (Eds.), *Race, culture, and identity in second language education: Exploring critically engaged practice* (pp. 64–80). New York: Routledge.

Train, R. (2007). "Real Spanish": Historical perspectives on the ideological construction of a (foreign) language. *Critical Inquiry in Language Studies, 4,* 207–235.

Wong, S. (2006). Perpetual foreigners: Can an American be an American? In A. Curtis & M. Romney (Eds.), *Color, race, and English language teaching: Shades of meaning* (pp. 81–92). Mahwah, NJ: Lawrence Erlbaum Associates.

8

Critical Multiculturalism and Cultural and Media Studies

SANJAY SHARMA

Questions of identity, difference and representation have been key pedagogic concerns for both critical multiculturalism and cultural/media studies. The politics of teaching and knowledge continue to be central to their projects, especially through engagements with popular media culture and "diversity" (Grossberg, Nelson, & Triechler, 1992; McRobbie, 2005). The inclusion of texts marked by cultural diversity has attempted to transform a Eurocentric curriculum, and acknowledge the contested issues of "race" and difference. The new-found legitimacy of "minority/non-white" texts proffered by cultural/media studies has led to, for instance, the inclusion of Latin American literature, African-American hip-hop music, or diasporic South Asian film. These texts have been used to analyze racial power and whiteness, deconstruct identities, or offer modes of resisting domination. Alongside critical multiculturalism, cultural/media studies has shared a will to overcome liberal multicultural celebrations of diversity of ethnic others. However, the efficacy of cultural/media studies pedagogies which turn to "difference" has received little self-scrutiny: What are the limits of using "multicultural" texts? What kinds of student antiracist subjectivity (agency) is assumed? And what kinds of ethical encounters with "otherness" do critical multicultural pedagogies engender?

This chapter focuses on the critical multicultural praxis of cultural/media studies.[1] My approach considers the conjuncture of cultural/media studies, critical multiculturalism and critical pedagogy in relation to the challenge of pedagogically *engaging* with multiple forms of difference. I will contend that the charged arena of "race" and difference compels us to rethink the *agency* of the student, and the curriculum practices of representation and knowledge of otherness. While there has not been an orthodoxy in tackling questions of "race" and representation in these various educational disciplines, anti-essentialist and intersubjective theorizations of identity and difference have been particularly influential (Hall, 1997). What is of interest is that the frameworks of difference employed have not been sufficiently interrogated in relation to the question of student agency when encountering otherness.

As an example, this chapter considers the challenge of deploying the celebrated British-South Asian film *Bend It Like Beckham* (dir. Gurinder Chadha,

2002). It explores the *praxis* of a critical multicultural pedagogy by focusing on key ethical and political difficulties raised by utilizing this kind of "multicultural" cinema. The aim is to question pedagogic orthodoxies which valorize cultural difference, border crossing and representation at the expense of examining a politics of *alterity* (cf. Nealon, 1998). Alterity refers to the possibility that the differences of those marked as *other* can be ethically encountered, without the other being dominated or reduced to stereotypical representations. The educational turn to difference has scarcely considered on what *ethical* grounds otherness has been engaged, if at all. To *include, deconstruct,* and *re-present* the minority subject is confronted by the risk of domesticating their otherness (cf. Lea, this volume). Undertaking a critique of cultural/media studies approaches explores their potential limits, and offers alternative practices for an *alterity pedagogy*. My intention is to mobilize students towards an "ethical encounter" with difference, rather than demand that they acquire supposedly emancipatory antiracist knowledge about otherness.

Multicultural Diversity

In recent years, developments in cultural/media studies have been increasingly influenced by critical multicultural and feminist pedagogies' engagements with questions of difference (Sleeter & Delgado Bernal, 2004). In particular, the ascendancy of a *critical multiculturalism* has confronted the hegemony of a liberal multicultural education which continues to objectify otherness. The earlier antiracist critiques of the ideology of "cultural diversity" have been superseded by a "critical multiculturalism" which directly grapples with the *cultural* politics of identity, difference, and representation (May, 1999).

Homi Bhabha (1994) advanced an influential account for rethinking "cultural difference" against the pernicious liberal multicultural management of otherness. He contended that the ideology of "cultural diversity" seeks to control and repress cultural difference. The containment of difference constructs "cultural diversity" as an "object of knowledge," compelling it to be encountered as a category to be discovered, *observed, evaluated.* The appreciation and knowledge of *other* cultures, or the inclusion of cultural diversity in the curriculum is manifested as a difference against an invisible Eurocentric frame of reference. An example of this is a focus on the cultural characteristics of ethnic others—their food, clothes, rituals—without exploring how the norms of whiteness remain dominant.

In contrast, Bhabha locates the problem of cultures at their *boundaries,* at points of political conflict and crisis. The articulation of culture is possible because it is lived out through unfinished forms of representation. It is at the borders where these cultural practices are contested, and as a form of difference "gives rise to something different . . . a new area of negotiation of meaning and representation" (Bhabha, 1994, p. 211). Bhabha stresses the *conditions* in which a particular "culture" and "identity" *emerge* (and not their "contents" or "characteristics" which has been reified by the ideology of liberal multiculturalism; see May & Sleeter, this volume). It is the negotiations, dissonant exchanges, and struggles over power, which mark those conditions and inscribe particular differences that can inform a critical multicultural practice. Rather than simply focus on the characteristics of so-called "other cultures," the question of how these cultures come to *be known and represented as other* needs to be made clear (Sharma, 2008).

Pedagogy and Difference

The necessity of deconstructing cultural identity and its operations of power has been taken up by a number of critical educationalists. Bhabha's account of cultural difference has impacted on the development of a "border pedagogy" (see Giroux, 1994; Giroux & McLaren, 1994). Henry Giroux originally coined the term "border pedagogy" for redefining a radical educational praxis in order to attend to the shifting configurations of power and the complex discursive sites of identity formation.

Notably, a persistent criticism against the conceptually driven work of critical pedagogy has been its lack of application to the "messy realities" of teaching. Elspeth Probyn (2004) has complained about the difficulty of putting into practice some of the abstruse concepts of radical pedagogies. Critical pedagogy continues to be challenged by the "gap" between theory and classroom practice. For anyone who has experience of antiracist teaching, the repetition of the classroom incantation, "*race is a social construct*" has a dubious impact upon students' racialized subjectivities.

Stephen May has highlighted what is at stake for a "border pedagogy":

> students who can engage critically with all ethnic and cultural backgrounds, including their own. Such an approach would allow both minority and majority students to recognize and explore the complex interconnections, gaps and dissonances that occur between their own and other ethnic and cultural identities …
>
> (May, 1999, p. 33)

While there is no single pedagogical approach for realizing a critical multicultural practice, it is unsurprising that in cultural/media studies the work of "non-white" artists has been utilized as a *pedagogic* resource. Kobena Mercer (1994) has highlighted the cultural productions of British-Black/South Asian artists for opening up complex questions of identity, difference, and belonging (cf. Hanley, this volume).

Teaching with *Bend It Like Beckham*

By way of identifying a common critical multicultural cultural/media studies practice, it is productive to examine how an internationally popular film such as *Bend It Like Beckham* can be used to explore and deconstruct identity formation.

Over the last few decades, a significant number of British-South Asian films have been produced, including *My Beautiful Laundrette* (1985), *Bhaji on the Beach* (1993), and *Bend It Like Beckham* (2002). These films have achieved "mainstream" success, as well as receiving international critical acclaim. What makes these films distinct is their interrogation of diasporic "South Asian" cultural identity, by utilizing popular narrative formats, particularly a comedic genre. The films have not relied simply on countering or inverting "negative" Asian stereotypes circulating in dominant media culture, although what makes these diasporic films politically "ambiguous" is the use of "popular" film genre. Films such as *Bend It Like Beckham* operate ambivalently within, as well as struggle against, the master-codes of "race," ethnicity, and gender.

The plot of *Bend It* revolves around the female character, Jess (Parminder Nagra), a 17-year-old British-Asian living in West London, yearning to become a professional women's soccer player, alongside her white friend, Jules (Keira Knightley). The contention of the film is that Jess's family do not share this desire and wish her to attend university, train as a medical doctor, and marry as so-called "tradition" dictates. Much of the source of comedy is based on Jess deceiving her parents and continuing to play soccer against their demands.

The director, Gurinder Chadha, avoids depicting a patriarchal South Asian family environment or a despotic father, which have been common stereotypes of such families. In some respects, the generational tensions between Jess and her parents are those experienced by many young people. The director attempts to present a nuanced representation of the family, which is sympathetic to the parents as well as celebrating Jess's autonomy and right to choose her destiny. Chadha's intent is to depict a young British-Asian female who is alienated from neither her South Asian "roots," nor British culture. The familiar "clash between cultures" thesis of young South Asians unable to negotiate their so-called *traditional* home environment with the *modern* British (white) ways of life is contested in the film.

Bend It Like Beckham offers a plethora of composite representations of difference and ethnicity. The use of comedy, however, highlights the film's ambivalent status when operating in the terrain of a racialized popular culture. "Ethnic humor" raises the question whether dominant white audiences are laughing along *with* "minorities" or *at* them (Sharma, 2006b). While most comedies necessarily trade on forms of stereotypes as sources of humor, Chadha is aware of presenting a diversity of South Asian identities, which capture everyday nuances of living in an urban multicultural space. For instance, Jess's gay friend, Tony (Ameet Chana), and sister, Pinky (Archie Panjabi), are characters who express the multifarious and sometimes conflicting desires of youth.

In particular, the film's sexual politics seeks to contest the confines of an "appropriate" femininity for both Jess and Jules. While its ideology of sexual difference is open to further contestation in terms of how lesbian sexuality is utilized as a central narrative device, lesbianism ultimately remains marginalized. After prying relatives mistakenly spot Jess being overtly affectionate with Jules in the street, Jess's parents conclude that their daughter is a lesbian, which would bring disrepute upon the family. Similarly, Jules's aspirational white working-class mother considers soccer as wholly unfeminine, and also believes her daughter is a lesbian after eavesdropping upon a heated conversation between the two young women. From a critical standpoint, arguably the film sidesteps undertaking an exploration of lesbian sexuality. Moreover, as reported in subsequent interviews with cast members, a lesbian storyline between the two main protagonists was originally planned, whereas in the final narrative it is reduced to a source of innuendo and humor.

The *repressed* lesbianism of the text may lend itself to reinforcing it as a deviant subjectivity in the face of the continuing hegemony of heterosexuality in popular (South Asian) culture. However, more than one interpretation of this film is possible. To accuse the film of offering a suspect sexual politics limits its alternative registers of meaning. Notably, *Bend It Like Beckham* was one of two films selected for the "Outstanding Film" category in the 15th Annual Gay & Lesbian Alliance Against Defamation (GLAAD) Media awards in Los Angeles.

Thus, the point of offering a critique of *Bend It* is not simply to admonish the film's sexual politics. Rather, it is to valorize the grounds upon which a critical multicultural pedagogy could be performed. One of the intentions of the film's representational strategies was to promote a diversified set of identities which *pluralize* Asian subjectivity, outside of a discourse of positive/negative images (Hall, 1997). Nevertheless, a pedagogy exploring the film's politics of identity can conclude that the repressed lesbianism of the film was a missed opportunity for opening up the identity-differences of minority South Asians. The film may be considered to have failed to explore lesbian sexuality at a discursive level, and even buttress a heterosexual matrix (Fitzpatrick, this volume). Moreover, by offering such a critique, a critical pedagogy could further deconstruct South Asian subjectivities by opening up the question of alternative racialized sexualities.

Deconstructing "Race" and Identity?

A deconstructive reading of *Bend It Like Beckham* offers a means for teaching to grapple with the contradictory grounds of identity and racialization. However, this kind of critical practice also incites the problem of textual ambiguity for pedagogies of representation. That is, *more than one* interpretation of the film is possible, and a pedagogy of *Bend It* easily falls prey to advancing a de rigueur counter-hegemonic reading which pursues the hybrid, contested identity-differences of minority subjects (cf. May & Sleeter, this volume). What can remain foreclosed is *why* such interpretations of the film arise in the first place, and *what students do* with such knowledge about racialized others. It is worth probing Hall's (1997) influential essay, *The Spectacle of the Other*, as it continues to exemplify the potential "limits" of critical "race" work in cultural/media studies.

Hall interrogates the representational practices of racial otherness circulating in contemporary culture. He acknowledges that the question of representation "engages feelings, attitudes and emotions and it mobilizes fears and anxieties in the viewer" (Hall, 1997, p. 226). His analysis of racial imagery is framed by the proposition "that meaning can never be finally fixed" (p. 270). The practice of "trans-coding"—the counter-strategy of challenging existing racialized representations in the making of new possible meanings—is understood in terms of the insight of the plasticity of meaning.

Hall offers an example of the politically indeterminate nature of Robert Mapplethorpe's photography of black gay men, as emblematic of how *interpretation* and *judgment* pervade the reading of contradictory racialized representations. Notwithstanding that his stress on the indeterminacy of meaning is located in extant social struggles, the limit of such an approach is that the *exposition* of the ambivalences of racialized textual meaning-production has become a dominant *pedagogic* mode of engagement. In terms of cultural studies classroom practice, there is an implicit assumption that by problematizing the representations of difference, students are offered the "correct" analytical tools to explore and contest dominant racialized imagery. What is *pedagogically* underplayed is not only the grounds on which knowledge-production—a particular interpretation, judgment or exposition—takes place and *why*, but also *what* this knowledge about otherness "can *do*".

Eve Sedgwick (1997, p. 3) claims that critical practices are governed by an "extraordinary stress on the efficacy of *knowledge per se*". Exploring how dominant ideologies are contradictory, meanings unfinished or that identities are discursively constructed, gives no guarantee of producing emancipatory knowledge effects. Orthodox *practices* of critical multicultural pedagogy in cultural/media studies have paid scant attention to activating alternative "ethical" engagements with otherness that surpass extant frameworks of knowledge and representation.

The Politics of Alterity

There exists a gap between conceptualizing an "ethical encounter" and its concrete realization. Ethics has traditionally belonged to the realm of Western philosophy and a fundamental issue has been how "difference" as "Otherness" has been conceived. Following thinkers such as Foucault (1984), the ethical can be grasped not as a universal prescriptive set of moral principles or foundational rules by which to abide. The Occidental quest for Western knowledge outside of itself—the process of incorporating the other—has been structured by an epistemic violence. Notably, the emergence of cultural studies has turned to "otherness," not as a philosophical inquiry for Western knowledge, but to Europe's "actual others," forged by a history of violent colonial encounters (Chow, 1998). Nevertheless, a problem remains that the "actual other" is entangled with the philosophical Other of knowledge. Thus, the difficulty of posing the apparently Eurocentric question of "can we know the other?" conflates actual others, with Otherness as a marker of the limit of Western knowledge.

However, it does not follow that there can be no encounter with the actual other, outside of domination. Yet, nor does this mean that the alterity of the actual other can be wholly "known" within existing regimes of power/ knowledge. For instance, when Edward Said (1987) declared that the "Orient does not exist," he was pointing to the "im/possibility" of representing a specific historical minority subject outside of a discourse of Orientalism. An "actual other" refers to a social agent whose own difference or *alterity* has been historically subordinated. If a critical multicultural pedagogy is to address this subordination, it must engage the alterity of the other (Nealon, 1998), outside of a pedagogical relationship of appropriation, domination, or assimilation. Engaging alterity is not an easy activity, and requires rethinking student agency and moving beyond only representational forms of knowledge about otherness.

Christopher Falzon (1998) highlights the im/possibility of the ethical as a socially *grounded* relation through a notion of "social dialogue". Encounters with others are historically forged and an inescapable fact of human existence. Forms of ordering and domination emerge when social dialogue is *arrested* in the attempt to domesticate the other (which is incomplete, else the other as an actual social being would not exist). However, appropriation or domination are not the only types of encounters that are possible. While encounters with the other involve judgment and the imposition of categories, this "is not a final under-standing, but only the beginning of an open-ended process" (Falzon, 1998, p. 93). Dominant ways of knowing are not absolute, but historically specific because they have emerged from encounters with others in the first place. It means that ongoing social dialogue allows the possibility of the transformation of these frameworks, leading to "new forms" and *ethical* "ways of knowing". Mary Louise Pratt's account of "contact zones" usefully elaborates these encounters: "social spaces where disparate cultures meet, clash, and grapple with each other in often highly asymmetric relations of domination and subordination" (Pratt, 1992, p. 4). She points to the frissons of difference and its everyday realities, which can be mutually enriching for different groups.

As noted earlier, border pedagogies of cultural studies advance intersubjective theorizations of identity formation. However, the notion of identity that these pedagogies of difference work from has been unable to resolve the challenge of otherness (Grossberg, 1994). Intersubjective accounts of identity highlight the relationality of all identities, vis-à-vis a dependency between self and other: an identity relies on the othering or *negation* of difference—what it is not—to secure its self-certainty: "I'm straight (because I'm not gay)" (Brown, 1995). The interdependence on the other has led to an understanding that identities are in constant negotiation with other differences, and cannot be complete in them-selves. In the roll call of identity differences, "race, gender, class, sexuality...," we are left with an "exasperated etc."—an excess of difference. This excess (incompleteness) seemingly haunts identity (Nealon, 1998).

Intersubjective identity is founded on a "lack of wholeness" or a certain kind of "failure" to be whole: otherness is required in order for the subject (self) to be complete. But this is not possible because of the excess of difference, there-fore we share this "lack," and it is this groundlessness, which supposedly struc-tures all forms of identity. Identity or more precisely, *agency* of the subject is founded upon this "lack." The "logic of identity" cannot adequately respond to alterity (Nealon, 1998). Thus, a fundamental educational challenge for a criti-cal multiculturalism is, as Cameron McCarthy (1998, p. 92) writes, "defining iden-tity in ways other than through the strategy of negation of the other." He highlights that the "paradox" of requiring otherness—the dis/avowal of difference—can lead to *ressentiment* rather than an increased tolerance of others.[2]

If we return to the analysis of the film *Bend It Like Beckham,* arguably the repressed lesbianism of the film is not just an ideological shortcoming of the text, but is symptomatic of identity being predicated upon the agency of the student as being structured by a lack. Yet, how can the agency—as lack—of the student be mobilized to encounter the alterity of the "Asian-other"? It is not the case that a representational pedagogy of difference is simply flawed in reading *Bend It.* Rather, such a teaching practice finds it difficult to activate an ethical encounter with "Asian" alterity because it cannot overcome the excess of difference, yet presents the other's differences as already knowable for antiracist teaching. The pursuit of deconstructing South Asian identity by pluralizing or complicating its ethnic, sexual, or class differences, or valorizing a radical lesbian subject position, does not necessarily undermine the structure of Orientalism, which continues to govern how the South Asian subject is made into an ethnicized object of knowledge (e.g., passive, feminized, or exotic). Within the discourse of Orientalism, the Asian subject can be no more than its identitarian ethnicity, however much we may attempt to explicate, proliferate its differences, or complicate its representations in the classroom (Sharma, 2008; Sharma & Sharma, 2003).

Alterity Pedagogy

There is no easy method of realizing an alterity pedagogy, because there is no simple solution to overcome existing relations of power and representation, both inside and outside the classroom setting. Nevertheless, we can begin by engaging with how student agency can be *mobilized* otherwise, beyond merely presenting them with knowledge and meaning about otherness (Probyn, 2004). Student agency can be grasped as a site (set of places) in which specific affective investments can be articulated and enabled: "how one can and does invest, and where and how one is empowered, made into an agent" (Grossberg, 1993, p. 101). The task is to struggle over the articulation of places and students' affective investments in a bid to move or "win them over"—by *mobilizing* their desires (Giroux, 1993)—to another set of places or sites of investment.

An alterity pedagogy encourages students to encounter difference from standpoints that interrogate the frameworks of understanding being used in the classroom. For example, instead of asking whether the film *Bend It Like Beckham* positively (or negatively) portrays South Asian culture, we can inquire what repertoire of representational frameworks are available for encountering this "culture." Similarly, instead of focusing on how the film is challenging (or reinforcing) notions of "tradition" in South Asian culture, we can consider how and why "tradition" is attached to other cultures. Therefore, the focus shifts from "knowing" about other cultures. A more productive practice involves rethinking what is *un/knowable* about the other.

Elizabeth Ellsworth (1992) raises the challenge of what is "unknowable" in relation to the production of classroom knowledge. Her contentions highlight the multiplicity of alternative ways of knowing, which cannot be wholly rendered by existing curricula master discourses. She suggests that pedagogic practices are confronted by and contingent upon the "outside," that which lies beyond existing frameworks of (representational) knowledge. This points to an open-ended pedagogy which seeks to make connections and mobilize students' affective investments, rather than compelling them to acquire "emancipatory" knowledge about otherness by occupying prescribed "antiracist" subject-positions—a practice which more than often "fails." What teachers may experience as silence, resistance, or the cynical-knowing student is indicative of the refusal of a pedagogy implicitly governed by a demystification of the other. As Simon (1992) suggests, knowledge production in the classroom needs to exceed merely asking whether the meanings of a text are ideologically suspect or racist, for example.

The *irreducibility* of the multiplicity of classroom knowledges points to a pedagogy of *Bend It Like Beckham* that does not seek to produce *more* knowledge about what it means to be a British Asian. Neither would it make the unknowable something that is a function of what is already, or can be, known. An ethical encounter is a site-specific event, often fleeting and momentary. And an alterity pedagogy is haunted by the *im/possibility* of its encounter with otherness outside of domination. Thus, a challenge for critical multiculturalism is to *activate* the conditions for such events, and to resist the institutionalization of practices which ultimately reify or explicate the other.

In more concrete terms, and against the drift towards a rational packaged curriculum and measurable learning outcomes (see also Locke, this volume), students would be encouraged to be exploratory, and creatively *make* and *multiply* connections beyond their everyday common-sense experiences and knowledge—connections which may appear unexpected, anomalous or even aberrant (Grossberg, 1994). This could involve something as modest as students writing (or role playing) alternative endings, or gathering and inventively responding to reviews of the film. We could explore and experiment by deploying *Bend It Like Beckham* in a manner that juxtaposes illegitimate or unexpected knowledges about difference. It may create possible transformations of the self through ethical openings towards otherness—a risky venture for *both* the teacher and student. The contradictions of the text would be a point of departure, rather than only a point of contestation. It would be a practice that neither seeks closure nor is determined by a single strategy or method.

Conclusion

The pedagogic challenge of multiple differences necessitates moving beyond (though not abandoning) representational teaching strategies that only pursue struggles over meaning or accentuate the textual ambivalences of racialized and gendered representations. The ethical provocation of alterity has been met by a curious silence by critical multiculturalism and cultural/media studies, even with all their zeal for student-centered libratory educational practices. However, to claim that an alterity pedagogy can simply escape the ideological markers of identity would be at best naive, and at worst, in danger of erasing the forces of difference, desire, and power.

A critical multicultural pedagogy for alterity seeks to activate the affective investments of students by making connections that offer the potential of other ways of living with difference. It would be an experimental and *risky* practice, likely to unleash the dissonances, contradictions, and conflicts in the teaching of "race." Why should we expect the antagonisms of "race" and "culture" not to be also played out in our classrooms? Moreover, because there is no general other (only specific subordinated social agents), it follows that there is no universal pedagogy for alterity. An attempt to prescribe a methodology in advance fails to consider that an ethical encounter is a *site-specific* production of social relations. An alterity pedagogy is a transformative critical multicultural practice which attempts to create the *conditions* for pursuing the ethical: a practice of the im/possible.

Notes

1 This chapter is based on earlier work; see Sharma (2006a, 2006b, 2008).

2 The Nietzschean term of *ressentiment* is usefully elaborated by Brown as follows: "it delimits a specific site of blame for suffering by constituting sovereign subjects and events as responsible for the 'injury' of social subordination. It fixes the identities of the injured and the injuring as social positions" (1995, p. 27).

References

Bhabha, H. (1994). *The location of culture.* London: Routledge.

Brown, W. (1995). *States of injury: Power and freedom in late modernity.* Princeton, NJ: Princeton University Press.

Chow, R. (1998). *Ethics after idealism.* Bloomington and Indianapolis: Indiana University Press.

Ellsworth, E. (1992). Why doesn't this feel empowering? Working through the repressive myths of critical pedagogy. In C. Luke & J. Gore (Eds.), *Feminisms and critical pedagogy* (pp. 90–119). London: Routledge.

Falzon, C. (1998). *Foucault and social dialogue.* London: Routledge.

Foucualt, M. (1984). Space, power, knowledge. In P. Rabinow (Ed.), *The Foucault reader* (pp. 239–256). New York: Patheon.

Giroux, H. (1993). Reclaiming the social: Pedagogy, resistance and politics in celluloid culture. In J. Collins, H. Radner, & A. Collins (Eds.), *Film theory goes to the movies* (pp. 37–55). London: Routledge.

Giroux, H. (1994). *Disturbing pleasures: Learning popular culture.* London: Routledge.

Giroux, H., & McLaren, P. (Eds.). (1994). *Between borders: Pedagogy and the politics of cultural studies.* New York: Routledge.

Grossberg, L. (1993). Cultural studies and/in new worlds. In C. McCarthy & W. Crichlow (Eds.), *Race, identity and representation in education* (pp. 89–105). London: Routledge.

Grossberg, L. (1994). Introduction: Bringin' it all back home—pedagogy and cultural studies. In H. Giroux & P. McLaren (Eds.), *Between borders: Pedagogy and the politics of cultural studies* (pp. 1–28). London: Routledge.

Grossberg, L., Nelson, C. & Triechler, P. (Eds.). (1992). *Cultural studies.* London: Routledge.

Hall, S. (1997). The spectacle of the 'other'. In S. Hall (Ed.), *Representation: Cultural representations and signifying practices* (pp. 223–290). Milton Keynes, England: Sage/Open University.

May, S. (1999). Critical multiculturalism and cultural difference: Avoiding essentialism. In S. May (Ed.), *Critical multiculturalism: Rethinking multicultural and antiracist education* (pp. 11–41). London: Falmer.

McCarthy, C. (1998). *The uses of culture: Education and the limits of ethnic affiliation.* London: Routledge.

McRobbie, A. (2005). *The uses of cultural studies*. London: Sage.

Mercer, K. (1994). *Welcome to the jungle: New positions in black cultural studies*. London: Routledge.

Nealon, J. (1998). *Alterity politics: Ethics and performative subjectivity*. London: Duke University Press.

Pratt, M. L. (1992). *Imperial eyes: Studies in travel writing and transculturation*. London: Routledge.

Probyn, E. (2004). Teaching bodies: Affects in the classroom. *Body & Society, 10*(4), 21–43.

Said, E. (1987). *Orientalism*. London: Penguin.

Sedgwick, E. (1997). Paranoid reading and reparative reading; or, you're so paranoid, you probably think this Introduction is about you. In E. Sedgwick (Ed.), *Novel gazing: Queer readings in fictions* (pp. 1–37). London: Duke University Press.

Sharma, S. (2006a). Teaching diversity: Im/possible pedagogy. *Policy Futures in Education, 4*(2), 203–216.

Sharma, S. (2006b). *Multicultural encounters*. London: Palgrave.

Sharma, S. (2008). Teaching representations of cultural difference through film. In M. Pollack (Ed.), *Everyday antiracism: Getting real about race in school* (pp. 186–190). New York: The New Press.

Sharma, S., & Sharma, A. (2003). White paranoia: Orientalism in the age of empire. *Fashion Theory, 7*(3/4, double issue: Fashion & Orientalism), 301–318.

Simon, R. (1992). *Teaching against the grain: Texts for a pedagogy of possibility*. London: Bergin & Garvey.

Sleeter, C., & Delgado Bernal, D. (2004). Critical pedagogy, critical race theory, and anti-racist education: Implications for multicultural education. In J. Banks & C. Banks (Eds.), *Handbook of research on multicultural education* (2nd ed.) (pp. 240–258). San Francisco, CA: Jossey Bass.

III
Critical Multiculturalism in Mathematics/Sciences

9

Critical Multicultural Approaches to Mathematics Education in Urban, K-12 Classrooms[1]

ERIC GUTSTEIN

Critical multiculturalism and *critical mathematics* (or *mathematics for social justice*) have several common aspects. These include an acknowledgment of the importance of culture in education (in all its complexity and contestedness); a "critical" perspective on relations of power; and a commitment that education should prepare students to critique, challenge, and question the existing social order so that they can participate in the struggle for a more just world. In this chapter, I focus on the latter two and describe our critical mathematics theory and practice in an urban public high school in Chicago.

I draw heavily on Paulo Freire, who left us many things from which to learn. Foremost is that education explicitly needs to serve the people, standing firmly with the oppressed against capitalism and neoliberalism (1994, 1998, 2004). Though Freire acknowledged that education alone could not change society, he believed that social transformation was impossible without education. For him, education needed to be for liberation rather than for domination and submission—its current function in urban U.S. schools (and elsewhere). His terms, *reading the world*, or developing a deep sociopolitical consciousness of relations of power and the genesis of structural oppression, and *writing the world*, or taking one's own destiny into one's hands to make history, are useful ways of framing education's relationship to social reality.

Second, he argued that teachers and students need to be partners, learning from each other, including in anticolonial, independence struggles (e.g., Guinea-Bissau, Freire, 1978), adult literacy campaigns (e.g., Brazil, Nicaragua, and Grenada, Freire, 1994), and schools (e.g., São Paulo, and the United States, Freire, 1993; Freire & Macedo, 1987). Teachers should view students as allies in common struggles for social justice; this perspective echoes the long history and tradition of African American education for liberation (Anderson, 1988; Perry, 2003; Siddle Walker, 1996; Woodson, 1933/1990).

Third, he saw history "as possibility" (1994, 1998, 2004). By this he meant, "the future does not make us. We make ourselves in the struggle to make it" (Freire, 2004, p. 34). He argued that humans are *conditioned*, but not *determined*, by structural and institutional forces. That we are conscious of that conditioning means we can transcend it. He believed that human "unfinishedness" implied our constant search for deeper understanding and social and individual transformation.

Fourth, Freire deeply appreciated what he called "popular knowledge," the knowledge of the "popular classes" (1978, 1994). His writings are full of vignettes of how he learned from workers, peasants, fisherpeople, and other "ordinary" people. He came to understand the limitations of his own class position and the meaning of "class suicide" (1978), and to appreciate the perspectives, analyses, values, beliefs, and hopes of the oppressed (1994). In discussing his work, he wrote:

> In the beginning of my work, my surprise in the face of the critical positions assumed by these unschooled workers arose from the perception that I had up to that time that these were positions held exclusively by university students. My surprise had its origin in my own class position, increased by my university training—perhaps, to be more accurate, I should say by my elitist university training.
>
> (1978, pp. 116–117)

Freire believed that educational programs needed to build on this community knowledge. He argued "the starting point for organizing the program content of education or political action must be the present, existential, concrete situation, reflecting the aspirations of the people" (1970/1998, p. 76). In his work, these contexts were uncovered by studying the people's *generative themes* (the dialectical interrelationship between key social contradictions in their lives and how they understand and interact with them). Teachers in various settings have developed curriculum from such themes (Camangian, 2006; Freire, 1993; Gandin, 2002; O'Cadiz, Wong, & Torres, 1998).

Finally, although Freire's work covered many other ideas, a central one was that political experiences are essential to develop political consciousness, and this conscientization is key to learning to read—or to do mathematics. People's involvement in political struggles and social movements can lead to deeper understandings of relations of power and how people themselves make history. Furthermore, and dialectically, this increased awareness can then lead to more involvement in and commitment to transforming society. Since Freire was involved in literacy campaigns in which people were learning to read both the *word* (acquire textual literacy) and the *world*, a fundamental question was: Why should people learn to read—or, in our case, to do mathematics?

Freire's (1970/1998, 1978, 1994; Freire & Macedo, 1987) experiences in Brazil, Guinea-Bissau, Chile, and Nicaragua taught him that the response was related to how people understood the political necessity to be literate. Commenting on Brazil's literacy campaigns, he wrote, "between acting in an area where popular consciousness was still buried and one where popular rebellion was visible, we did not hesitate in choosing the second" (1978, p. 111). The relationship of political engagement to the demand for literacy was clear: "In Brazil ... literacy in rural areas ... made sense only to those within the peasant population who were involved in situations of conflict and who saw within them one more tool for their struggle" (p. 112). Others concurred. Describing a 1975 UNESCO study on literacy, Freire & Macedo (1987) wrote: "the relative success of literacy campaigns evaluated by UNESCO depended on their relation to the revolutionary transformations of societies in which the literacy campaigns took place" (p. 108). Freire believed that people develop sociopolitical consciousness through acting to change society. He described Nicaragua after the Sandinista revolution:

> Literacy in ... Nicaragua started to take place as soon as the people took their history into their own hands. Taking history into your own hands precedes taking up the alphabet. Anyone who takes history into his or her own hands can easily take up the alphabet. The process of literacy is much easier than the process of taking history into your own hands, since this entails the "rewriting" of your society. In Nicaragua the people rewrote their society before reading the word.
>
> (Freire & Macedo, 1987, pp. 106–107)

How is this relevant to U.S. urban mathematics education? Freire worked mainly with adults—volunteers, in economically developing countries, on literacy campaigns, with no high-stakes tests, and with curriculum created from learners' generative themes. In contrast, we work with youth in a Chicago public high school—mostly not volunteers, in an "advanced" capitalist country, on mathematics, with high-stakes tests, and mostly with curricula irrelevant to our students' lives. What can we learn from his experiences and from those who have tried to actualize his theory, and how can we apply this to our contexts? In the rest of this chapter, I address these questions. My understanding of how to enact critical mathematics involves engaging youth in political experiences similar to those that Freire found important in learning to read and write the world.

First, some caveats—this is not to "import" Freire. He consistently argued this was impossible, that the particularity of local contexts was fundamental. As he put it, "In order to follow me it is essential not to follow me!" (Freire & Faundez, 1992, p. 30). "Reinventing" Freire (his word) means to concretely analyze one's own specific conditions. Second, Freire did not write much about certain contradictions in Brazil, let alone in the United States. Several African American scholars (e.g., Haymes, 2002), while upholding Freire, noted his lack of analysis of racism in Brazil (the country with the second largest number of people of African descent). None doubted Freire's commitment to antiracist politics, but his overall focus on social class and oppression, and lack of attention to racialization, seem problematic. At the very least, in the United States, we have to turn elsewhere on these issues (see May & Sleeter, this volume). For me, the history of African American education for liberation is a major source of inspiration, theoretical clarity, and practical direction (Anderson, 1988; Harding, 1990; Perry, 2003; Siddle Walker, 1996; Watkins, 2001; Woodson, 1933/1990). Third, some have critiqued or extended Freire's treatment of gender (Weiler, 1991), although bell hooks (1994) and Freire himself (1994, 2004) clarified that his weaknesses reinforce the notion of human unfinishedness. Finally, Freire's scathing condemnations of capitalism and neoliberalism (1994, 1998, 2004) dealt more with ideology than structure; he wrote little about political economy, which, for me, is essential to understanding sociopolitical contexts. Those points notwithstanding, as we try to grasp his theory and how it emerged from and guided his practice, Freire is extremely important for developing political orientation for our U.S. urban work and for critical multiculturalism more generally.

Teaching Mathematics for Social Justice: Providing Opportunities for Political Experience

I have worked with Chicago public schools for the last 15 years, first for 10 years with Rivera elementary school (a pseudonym), in a low-income Mexican immigrant community where I taught seventh- and eighth-grade mathematics for four years (one class a year, as part of how I defined my work as a university professor). For the past five years, I have worked with a new high school in a similar community whose students are 30% African American and 70% Latino (mainly Mexican), and 98% low income. That school is the Greater Lawndale/Little Village School for Social Justice (called "Sojo"). I support the mathematics teachers, work with students, develop critical mathematics curriculum, and co-teach social justice mathematics projects (ranging from a few days to two weeks). As I write this (July 2009), I just finished teaching a twelfth-grade class in which all contexts that students studied and from which they learned mathematics were real-world ones related to their lives. In both settings, I studied the process as it unfolds, with students and teachers as coresearchers (Gutstein, 2006, 2007, 2008).

Briefly, I understand critical mathematics education to be when teachers and students collaborate to afford students opportunities to read and write the world with mathematics (Brantlinger, 2005; Frankenstein, 1987; Gutstein, 2006). These ideas derive largely from how I interpret Freire's work and African American liberatory education. My goals include that students learn both mathematics and about the world. They should develop deep sociopolitical consciousness of their immediate and broader contexts and see themselves as capable of changing the world. In the process, they should develop strong cultural and social identities, be rooted in who they are as a people, and develop the confidence to stand up for their beliefs. They should learn rich mathematics so that they have opportunities to study, pursue meaningful lives, and support their families and communities, but even more, to use mathematics to fight injustice and improve society. Finally, we want students to realize that mathematics has real meaning in life and can *specifically* be used to read and write the world.

I am well aware that at Sojo and Rivera, I am an outsider to the local neighborhoods, languages, and cultures. However, I am a close outsider because I have substantive experience in such communities, and I consciously try to stand in solidarity with the people there. Nonetheless, teaching for social justice is complicated enough, and attempting it with "other people's children" (Delpit, 1988)—crossing lines of social class, race, age, gender, culture, language, ethnicity—is even more complex. Although I do not have space here, this is important to my story (see Gutstein, 2006).

My data suggest that the above goals can be partially realized—that is, youth can *begin* the process of reading and writing the world with mathematics, while learning mathematics—but the work is complicated, slow, and difficult. At Sojo, there is evidence that the school's first graduating class (June 2009, about 75 students) normalized critical mathematics. This is not surprising, given that the school attempts to provide a "social justice" education, although that means diverse things for different teachers, administrators, students, and parents. But it is also because since that class entered Sojo, the teachers and I taught critical math projects. Students may have learned about social justice ideas across the curriculum, but they only encountered critical mathematics in their math classes. And although we spent perhaps only 10–15% of our time on two to four such projects a year, these were evidently sufficiently meaningful and memorable that, in focus-group interviews with the majority of the grade, no student reported it unusual to consider "mathematics as a weapon in the struggle for social justice."

Critical Mathematics Projects—Examples and Lessons

When the school's first graduating class was in tenth grade, students completed two critical mathematics projects, including "Reading Hurricane Katrina with Mathematics." It began: "This is an investigation into Hurricane Katrina [in August, 2005]. The main question we are asking is: What story can mathematics tell us about what happened with Hurricane Katrina—and who did it happen to and why?" Students examined demographic data and pictures of displaced African Americans who were trapped in the Superdome (a sports stadium). The project asked, "This picture looks like only African Americans were in the Superdome, so maybe only African Americans lived in New Orleans. Is that true? Or maybe they were the only ones who stayed/got left behind? We will investigate these questions." The assignment's final part was:

> Now that you've done all this investigation, it's time to pull together the story that your data tell. Write a good, solid essay explaining your analysis of Hurricane Katrina on the people of New Orleans. You *must* use mathematical arguments from your work here and create one (or more) *well-labeled* graphs to present your data/mathematical arguments. Here are some questions to help you:
>
> a) What data are most convincing and what do they tell you? Why are these data convincing to you?
> b) How do the data help explain the story? Could there be other explanations?
> c) What other data would you need to know or do you want to know? What questions do *you* have?

Using a confusing *New York Times* graph, students had to understand that the ratio of *poor-African-Americans-with-no-car* to *poor-whites-with-no-car* was relevant and key to arguing why more African Americans numerically and proportionally were stranded than whites. Students' essays were emotional, strongly worded, but uneven analytically. They generally argued mathematically, but with some errors and weaknesses.

Gregory, an African American male, wrote:

> The most convincing piece of data was that it was 3.2 × more likely to be a poor black in New Orleans than white. This basically tells me that it is more likely for you to see a poor black than a poor white [in the Superdome]. This data is the most convincing because I saw a lot of this on TV. This helps to tell the story because when you look at the pictures, that is all you see.

Mirella, a Latina, who did a lot of careful mathematical analysis, wrote:

> Mathematics helped me make a realistic picture, how many black people were left behind because they didn't have any type of transportation. I think using math was an amazing way [of] dealing with huge problems around the world. You could use mathematics for almost anything in the everyday world. Projects like this keep people aware [of] what's going on.

These responses are typical of students' writings on critical mathematics projects. An obvious goal is that students build coherent defensible arguments using, but not limited to, mathematical analyses. This takes time because students have rarely been taught how to do this. Yet we see evidence of it in Sojo students' writings. We also recognize that teachers need to provide students opportunities to see and critique others' mathematical arguments, while being explicit that students need to develop the capacity to do so themselves.

We began the 2007–08 school year (when the just-graduated students were juniors) with a two-week project about the criminalization of youth of color, specifically about the *Jena Six*, six African American male high-school students from Jena, Louisiana (a small town in the southern United States). In December 2006, they were initially charged with attempted murder in a schoolyard fight that developed out of a racist incident a few months earlier, when white students hung three nooses in a tree on school grounds (reminiscent of lynchings of African Americans). The first of the six (Mychal Bell) was tried and convicted by an all-white jury in June 2007 and awaited sentencing in September 2007, the beginning of the school year. Our focus question was: Given Jena's demographics (85.6% whites; 2,154 adults), what was the probability of randomly choosing an all-white (12-person) jury for Mychal Bell? After students completed the project, on Mychal Bell's sentencing day, about 40 walked out of school and organized an impromptu solidarity protest on a nearby street corner. This happened when they discovered that a local black college was holding a rally, but the school principal was unable to satisfy their demand for a bus to the rally.

This project resonated strongly with students because of its core themes: racism and the criminalization of youth of color. Jena may be 1,500 miles from Chicago, but the experiences of Sojo students, who live in a community with an astoundingly high incarceration rate, could not be closer. Furthermore, the issues impacted teachers as well. Although we only planned to teach the project in eleventh grade (at the time, the oldest grade in the school), Sojo's two other math teachers modified the project and taught it to their ninth- and tenth-grade classes. On Mychal Bell's sentencing day, before students walked out, the principal held a school-wide assembly to address student concerns. Sojo's administrators each noted that students had learned about Jena through their mathematics classes. Thus, this particular politicization moment for the whole school came through learning mathematics—unusual, to say the least.

This investigation helped some students connect mathematics to a political analysis—an explicit goal. When the seniors were in tenth grade, I formed a group to work as math and social justice advocates and co-researchers (the "crew"). On our way to a conference where the crew taught the project to mathematics teachers and others, we had a conversation. During the session, someone asked the students about their views. One (Rut) responded:

> we were in the car. And Mr. Rico [what students call me] asked us, "What did we think about this case." And I said I thought it was racist because he got an all-white jury out of a possibility of it being 15 percent. And then he said, "Well what if somebody else got an all-white jury, would that be racist?" And I was like, ok, well then that brings up more things … and I was like, well with his background, that the nooses were hung on the tree after the Black kids sat under the tree and all that, then—that's what makes the case seem racist, and the fact that the percent was only 15 of him getting an all-white jury.

Rut went on to explain that when she first heard that Jena was 86% white, it seemed quite reasonable that his jury was all white. But when she learned the probability of that occurring randomly was only 15%, it took her back. It made her rethink her assumptions and bring in sociopolitical and historical contexts to conclude that racism played a factor. This integration of mathematical and political analysis, in examining social reality, is a central aspect of critical mathematics.

Conclusion

If, as Freire argued, political experiences can lead to political consciousness, then is student participation in critical mathematics such an experience? Consider what Vero, a crew member, said in a 2008 focus group discussion:

I've learned to question how and why. Mr. Rico told me that I was just giving people the mathematical answers [when the crew taught projects to adults]. I went from questioning things in math to questioning things in life. Now I question everything and everyone. [I asked: Why?] Because we're taking [pause] regular math and implementing it, we use our knowledge to address other issues that affect others, people of color, low-income people, etc.

A little later, in describing life in Sojo's two neighborhoods, she added:

The reason why some people act so aggressive is not because that's how we are, but because that's how we are meant to be because of what's happening to us. So like all the police and stuff, all these [local] North Lawndale shootings, Little Village shootings, another shooting, another kid dead, or something like that, it's just that that was led by something else. It's just not, people don't just pop out with a gun and start shooting. It's because something is going on that is leading people to do certain things. It's not a way of excusing it, but it's a way of addressing the question: Why?

I argue that Vero exemplified Freire's (1970/1998) point, "No oppressive order could permit the oppressed to being to question: Why?" (p. 67). Her developing political consciousness is related to her experiences in teaching adults at crew presentations about using mathematics to study injustice, as well as to her critical mathematics classrooms. These opportunities have influenced her to begin to question both mathematical ideas and subsequently (or perhaps simultaneously) political ones. This year (2008–09), she and 20 other seniors were in the "math for social justice" class I taught, where our whole focus was on studying social reality, using and learning college-preparatory mathematics. In that class, students explicitly and continuously learn to read and write the world through mathematics. As Channing, one crew member wrote:

Reading and writing the world with mathematics is to look at important issues that we are faced with in the world and try to understand them using mathematics. It is to try and have a bigger picture of why and how things may have gone wrong or why there are injustices in certain situations. With mathematics, things can become more clear, especially when dealing with situations that are based on quantity or the amount of something or somebody. Once we understand these things, we take it out to the world. We use our knowledge to let others know what we know. We do this because too many of the problems in this world are happening with our people. We have looked at so many injustices that are done to our people. We want our people to know what is being done to them and what they can do to avoid these things from happening. We want them to be able to collectively think of some solutions to the issues that they are faced with.

These experiences are political, because they are about questioning the status quo, relations of power, roots of injustice, as well as about envisioning and taking action. These are goals of critical education, generally, and critical multiculturalism, specifically. Framing mathematics as a weapon in the struggle for social justice explicitly politicizes mathematics education in particular, and school in general. Freire (1978) wrote of the clear choice between working with people whose consciousness "was still buried ... [as opposed to] where popular rebellion was visible" (p. 111). One has to create opportunities for youth to be involved in political experiences and social movements, in appropriate and various ways, both directly and vicariously.

The mathematics curriculum at Sojo and Rivera and the crew's activities are political experiences, fitting for youth in urban U.S. schools. Critical mathematics is, in Perry's (2003) words, "linked to and address[es] one's status as a member of a historically oppressed people." It positions learning mathematics as a liberatory tool that provides students with deeper understandings of Hurricane Katrina, racial profiling, conditions of immigrant agricultural workers, disparity in mortgage rejection rates, wealth inequality, the cost of the Iraq War, the impact of different world map projections, gentrification, and many other issues that we studied. These matter to Sojo and Rivera students because of the righteous anger and powerful sense of justice that they bring into the classroom due to their location in an oppressive society. Furthermore, the projects at times give them ways to begin to see themselves as agents of change, whether through demonstrating in support of the Jena Six, attending city hall hearings about displacement, teaching adults about critical mathematics, or just coming to know that, although they have the capacity to do so, their prior schooling has not prepared them to read and write the world.

Some students at Sojo understand that they have been profoundly "miseducated" (Woodson, 1933/1990) in U.S. schools that prepare them mostly for low-skill service-sector jobs, prison, the military, or the grave (Lipman, 2004). In North Lawndale (the African American community), the mathematics is grim—two males for every three females, because, to quote one male student from the community, "all the brothers [Black men] are locked up or in the ground." This realization of their incomplete, mis-education—which one student, Charles, wrote about on a project, "It makes me feel like I was lied to all these years"—is related to what a farmer in postcolonial Guinea-Bissau told Freire: "Before [liberation], we did not know that we knew. Now we know that we knew. Because we today know that we knew, we can know even more" (Freire & Macedo, 1987, p. 114). Rigoberto spoke to this well, on a project about different world map projections:

> I feel as if someone was trying to take advantage of me as a student. That just because I am a student, that I should believe anything that I was told.... The project really made me think more about the information being provided in many schools. I now start to question the material being taught. I really enjoyed doing the project because now I can think about maps and their differences. I can also see the differences in peoples' different point of views. I can imagine what other people think and see about how the globe and world really is.

This broader consciousness, gained through the political experiences of reading and writing the world with mathematics, will be necessary for Rigoberto, other Sojo students, and youth like them to become effective change agents in the larger historical motion. Their critical mathematics education *can* contribute to this process. I end this chapter with Rogelio's words, also a crew member:

> Before this [the crew], everything was like a black and white picture. I just went to school, like I was a student soldier doing the same thing over and over, just went to school, came home, did my homework and didn't care about anything. But now, when I started doing this, everything started getting full with color, being understanding and getting ideas and not just learning the same things, but pushing it to the limit into what a person can do and actually understanding what's really going on in the world.

Note

1 All names are pseudonyms except student "crew" members.

References

Anderson, J. (1988). *The education of Blacks in the south, 1860–1935.* Chapel Hill: University of North Carolina Press.

Brantlinger, A. (2005). The geometry of inequality. In E. Gutstein & B. Peterson (Eds.), *Rethinking mathematics: Teaching social justice by the numbers* (pp. 97–100). Milwaukee, WI: Rethinking Schools, Ltd.

Camangian, P. (2006, March 30). *Transformative teaching and youth resistance.* Talk given at DePaul University, Chicago, IL.

Delpit, L. (1988). The silenced dialogue: Power and pedagogy in educating other people's children. *Harvard Educational Review, 58,* 280–298.

Frankenstein, M. (1987). Critical mathematics education: An application of Paulo Freire's epistemology. In I. Shor (Ed.), *Freire for the classroom: A sourcebook for liberatory teaching* (pp. 180–210). Portsmouth, NH: Boyton/Cook.

Freire, P. (1970/1998). *Pedagogy of the oppressed* (M. B. Ramos, Trans.). New York: Continuum.

Freire, P. (1978). *Pedagogy in process: The letters to Guinea-Bissau* (C. St. John Hunter, Trans.). New York: Continuum.

Freire, P. (1993). *Pedagogy of the city* (D. Macedo, Trans.). New York: Continuum.

Freire, P. (1994). *Pedagogy of hope: Reliving pedagogy of the oppressed* (R. R. Barr, Trans.). New York: Continuum.

Freire, P. (1998). *Pedagogy of freedom: Ethics, democracy, and civic courage* (P. Clarke, Trans.). Lanham, MD: Rowman and Littlefield.

Freire, P. (2004). *Pedagogy of indignation.* Boulder, CO: Paradigm.

Freire, P., & Faundez, A. (1992). *Learning to question: A pedagogy of liberation* (T. Coates, Trans.). New York: Continuum.

Freire, P., & Macedo, D. (1987). *Literacy: Reading the word and the world.* Westport, CN: Bergin & Garvey.

Gandin, L. A. (2002). *Democratizing access, governance, and knowledge: The struggle for educational alternatives in Porto Alegre, Brazil.* Unpublished doctoral dissertation. Madison: University of Wisconsin.

Gutstein, E. (2006). *Reading and writing the world with mathematics: Toward a pedagogy for social justice.* New York: Routledge.

Gutstein, E. (2007). Connecting *community, critical,* and *classical* knowledge in teaching mathematics for social justice. *The Montana Mathematics Enthusiast, Monograph 1,* 109–118.

Gutstein, E. (2008). Developing social justice mathematics curriculum from students' realities: A case of a Chicago public school. In W. Ayers, T. Quinn, & D. Stovall (Eds.), *The handbook of social justice in education* (pp. 690–698). New York: Routledge.

Harding, V. (1990). *Hope and history: Why we must share the story of the movement.* Maryknoll, NY: Orbis.

Haymes, S. N. (2002). Race, pedagogy, and Paulo Freire. *Philosophy of Education,* 151–159.

hooks, b. (1994). *Teaching to transgress: Education as the practice of freedom.* London: Falmer.

Lipman, P. (2004). *High stakes education: Inequality, globalization, and urban school reform.* New York: Routledge.

O'Cadiz, M., Wong, P., & Torres, C. (1998). *Education and democracy: Paulo Freire, social movements, and educational reform in São Paulo.* Boulder, CO: Westview Press.

Perry, T. (2003). Up from the parched earth: Toward a theory of African-American achievement. In *Young, gifted, and black: Promoting high achievement among African-American students* (pp. 1–108). Boston: Beacon Press.

Siddle Walker, V. (1996). *Their highest potential: An African American school community in the segregated south.* Chapel Hill: University of North Carolina Press.

Watkins, W. (2001). *The white architects of black education.* New York: Teachers College Press.

Weiler, K. (1991). Freire and a feminist pedagogy of difference. *Harvard Educational Review, 61,* 449–474.

Woodson, C. G. (1933/1990). *The mis-education of the Negro.* Trenton, NJ: Africa World Press.

10
Digital Stories for Critical Multicultural Education
A Freireian Approach

JAMES C. McSHAY

Introduction

Liberal conceptions of multicultural education continue to be very popularly held in a majority of teacher education programs throughout the United States (Kincheloe & Steinberg, 2002; McLaren, 2000; Sleeter & Grant, 2003). Many critical multicultural scholars have strongly criticized these programs with regard to the ways in which their curricular and pedagogical practices have had a very limited impact on helping prospective and practicing teachers develop critical literacies surrounding identity, difference, and power and their relationship to understanding unequal educational outcomes for K-12 students based on their social identities. Against this backdrop, the push for teacher education programs to also prepare students to acquire digital literacies for the new information age and understand how to infuse them across a range of academic content areas has greatly intensified (Kim, Sharp, & Thompson, 1998; Rasmussen & Norman, 1998).

Out of these often-times separate discourses in teacher education, new questions have emerged about how digital learning technologies can be harnessed effectively to support the production of critical literacy-based learning outcomes for teachers and their students (see also, Locke, this volume). These questions tend to reflect the concerns of Shulman (1986), who expressed the need for teacher educators to ensure that there is always a purposeful, substantive, and synergetic connection between content and pedagogical knowledge. Even though an increasing amount of scholarly literature has highlighted collaborative efforts occurring between these two areas within teacher education (Damarin, 1998; Gorski, 2001; McShay & Leigh, 2005; Sleeter & Tettagah, 2002), it is still unclear what are ways in which pedagogical frameworks grounded in critical multicultural theory can be used to conceptualize and develop the types of technology-based learning tools often introduced to students. It is my contention that without an understanding of the theoretical tenets of critical multicultural pedagogy and how they can be methodically reflected in the design and implementation of technology-based learning applications, technology-mediated learning will continue to be under-theorized and poorly conceptualized, often used in classrooms as a means of drill and practice rather than for substantive meaning-making.

In this chapter, I explore how one such technology-based application, "new media narratives," more commonly known as digital stories, can be used as a learning tool to promote Paulo Freire's conception of critical pedagogy. Using a Freireian lens, I am interested in how these media-based narratives can create powerful learning opportunities for teachers to develop new critical perspectives about how U.S. history, ideology, and its institutions work to shape their own self-knowledge, social location, and societal participation, and also impact understandings about teaching and learning in K-12 schools. In an effort to carry out this exploration, this inquiry will be guided by the following questions: How can an analysis of Paulo Freire's use of the dialogical method of inquiry with oppressed African Brazilians in the mid twentieth century help us to understand how to build critical literacy? How can this inquiry method be a central consideration in the design of digital stories? What specific elements and uses of digital stories align most effectively with the dialogic method? And finally, what are potential learning implications for critical and digital literacy development as it pertains to transformative multicultural teacher preparation and multicultural classroom teaching?

What Are Digital Stories?

There is a growing body of literature about digital stories and their use in education (Lambert, 2007; Ohler, 2008; Robin, 2008). According to Ohler (2008), digital stories rely on relatively inexpensive personal forms of digital technology that use an array of media such as video, music, computer-generated graphics, and narration to construct a coherent three- to five-minute narrative. Typical uses of digital stories in education classrooms include the development of personal narratives, historical documentaries, or instructional presentations (Robin, 2008). Lambert (2007) has identified seven essential elements of digital stories which will be elaborated in detail later in this chapter: point of view, a dramatic question, emotional content, personal voice, soundtrack, economy, and pacing (refer to Table 10.1). What typically differentiates digital stories from other multimedia-based applications is that the student user has complete creative license in its development, similar to how a screenwriter, producer, or computer programmer makes design decisions in her or his respective areas of work.

Digital stories' use of visual and textual images aids in making abstract concepts easier to interpret, therefore enhancing student acquisition of new knowledge (Robin, 2008). Also, the students' voice plays a central role in the development of the digital story, resulting in a potentially profound impact on their learning (Robin, 2008; Kajder, 2004). In support of this claim, Ohler explains the following:

Table 10.1 Seven Main Elements of a Digital Story

Elements	Description
Point of View	Students' stories are constructed from their own experience and understanding; highly values personal expression
A Dramatic Question	Student poses a compelling question that evokes interest and commitment
Emotional Content	Digital stories are designed in ways that incite emotion and reaction from the audience
Gift of Your Voice	Considered to be an essential element, students' voice can convey personal meaning and purpose in a way not fully achieved by other elements
Power of the Soundtrack	Students can use music or lyrics to help add complexity and depth to the narrative
Economy	Students intentionally limit the amount of visual imagery and audio, and special effects as a way to communicate more effectively the intended meaning
Pacing	Students regulate the story progression as a way to enhance audience comprehension and interest

Source: Lambert (2007).

As students hear themselves via recorded media for the purpose of listening, self-assessment, and rewriting and/or speaking or recording—the re-narration process, the power of hearing oneself for self-assessment purposes can't be underestimated. It's as though the process of getting words out of one's head and out in the open air exposes them to a quality of critique not available within the confines of one's internal landscape, even if the only people reviewing the narratives are the authors themselves.

(p. 58)

Ohler's comments are significant with regard to the learning benefits of "new media narratives," as well as other digital learning tools, due to how they work to situate the learner in a context that maximizes opportunities for critical analysis and interpretation. Barab, Hay, and Duffy (1998) refer to this form of learning as "grounded constructions." This idea is driven by the belief that student learning can be facilitated in ways that help them to develop complex understandings about a particular problem or issue, if properly grounded within an inquiry-based context. Within this conceptual frame, I contend that digital stories can achieve two goals: first, to construct experiences for prospective teachers as well as their students that enable them to examine how historical, ideological, and institutional forces work to shape identity as it relates to race, gender, class, religion, language, and ability, and how these influence teacher decision-making; second, to develop a process for enhancing their proficiency in technology use and integration. In an effort to better understand how to achieve these educational outcomes, I will focus my discussion on the influential work of Paulo Freire

(Freire, 1972, 1974; Shor & Freire, 1987; see also Gutstein, this volume), who was concerned with helping members of historically oppressed groups acquire tools for developing a social consciousness that would lead to political action. This exploration will help to illuminate new possibilities for using digital stories in ways that help educators to acquire a critical literacy of education, which is necessary for enacting a K-12 curriculum that is equitable and liberatory.

Freire's Brazil and Critical Literacy

Paulo Freire, a Brazilian philosopher, scholar, and activist has written extensively about how historically situated economic, political, and social structures and practices have collectively subjugated African Brazilians, therefore, creating their present-day social reality (Freire, 1972, 1974; Shor & Freire, 1987). In an effort to help Blacks create a more equitable and just reality for themselves, Freire sought to help them develop literacy skills and simultaneously construct a critical awareness of the ways in which the governing elite regulated their access to the larger Brazilian opportunity structure. He advocated that to become literate both mechanically (read and write) and critically (social awareness) are essential skills for one to gain full participation in a democratic society (cf. Locke, this volume). Freire articulated the following about the meaning of literacy:

> [As a narrative for agency], literacy becomes synonymous with an attempt to rescue history, experience, and vision from conventional discourse and dominant social relations. It means developing the theoretical and practical conditions through which human beings can locate themselves in their own histories and in doing so make themselves agents in the struggle to expand the possibilities of human life and freedom.
>
> (Freire & Macedo, 1987, p. 10)

Many scholars have referred to this attempt to help members of oppressed groups and their political allies rescue history, experience, and vision within an educational context as a form of critical pedagogy. Giroux (cited in Duarte & Smith, 2000) explains that pedagogy is removed from its exclusive emphasis on management and is defined as a form of political leadership and ethical address (p. 199). Kincheloe and Steinberg (2002) seek to expand upon the goals of critical pedagogy within a learning context. They suggest that teachers should be able to help students overcome social barriers by engaging the students in the exploration of different ways of critically examining their work, methods of resisting oppression, and vision of progressive democratic communities. The goal of critical educational approach is to prepare students to see themselves as sites of political struggle in relation to oppressive and democratic forces, and move them to a recognition of the forces that shape their identity, the various stages of reflective self-awareness, and the strategies their personal empowerment demand (Kincheloe & Steinberg, 2002; see also Gutstein, this volume).

Freire's use of critical pedagogy was best exemplified with his work using Culture Circles to help African Brazilian workers and other poor working-class adults not only learn how to read and write but to break the psychological and material chains that held them in a economic and social purgatory. Culture Circles grew out of an Adult Education project of the Movement of Popular Culture in the 1950s. Freire referred to this project as Culture Circles instead of schools because he wanted to challenge the discursive meanings and practices that convey conceptions of authority and dominant epistemologies often promoted by schools. This notion about the need to resist the oppressive language of schooling was also reflected in how the roles of teacher, students, and their practices were constructed. In this instance, teachers were referred to as coordinators, students were called group participants, and the method by which they interacted was called dialog. This method, Freire termed it dialogic inquiry, created a context for group participants to meet to reflect on their reality as they make and remake it (Shor & Freire, 1987, p. 98). It was through this process of dialog that Freire sought to help Blacks interrogate critical forms of knowledge and understandings about their own historical reality and acquire tools for dismantling oppressive structures and practices firmly embedded in Brazilian life and society.

The question remains, how does the history of African Brazilians and Freire's use of Culture Circles help to offer new perspectives about how digital stories can be used as tools of pedagogy of critical literacy?

Freireian Perspectives About Digital Technology

Freire's aforementioned dialogical inquiry process provides a framework for understanding how technology can play a role in supporting pedagogies that create opportunities for emancipatory learning. According to Sleeter and Bernal (2004), there are four major components of Freire's dialogical process:

1 Supports a pedagogy of empowerment in which the teacher acts as a partner with the students;
2 Uses problem posing as a way to help students critically examine their own experience and historical location;
3 Students are creators of knowledge and their classroom practices reflect democratic ideals;
4 Class materials are used as tools for expanding students' analyses.

All four of these components were reflected in the pedagogies Freire used in his adult literacy project in Brazil, not only as a means to help African Brazilians learn to read and write, but to develop a critical understanding about their own social reality. In order to support and enhance learning, Freire introduced the use of slide projectors in these Culture Circles. Freire showed participants in the Culture Circle, via the slide projector, images depicting their communities and used them to facilitate critical exchanges about how their identities and experiences were mediated by various ideological, institutional, and historical forces.

Moreover, tied to this analysis, were dialogs that helped form the foundation for learning about phonemics, grammar usage, and syntax. According to Kahn and Kellner (2007), Freire viewed the use of technology as essential in helping to foster a collective learning environment and amplify reflective distancing (p. 435). His prescient understandings about technology use is reflected in the work of Gorski (2001), written nearly 50 years later, who asserted that digital learning technologies can be powerful tools that support collaborative teaching and learning, and student mastery of skills and acquisition of knowledge, all of which are key components of effective critical pedagogy.

Another major goal of technology use within the Culture Circles was to build capacity for political agency within African Brazilian communities. Kahn and Kellner (2007) elaborated the following regarding Freire's vision for technology use as a way to support this form of critical learning: "He argued for the importance of teaching media literacy to empower individuals against manipulation and oppression, and of using the most appropriate media to help teach the subject matter in question" (p. 435). Whereas Freire's notions about ways technology can be used to support critical education are clear, it too, should be understood that he was keenly aware of the propensity for technology to be used as a tool for domination and dehumanization (Freire, 1972). More specifically, Freire envisioned how technologies (both analog and digital) would help reproduce and sustain Brazil's social and economic class structure. As a way to assist in this process of economic stratification, the governing elite situated matters concerning technology within a depoliticized discourse by solely hailing its remarkable ability to advance the economic development of Brazil. Therefore, notions about the value of technology use, shaped by globalism and in the name of market dominance, would likely continue to only benefit a wealthy few at the expense of the majority who were poor and working class (cf. May & Sleeter, this volume).

Freire's views about the social consequences of technology help to shed light on the challenges of successfully creating technology-facilitated learning experiences for students that are both equitable and emancipatory. In order to meet these challenges, teachers must create ways for students to systematically couple pedagogies of critical multiculturalism and technology education as to bring about a transformed critical literacy in these areas. Toward this end, I argue that digital stories are one such possibility for helping educators to enact teaching that is emancipatory and technology facilitated.

Dialogic Inquiry and Digital Stories

Understanding how Freire's dialogic method of inquiry can be embedded in the design structure of digital stories creates new possibilities for helping teachers to acquire a critical literacy of education, which is necessary for enacting a school curriculum that is equitable and emancipatory for K-12 learners. As displayed in Figure 10.1, elements of digital stories (DST) and critical pedagogy (CP) can be aligned in ways that simultaneously support learning in critical multiculturalism and technology education. Each oval represents how learning aspects of

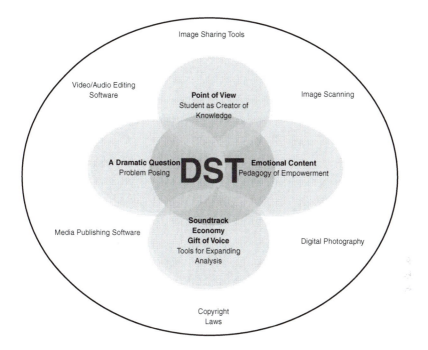

Figure 10.1 CP Elements Reflected in Digital Stories.

critical pedagogy can be achieved through the typical design structure of digital stories. The outer area represents various digital tools or computer-related topics teachers will become familiar with as they create a digital story project. The question remains as to what is the conceptual relationship between these aligned elements, as well as how they translate into instructional goals within multicultural teacher education and teacher practice. The following discussion highlights ways that digital stories can be used to reflect the key elements of a Freireian critical pedagogy, consonant with a wider critical multiculturalism.

Student as Creator of Knowledge/Point of View

A central goal of Freire's dialogic method is to create opportunities for students to examine their own positionality and understand the ways in which one's social reality impacts views about self, others, and society. A corresponding goal, referred to by Lambert (2007) as *Point of View*, allows the student to situate his or her experience within the center of the story and use it as point of critique and analysis. I contend that this particular use of digital stories can help develop teachers' capacity for critical self-reflection. According to King and Baxter Magolda (2005), underlying dimensions of critical self-reflection center on how one understands one's beliefs, values, and sense of self, and uses these to guide choices and behaviors. Furthermore, they assert that another dimension of critical self-reflection is how one views oneself, in relationship to and with other people, and makes choices in social situations (p. 574).

Digital stories can help students develop critical self-reflective orientation in ways that would have important implications for critical literacy in education. Acquiring a critical self-reflective orientation would help students to develop a flexible belief system that would support their ability to adapt to diverse social and cultural situations (King & Baxter Magolda, 2005). This way of thinking can help learners resist using an ethnocentric lens to interpret various social realities (see also, Flynn; Lea, this volume). Instead, a self-reflective individual can often suspend judgment and "try on" a new perspective in an effort to broaden one's own understanding about a particular condition or circumstance.

Incorporating digital stories into a cooperative learning activity, students can collectively explore and analyze one another's stories as a way to broaden one's own perspective. Presenting multiple perspectives to the student creates new opportunities for them to facilitate learning of complex knowledge with regard to an issue or problem related to critical literacy. When students are able to examine multiple viewpoints, it encourages reflection upon their own belief structures and supports the development of respect and appreciation toward beliefs that are divergent from their own (Pang, 2004). This quality is an essential building block for engaging in critical literacy.

Problem Posing—A Dramatic Question

According to Shor and Freire (1987), dialogical inquiry must emerge directly from the lived experience of students which are mediated by their own economic, political, and cultural realities. Moreover this method uses students' personal stories as pedagogy to assist them in identifying problems, issues, and themes central to understanding factors that affect their own societal participation. A main goal is for students to construct questions that will work to illuminate new pathways for challenging and resisting practices that seek to limit their potential and maintain the status quo. Freire referred to this concept of problem posing as generative thematics. Petersen (cited in Darder, Baltadano, & Torres, 2003) explains the following:

> A generative theme is an issue or topic that catches the interest of students in such as way that discussion, study, and project work can be built around it. Themes may come from an incident in a particular student's life, a problem in the community, or an idea that a student latched onto from the media, the news, or a classroom activity.
>
> (p. 368)

Self-exploration, guided by a compelling and thought-provoking question, or as Lambert (2007) refers to them, *A Dramatic Question*, is often the cornerstone of digital stories. Questions that stem from students' exposure to societal discourses such as poverty, hate crimes against members of the lesbian, gay, bisexual, and transgender community, gang violence, and interracial dating, can prompt critical personal exploration of one's own class, sexual, peer, and race identities. Using Freire's problem posing approach in digital stories can create a context for generating and examining personally meaningful questions that impact understandings about the deployment of identity and how it is implicated in school leadership and community involvement.

Emotional Content—Pedagogy of Empowerment

As described earlier in this chapter, Freire's use of the dialogic inquiry method in his literacy project with African Brazilians in the mid twentieth century was critical in helping them not only to learn how to read and write, but also to gain the political skills necessary for dismantling structures that oppressed them. I argue that the most significant achievement of Freire's approach was his participants' engagement in collective action as a way to alter positively their social reality. This notion for teachers and students to make an emotional investment and commitment to engage in social action is not an expectation in their traditional school roles and activities. This emotional investment is exemplified in teachers feeling compelled to dream about the promise of a true democracy, and uses their leadership role in schools to direct efforts that work toward that dream (Gale & Densmore, 2003; Shor & Freire, 1987; cf. Fitzpatrick; Flynn, this volume). For teachers to be strong advocates of equity and social justice, their emotions, not just their knowledge base, must be developed. Goodman (2001) comments on this notion further:

> Meaningful social justice education is inherently an emotion-laden process. For students to be connected to the content, there needs to be an emotional link. For them to stay engaged in a process of growth and change, we need to help them work through their feelings. We can intentionally structure into the class or workshop opportunities for people to appropriately deal with their emotions.
>
> (p. 39)

The *Emotional Content* element of digital stories can be an effective way to process one's feelings about a social issue or topic for both the story composer and the audience member. A carefully constructed story can raise awareness about a social issue or concern, compel individuals to dream of their role in creating new socially just realities, and possibly act in ways to help realize their dreams. I argue that affective learning approaches can have a potentially strong impact on one's engagement in critical literacy with respect to the teaching and learning process. Using digital stories can catalyze dialog about questions such as: What perspective did you gain after viewing the story and how did it help you to see things differently? How did that make you feel? What unanswered questions do you have? How do I feel about this issue now and how might that change? Facilitating discussions, either among students in the classroom or among prospective teachers, that incorporate responses to these questions can promote opportunities for personal growth, change, trust, and friendship.

Tools for Expanding Critical Analysis—Voice/Soundtrack/ Economy/Pacing

Freire referred to his use of technology with his adult literacy project in Brazil as liberatory media (Kahn & Kellner, 2007). While working with African Brazilians, Freire was able to use analog media to provide authentic representations of their social realities in ways that incited them to question their world and compelled them to engage in liberatory action. Creating digital stories requires that the student employ various tools that convey the authenticity and diversity of the human experience. Depicting one's lived experience in this manner can create a generative space for prospective and practicing teachers that leads to critical reflection, analysis, and dialog about issues of diversity, equity, and social justice. Use of voice, music, carefully chosen special effects, and attention to story progression can all be used in ways that bring realism to one's story, therefore, creating context for meaningful critical multicultural learning to take place (cf. Hanley; Morton, this volume).

It is my contention that even though each one of the aforementioned aspects of digital stories has unique qualities that support Freire's dialogic method of inquiry, the element of voice has special relevance for this discussion. Freire and Macedo (1987) argue that the theory of critical literacy is informed by a dialectical theory of voice and empowerment. Their postulation helps explains how hegemonic structures work to shape schooling organizational practices, namely the curriculum. Freire and Macedo contend that the U.S. school curriculum often represents the dominant *voice* of society. Through this curriculum, students are exposed to narratives that construct a worldview constituted by mainly White, male, middle-class, Christian, heterosexual, and able-bodied identities. This has unfortunate consequences for students that are in need of knowledge, skills, and dispositions necessary to successfully participate in an increasingly interdependent world. Similar to how school curriculum can be read as a text that tells the story of the dominant group; teachers' use of voice in digital stories can help them analyze ways in which their own histories and self-knowledge can be reflected through personal narrative.

Implications for Digital and Critical Literacy in Teacher Education

Digital stories can be used as a platform to support not only critical multicultural learning for teachers but digital learning as well. Constructing a well-developed digital story requires that teachers learn how to use a range of technology-based applications to enhance teaching and learning in K-12 classrooms. During this development process, students acquire proficiency in using editing software to embed audio and video files, image sharing tools, media publishing software, and digital cameras or scanners to capture images, and also learn about pertinent copyright regulations. As teachers acquire these new digital literacies, they will be better positioned to enhance student learning for a new generation of K-12 students that are more adept at using digital technologies both in and outside of the classroom.

Teacher education programs play a critical role in shaping both practicing and prospective teachers conceptions about the use of multicultural technology in K-12 education. Therefore, it is essential for educators who are concerned with multicultural and technology education be offered new ways of thinking about how, why, and under what conditions critical multicultural learning can take place through the use of technology. As teachers study across the disciplines of critical multicultural education and educational technology, they must continually examine ways in which such interdisciplinary experiences can create opportunities to promote transformative critical and digital literacy outcomes for their students. To this end, and using digital stories as an example, educators should be intentional in their efforts to ensure that the theoretical tenets of critical multicultural pedagogy are methodically reflected in the design and implementation of technology-based learning applications used in the classroom.

References

Barab, S., Hay, K., & Duffy, T. (1998). Grounded constructions and how technology can help. *Techtrends, 43*(2), 15–23.

Damarin, S. K. (1998). Technology and multicultural education: The question of convergence. *Theory into Practice, 37*(1), 11–19.

Duarte, E., & Smith, S. (Eds.). (2000). *Foundational perspectives in multicultural education.* New York: Longman.

Freire, P. (1972). *Pedagogy of the oppressed.* New York: Continuum.

Freire, P. (1974). *Education for critical consciousness.* London: Continuum.

Freire, P., & Macedo, D. (1987). *Literacy: Reading the word and the world.* Westport, CT: Bergin & Garvey.

Gale, T., & Densmore, K. (2003). *Engaging teachers: Towards a radical democratic agenda for schooling.* Philadelphia: Open University Press.

Goodman, D. (2001). *Promoting diversity and social justice: Educating people from privileged groups.* Thousand Oaks, CA: Sage.

Gorski, P. C. (2001). *Multicultural education and the internet: Intersections and integrations.* New York: McGraw Hill Higher Education.

Kahn, R., & Kellner, D. (2007). Paulo Freire and Ivan Illich: Technology politics and the reconstruction of education. *Policy Futures in Education, 5*(4), 431–448.

Kajder, S. B. (2004). Enter here: Personal narrative and digital storytelling. *The English Journal, 93*(3), 64–68.

Kim, M. K., Sharp, J. M., & Thompson, A. D. (1998). Effects of integrating problem solving, interactive multimedia, and constructivism in teacher education. *Journal of Educational Computing Research, 19*(1), 83–108.

Kincheloe, J. K., & Steinberg, S. R. (2002). *Changing multiculturalism.* Buckingham, England and Philadelphia: Open University Press.

King, P., & Baxter Magolda, M. (2005). A developmental model of intercultural maturity. *Journal of College Student Development, 46*(6), 571–592.

Lambert, J. (2007). *Digital storytelling: Capturing lives, creating community.* Berkeley, CA: Digital Diner Press.

McLaren, P. (2000). White terror and oppositional agency: Towards a critical multiculturalism. In E. Duarte & S. Smith (Eds.), *Foundational perspectives in multicultural education* (pp. 195–212). New York: Longman.

McShay, J. C., & Leigh, P. R. (2005). Reconceptualizing equity pedagogy in technology teacher education: A double infusion model. *Journal of Multicultural Perspectives, 7*(2), 10–19.

Ohler, J. (2008). *Digital story telling in the classroom: New media pathways to literacy, learning, and creativity.* Thousand Oaks, CA: Corwin Press.

Pang, V. (2004). *Multicultural education: A caring-centered, reflective approach.* Boston: McGraw-Hill.

Petersen, R. (2003). Teaching how to read the world and change it: Critical pedagogy in the intermediate grades. In A. Darder, M. Baltadano, & R. Torres (Eds.), *The critical pedagogy reader.* New York: Routledge.

Rasmussen, K., & Norman, S. (1998). Training teachers for success: Pre-service teachers and technology integration. *Canadian Journal of Educational Communication, 27*(1), 45–56.

Robin, B. (2008). Digital storytelling: A powerful technology tool for the 21st century classroom. *Theory into Practice, 47,* 220–228.

Shor, I., & Freire, P. (1987). *A Pedaogy for liberation.* South Hadley, MA: Bergin & Garvey.

Shulman, L. (1986). Those who understand: Knowledge growth in teaching. *Educational Researcher, 15*(2), 4–14.

Sleeter, C., & Bernal, D. (2004). Critical pedagogy, critical race theory, and antiracist education: Implications for multicultural education. In J. A. Banks & C. Banks (Eds.), *Handbook of research on multicultural education.* San Francisco, CA: Jossey-Bass.

Sleeter, C., & Grant, C. (2003). *Making choices for multicultural education: Five approaches to race, class, and gender.* New York: Merrill.

Sleeter, C., & Tettegah, S. (2002). Technology as a tool in multicultural teaching. *Multicultural Education, 10*(2), 3–9.

11

Knowing Our Place
Critical Multicultural Science Education

GEORGINA M. STEWART

Introduction

Multiculturalism has made less progress in science education compared with other curriculum areas, reflecting the abyss separating science and culture, and the adherence of school science to a traditional disciplinary view of the curriculum and the canonical science knowledge therein (Duschl, 1985). The nature of science knowledge, purposely aiming to exclude human dimensions such as aesthetics or history, precludes the options available for multicultural reform of the curriculum found in other subjects such as the arts, social studies, or English (cf. Hanley; Morton; Locke, this volume). The nature of science knowledge is also why the very idea of "multicultural science education" creates difficulty for many science educators. This chapter argues, first, that a critical perspective is essential for multicultural science education, and second, that a wider perspective including other traditions of science education reform may help to progress the debates.

The chapter title can be read in two ways. A place-based form of knowledge is central to an indigenous identity, and an important issue in multicultural science education, as discussed below. The title also evokes a socially imposed hierarchy of access to knowledge, and the multiculturalist repositioning of indigenous people and perspectives within that hierarchy (Tuhiwai Smith, 1999).

This chapter examines the complexities surrounding the application of critical multiculturalism to science education, arguing that terminological problems, amongst others, have contributed to the longstanding opposition between apparently incompatible perspectives (Tobin, 2008). Lack of resolution has contributed to disconnection between theory and practice, occluding the driving aim of equity for non-Western students behind a trenchant debate about indigenous knowledge. The most important differences between the positions in the research are in fact political, related to understandings of the links between science, science education, and power relations between different groups in society (Lacey, 2001).

The chapter brings a critical postcolonial lens to the relevant issues and literatures. The term "postcolonial" signifies the immigrant, imperialist history of societies such as the United States, Australia, and New Zealand, including implicit reference to the shifting binary of positions identifiable as "Western" and "indigenous" (or Oriental, Native, Black, etc.). The term "critical" refers to critical theory (Young, 1989), applied particularly to the critique of how science knowledge is deployed to support political powerbases in society, and how this affects indigenous and other marginalized students in science classrooms.

The next section introduces the issues in multicultural science education, revisiting the classic essay by Derek Hodson (1999), in the light of subsequent research. Comments follow on a specific indigenous science curriculum, then on links between multicultural science education and two other reform movements in science education, namely Science-Technology-Society (STS) and History and Philosophy of Science (HPS). The conclusion draws these discussions together to inform suggestions for change in classroom practice, and further research.

The Nature of Knowledge and Multicultural Science Education

The broad educational critique that goes under the banner of "multiculturalism" is concerned with embedded racism in schooling (McCarthy & Crichlow, 1993). As part of this, multicultural science education begins with recognizing the inequity of outcomes in science education for students from non-Western cultural backgrounds. Despite consensus of purpose, however, oppositional positions developed over certain key issues in multicultural science education, resulting in debates that have proved difficult to resolve, and which continue to drive much of the literature. These key issues are the nature of science and the nature of indigenous knowledge (IK), and their representations in school curricula.

Multicultural science educators, like other science educators, are concerned with how the nature of science is presented in school science curricula. The term "nature of science" can be understood either on a superficial descriptive level, or on a deeper philosophical level, although in school curricula (if the nature of science is included at all) the former interpretation dominates. To appreciate the concerns of multicultural science education, it is necessary to take a philosophical view. Through the course of the twentieth century, positivism was gradually displaced as the prevailing philosophy of science, and the criteria that define science also came into question. Increasingly, science became viewed as a human product (overturning an earlier conception of science as "pure knowledge") which develops within societies and cultures, so is subject to human errors and distortions (Cobern & Loving, 2008). The residue of outdated philosophies become "myths about science" (Hodson, 1999) left behind in the school curriculum, although discredited by contemporary philosophy of science. This recalls Glen Aikenhead's comments on the relationship between science and the science curriculum:

The twentieth century began with nature divided into physics, chemistry, biology and geology by an emerging community of scholars calling themselves scientists, but the century ended with nature viewed as a transdisciplinary collage by communities of engineers, technologists, scientists and funding agencies. The twentieth century began with the high-school science curriculum divided into the content of physics, chemistry, biology and geology, taught to an occupational elite. The century ended with a curriculum that adhered largely to its nineteenth-century roots, in spite of many innovative attempts to change it. In short, school science resisted coevolving with [W]estern science during the twentieth century. This successful resistance suggests that school science must somehow be serving the interests of dominant stakeholders who enjoy social, economic and political power in society.

(Aikenhead, 2000, p. 257)

In recent work, Aikenhead has even more explicitly challenged the way science education conceives of science knowledge, suggesting "objectivity has become the opiate of the academic" (Aikenhead, 2008). At first glance this is a surprising statement, since objectivity is widely regarded as one of the most important characteristics of science. Aikenhead clarifies, however, that he is identifying "objectivity" as part of "a positivist-like view of Eurocentric science" (p. 584)—as distortions, in other words, of science and objectivity, caused by scientism and Eurocentrism. These twin ideologies and their effects lead to greater debates in multicultural science education, compared with other curriculum areas.

Richard Boyd (2001) identifies the role of objectivity in science, while tracing the effect of "malignant" meanings in those parts of science most influenced by social ideologies, e.g., evolutionary biology. These result in "a sort of relativism about scientific rationality":

It is part of the stereotype of objectivity that objective methods are theory-neutral and thus immune to social ideology (and to individual idiosyncrasy as well). . . . the conception that science is 'objective,' and *thus immune from ideological influence,* itself serves the *ideological* function of enhancing the credibility of the political rationalizations produced by the sciences. There is, however, such a phenomenon as scientific objectivity [which] is a matter of the reliable operation of scientific methods to systematically produce real knowledge.

(p. 57, original emphases)

Boyd argues that "the ideological conception of ideology we have been discussing [is] constitutive of the conceptual meaning of the term 'objectivity,'" which creates a dichotomy between "the *concept* of objectivity, [which] is a tool of oppressors [in] politics and in the human sciences" and "the *phenomenon* of objectivity—the epistemically reliable deployment of scientific methods—[which] is essential to projects of social criticism and ideology critique" (p. 59).

His conclusion clarifies the link between this critical philosophical view of science and the political stance of critical multicultural science education:[1]

> In the human sciences and related domains, scientific objectivity cannot—absent wholesale political and economic change—be achieved within the normal workings of institutional science, except in rare contexts of sustained struggle. It can be obtained outside the normal workings of institutional science only in the contexts provided by oppositional movements. It is probably also true that only in the contexts provided by political struggle can the concept of objectivity be freed from its malignant meanings.
>
> (Boyd, 2001, p. 59)

Aikenhead's wry comment discussed above is thus a warning that the *concept* of objectivity becomes an opiate if it encourages us not to think about its reflection (or not) in real-world practices and their associated discourses. What is needed is stronger objectivity (Siegel, 2006), rather than its abandonment altogether. It is invalid (i.e., scientistic) to make blanket claims about science, such as "science is objective"; each aspect of science remains open to evaluation on all criteria considered essential for inclusion in the canon.

May (1999a) edited an early, influential, collection on critical multiculturalism. One of the chapters in that collection was an essay by Derek Hodson (1999), titled "Critical Multiculturalism in Science and Technology Education." A decade on, Hodson (1999) still provides a useful frame of reference on the issues that continue to be raised by multicultural science education research.

Hodson's chapter was organized around four themes—"the *personalization* of learning, the facilitating of *border crossings*, the *demythologizing* of science, and the *politicization* of science education" (p. 217, original emphases)—of which the latter two align with this discussion about the nature of science. Hodson argued that a key "myth about science" promulgated by school curricula is "science is a value-free activity," since "science and technology are driven by the needs, interests, values and aspirations of the society that sustains them" (p. 229). Giving examples of how "social and cultural influences can lead to distortion and misuse of science for political goals," Hodson noted "[f]rom here it is but a short step to consideration of scientific racism" (p. 230), and listed some associated questions, including:

> "What might African science, Māori science or Feminist science be like?" "Do these terms mean anything?" . . . "If science could be different, should it be different?" "Would these changes make it more accessible to students of ethnic minority cultures?" "Would these changes have beneficial effects on the environment or the social fabric?"
>
> (p. 230)

Hodson suggested that in "confronting these kinds of questions, students come to recognize that science is not the straightforward business that is part of its public image. Thus, they are empowered by the curriculum to challenge and, possibly, to change it" (pp. 230–231). But here Hodson alters, first, his target audience, since these questions arose from a discussion designed to challenge educators and curriculum developers, rather than students; and second, the aim of science education reform, earlier expressed as "provid[ing] better access [for non-Western students] to significant knowledge and, thereby, to enhance social mobility" (p. 228). Better results in science education for these students have thus far proved elusive. Thus, for these students to actually reform science, as this discussion implies, while a laudable aim, must be viewed as even more difficult to achieve, and dependent on the first objective, since informed critique obviously requires mastery of the material (Young, 1989).

Returning to his first two themes, Hodson used the notion of "personal frameworks of understanding" to extrapolate the constructivist influence in science education into an argument promoting "science education as enculturation," at first using "culture" in the sense of a "community of discourse":

> What is important is recognizing when particular meanings are appropriate and being able to use them properly within the appropriate discourse . . . [T]he aim of science education is not to eradicate the commonsense ways of understanding by imposing *the* scientific way as the one true and universally valid mode of explanation. Rather, it is to assist each learner to . . . know when and how to deploy scientific understanding.
> (Hodson, 1999, pp. 221–222, original emphasis)

Hodson went on to discuss "sociocultural factors in science learning," including the then-recent work on cultural world-views and border crossing in science education (Aikenhead, 1996), but the change in usage of "culture" (now meaning more-or-less the same as "ethnicity") went unremarked. Similar problems are evident in current work, helping to allow it to continue to remain at a politically "innocent" level (McKinley, 2001). Science educators working with non-Western students commonly allude to problems caused by world-views incompatible with science, but little of this work refers to world-view theory (Kearney, 1984), which underpins the notion of "science teacher as culture broker" (Cobern, 1991).

This notion of cultural broker has been widely supported, indeed, accepted as orthodoxy (e.g., Sutherland, 2002), despite lack of evidence of its fruitfulness in improving science education outcomes for non-Western students (Michie, 2004). Critique has identified the following limitations:

- Any [classroom] encounter can be simply "managed" as pedagogical moments requiring racial or cultural sensitivity.
- All science educators need to do is learn how to work their way through the differences.
- The acquisition and practice of cultural sensitivity can replace, for example, any concrete attempt to diversify the teacher population.

- Most teachers in places like New Zealand, the United States, and Britain are white and they get to interpret student actions in the classroom: thus a student not looking the teacher in the eye is interpreted as a "cultural response" in favor of a "power response" (McKinley, 2001, pp. 74–75).

The border-crossing/culture-broker work is important to counterbalance any "culture blind" assumption that all students are on a "level playing field" in the science classroom, but it is important to remember that the idea of "border crossing" between different "social worlds" is *metaphorical*. Despite the best intentions, reification of this notion, which leans towards "cultural monadism," i.e., viewing different ethnic cultures as closed off from each other, has often been apparent in multicultural science education (e.g., "distinctive social worlds," Hodson, 1999, p. 224). To insist that all students and all scientists live in the same *one* world underlines the political reality of unequal access to, and control over, science and its applications, which forms the legitimate target of critique for multicultural science education.

Inclusion of "African science" and "Māori science" in the above-quoted question was the only reference in Hodson's chapter to "indigenous science," although this is one of the most contentious issues in the research (Lacey, 2001). The term "indigenous science" and its correlates ("Native science," "Aboriginal science," etc.) originated in classical anthropology, where a Eurocentric delineation of the supremacy of "Western thought" took science as the paradigm (Scantlebury, McKinley, & Jesson, 2002), in contrast with "Native thought," where "Native" was a reified category of analysis, arising from a strong version of cultural monadism, under the then-pervasive influence of Social Darwinism (Salmond, 1985). This contributed to the wide acceptance of the term "Western science" that still prevails, along with its Eurocentric, scientistic undertones. In turn, this has catalyzed the strategic promotion of terms such as "Māori science" on political grounds, completing the construction of a reified binary, which although logically incoherent, has migrated from academic fields such as philosophy into areas such as education, where it continues to generate violent disagreements. This problematic dialectic appears in two sets of statements in Hodson's chapter—the first appearing to support the notion of "Western science":

> To say that scientific knowledge arises in a particular culture (the [W]estern scientific community) is not to discredit it . . . [W]estern science is 'biased' in the sense that it makes epistemological presuppositions that are cultural artefacts, and are not shared by some non-[W]estern cultures . . .
>
> (Hodson, 1999, p. 231)

In the next paragraph, an opposing view is expressed: "Another all-too-prevalent myth is that science is exclusively European or North American (i.e. white-ethnocentred)" (p. 231). Despite this inconsistent cultural/political stance on science, Hodson promoted politicizing science education to enable students "to use a range of powerful discourses, especially the discourse of science and technology, to effect social change" (p. 234). This crucial point is equally relevant today, with little sign that science curriculum development has overcome the depoliticizing tendencies of state education.

Hodson's chapter exemplifies multicultural science education research in the following ways:

- Written from a Western male academic point of view;
- Reviews and integrates a common set of themes in knowledge, language and politics;
- Shows occasional lapses in argument or political position, e.g. cultural monadism, Eurocentrism, scientism, etc.;
- Refers to the oppositional debates, including the vehement rebuttal of one's arguments by other scholars ("enraged," Hodson, 1999, p. 231);
- Curriculum proposals are not based on real-world programs or actual classroom data.

Hodson (1999) critically surveyed and synthesized the multicultural science education research, but like much of the literature, was unable to cross the divide from theory into practice. This has proved to be one of the enduring difficulties in the field. Many rehearsals of the issues are published, with suggestions for classroom practice, teacher education, and further research (e.g., Hines, 2003), but as yet there is little evidence that these measures have made a significant difference to the relative disparity in outcomes of science education for non-Western students.

Multicultural science education has become concerned with indigenous knowledge (IK) on ethical grounds, as a move towards "inclusiveness," but one that may not overcome inequities in science education of indigenous students. The dominant viewpoint in the literature favors including IK in the science curriculum (McKinley, 2007), since to advocate otherwise seems like a continuation of epistemic violence and Eurocentrist exclusion. Signs of frustration with the debate appeared in a recent special issue on IK:

> [T]here is a time where you need to stop philosophizing and try implementing an aspect of IK in the classroom. The reason I argue "just do it" is that the dialogue that will be most valuable in the development and implementation of local IK into the classroom will be the dialogue that takes place at level of the Indigenous community.
>
> (Dawn Sutherland in Keane, 2008, p. 619)

The answer may be that decisions on including IK in the science curriculum need to be made locally, rather than globally (McKinley, 2005). The following section comments from the perspective of one indigenous education context, namely Māori education in New Zealand (see also Bishop, this volume).

An Indigenous Science Curriculum: Pūtaiao

Specific contexts of indigenous politics bring together the debates in knowledge, language, and identity, and enable a more sustained application of critical theory and research methodology, by comparison with universalized discussions. In New Zealand, one such context is provided by the state-funded Māori-language schooling program, Kura Kaupapa Māori (KKM). In association with KKM, curriculum statements in Māori were produced in the 1990s, including the development of a full Māori-language alternative Science curriculum, known as Pūtaiao.[2]

The identity of teachers, students, and the overall school environment in KKM is Māori, so cultural alienation is minimized. Such schools value their IK knowledge base, seeing it as relevant across the whole curriculum, not just in science. Since KKM aims to overcome educational inequity for Māori students, moreover, these school communities are intensely aware of the disparity in outcomes in science education, and expect this to be addressed by Pūtaiao. These factors lessen the priority of including IK in the Pūtaiao curriculum, and increase motivation to teach science as successfully as possible in Pūtaiao classrooms.

It is easy to overrate the successes of KKM, however, including those of Pūtaiao. Some reports have focused on the radical novelty of Pūtaiao (Durie, 2005) and overlooked the lack of evidence of progress, both in the literature, and in terms of outcomes for students. Government monitoring shows that KKM students achieve school qualifications at rates similar to or better than Māori students in mainstream schools, but with different subject distributions. The disparity is greatest in Science/Pūtaiao: half of all KKM students who gain school qualifications do so without achieving any science credits at all. This is due largely to the closed circle of social and historical issues discussed above, resulting in a lack of qualified Māori-speaking science teachers.

The Pūtaiao curriculum has recently (2008) been revised as part of a wider national curriculum redevelopment. In the new version, two strands equate to chemistry and physics, respectively, while the largest Pūtaiao strand equates to more than one Science strand, since it contains biology, earth science, and astronomy. There is also a fourth strand whose title means "The philosophy and history of science," which goes beyond what is covered in the Nature of Science strand in the Science curriculum. Its inclusion is based on the above analysis regarding the political needs of Māori learners of science. Following local work on narrative pedagogy in science education (Barker, 2006), this strand could be taught using "teaching stories" from the history and current workings of science that illustrate aspects of the philosophical nature of science.

The point of these detailed comments is to provide a real-life example of the clashes and overlaps which arise when the rhetoric of multiculturalism is enacted in a modern multicultural country. Pūtaiao is an educational context brimming with conflict at all levels from the philosophical and symbolic, to linguistic, ethical, and exceedingly practical dimensions, debates which have been published elsewhere (Stewart, 2005). It provides a local lens on the universal significance of sociopolitical and philosophical dimensions for achieving equity of outcomes in science education for students with indigenous cultural identities.

Links With Other Traditions in Science Education: STS and HPS

There are commonalities between multicultural science education and two other traditions of reform and research in science education, which are also concerned to promote more authentic representations of the nature of science in the school curriculum. These are Science-Technology-Society (STS) and History and Philosophy of Science (HPS), each of which, like multicultural science education, has a voluminous ongoing research literature, replete with debate.

Congruence between the aims of STS and multicultural science education has long been acknowledged (Aikenhead, 1996). A recent paper, however, starts by observing, "For the most part, STS has not lived up to the expectations of its advocates. STS has turned 35 years of age and advocates are wondering what happened" (Nashon, Nielsen, & Petrina, 2008, p. 387). It concludes, "Perhaps, over the past three and one-half decades, HPS and STS enthusiasts developed a tremendous rationale for policy [but] left underdeveloped the will for practice" (p. 399). These authors trace the history of the division into STS1 (the academic version) and STS2 (or "activist STS"). HPS has been used to extend and operationalize STS1, and in that sense subsumes it. But the split along an "activist/academic" divide identifies the very problem (i.e., that these are seen as incompatible), hindering any emancipatory potential for groups disadvantaged by current ideological influences.

HPS also overlaps with multicultural science education research. For example, Cathleen Loving and Bernard Ortiz de Montellano (2003) critique currently widely used, culturally relevant materials, finding many based on "bad science," and suggest that "good culturally relevant science" consists of the "anthropology and history associated with a particular science phenomen[on]" (pp. 160–161).

The similar lack of progress or practical results in each of these research traditions—STS, HPS, and multicultural science education—hints at a cautionary tale for all three. The trend towards increasing specialization includes the recent "emergence" of CSSE (Culture Studies in Science Education) as a "hybrid field" (Tobin, 2008, p. 638) in its own right, inheriting the mantle of multicultural science education research. The analysis presented above suggests the need to move in the opposite direction, towards union with other traditions, or at least better collaboration.

Conclusion: Developing Critical Multicultural Science Educators

This chapter has argued that a critical multicultural approach to science education requires attention to the impact of political influences on science, science curriculum and classroom practices and resources, and the life experiences of non-Western students. This has implications for changes classroom teachers might undertake, as well as at the level of academic research on cultural issues in science education.

As a matter of ethical integrity, all teachers (including science teachers) should challenge their own and others' deficit thinking about culture, and maintain high expectations for all students. This is demanded by the multiculturalist critique of school education in general (cf. Bishop, this volume). Over and above this, however, science teachers who wish to be more effective in culturally diverse classrooms can benefit by developing their own understanding, first, at a theoretical level in two areas:

- The history and philosophy of science, including the historical relationship between science and imperialism;
- Cultural theory, including the concept of ethnicity, world-view theory, and the wider academic literature (beyond science education) on IK.

The second set of relevant teacher understandings to be promoted is more localized: it is appropriate for teachers to become familiar with the actual cultures of their students. Symbolic aspects (beliefs and values) are as useful, if not more so, than details of material culture.[3] As argued above, the history of an ethnic group's interaction with the dominant culture, including the role of science and technology in that history, is highly relevant to the current situation of students who identify with that ethnicity, and influences their attitudes towards education in general, and science in particular.

The learnings described above will contribute to the development of a politicized view of the educational problematic of ethnic minority inequity. Such politicization, necessary for a critical multicultural perspective, is an individual process involving challenging subjective as well as objective work.

Different cultures give rise to different world-views, but this does not in itself explain the longstanding inequity in science education for indigenous students around the world. The limitations of the notion of "science teacher as culture broker," with its implied support for "Western science" and "indigenous science," need to be more widely recognized. There is a need for further research into cultural epistemological diversity based on world-view theory, but whether this is strictly a concern for science educators is dubious.

Greater attention would be appropriate in science teacher education to the history and philosophy of science, science's role in the colonization and oppression of indigenous people, and the influence of social ideologies on science concepts. There is also a need for reform efforts in science education research, such as Science-Technology-Society (STS), History and Philosophy of Science (HPS), and Culture Studies in Science Education (CSSE), to become more unified, against current separatist trends, in order to maximize chances of change for greater equity.

Notes

1 Boyd's comments also clarify the significance of indigenous community schooling movements and of science curricula developed within those contexts (May, 1999b; see also below).

2 This chapter omits discussion of issues concerning the nature of the language of science, and its translation into an endangered indigenous language undergoing revitalization, since these are less applicable to the wider multicultural science education debate.

3 The values of IK, expressed through ethical narratives, are useful in science education for exploring the nature of knowledge about the natural world. It is important to resist scientistic urges to view IK as a body of facts, or systematize IK within the science curriculum (see, for example, Patterson, 1994).

References

Aikenhead, G. (1996). Science education: Border crossing into the subculture of science. *Studies in Science Education, 27*, 1–52.

Aikenhead, G. (2000). Renegotiating the culture of school science. In R. Millar, J. Leach, & J. Osborne (Eds.), *Improving science education—The contribution of research* (pp. 245–264). Buckingham, England and Philadelphia: Open University Press.

Aikenhead, G. (2008). Objectivity: The opiate of the academic? *Cultural Studies of Science Education, 3*(3), 581–585.

Barker, M. (2006). Ripping yarns: A pedagogy for learning about the nature of science. *New Zealand Science Teacher, 113*, 27–37.

Boyd, R. N. (2001). Reference, (In)commensurability and meanings: Some (perhaps) unanticipated complexities. In P. Hoyningen-Huene & H. Sankey (Eds.), *Incommensurability and related matters* (pp. 1–63). Dordrecht, The Netherlands: Kluwer.

Cobern, W. W. (1991). *World view theory and science education research*. Manhattan, NY: NARST.

Cobern, W. W., & Loving, C. C. (2008). An essay for educators: Epistemological realism really is common sense. *Science & Education, 17*, 425–447.

Durie, M. H. (2005). Pūtaiao: Tides of discovery. In *Nḡ tai matat: Tides of Māori endurance* (pp. 136–162). Melbourne: Oxford University Press.

Duschl, R. A. (1985). Science education and philosophy of science: Twenty-five years of mutually exclusive development. *School Science and Mathematics, 85*(7), 541–555.

Hines, S. M. (Ed.). (2003). *Multicultural science education*. New York: Peter Lang.

Hodson, D. (1999). Critical multiculturalism in science and technology education. In S. May (Ed.), *Critical multiculturalism: Rethinking multicultural and antiracist education* (pp. 216–244). London: Falmer Press.

Keane, M. (2008). Science education and worldview. *Culture Studies of Science Education, 3*(3), 587–621.

Kearney, M. (1984). *World view*. Novato, CA: Chandler & Sharp.

Lacey, H. (2001). Incommensurability and "multicultural science." In P. Hoyningen-Huene & H. Sankey (Eds.), *Incommensurability and related matters* (pp. 225–239). Dordrecht: Kluwer.

Loving, C. C., & Ortiz de Montellano, B. R. (2003). Good versus bad culturally relevant science: Avoiding the pitfalls. In S. M. Hines (Ed.), *Multicultural science education* (pp. 147–166). New York: Peter Lang.

May, S. (Ed.). (1999a). *Critical multiculturalism: Rethinking multicultural and antiracist education*. London: Falmer Press.

May, S. (Ed.). (1999b). *Indigenous community-based education*. Clevedon, England: Multilingual Matters.

McCarthy, C., & Crichlow, W. (Eds.). (1993). *Race, identity and representation in education*. New York and London: Routledge.

McKinley, E. (2001). Cultural diversity: Masking power with innocence. *Science Education, 85*(1), 74–76.

McKinley, E. (2005). Locating the global: Culture, language and science education for indigenous students. *International Journal of Science Education, 27*(2), 227–241.

McKinley, E. (2007). Postcolonialism, indigenous students, and science education. In S. K. Abell & N. G. Lederman (Eds.), *Handbook of research in science education* (pp. 199–226). Mahwah, NJ and London: Lawrence Erlbaum Associates.

Michie, M. (2004). Teaching science to indigenous students: Teacher as culture broker or is it something else? Retrieved from http://members.ozemail.com.au/~mmichie/teacher_cb.htm

Nashon, S., Nielsen, W., & Petrina, S. (2008). Whatever happened to STS? Pre-service physics teachers and the history of quantum mechanics. *Science & Education, 17*, 387–401.

Patterson, J. (1994). Māori environmental virtues. *Environmental Ethics, 16,* 397–409.

Salmond, A. (1985). Māori epistemologies. In J. Overing (Ed.), *Reason and morality.* London and New York: Tavistock Publications.

Scantlebury, K., McKinley, E., & Jesson, J. G. (2002). Imperial knowledge: Science, education and equity. In B. E. Hernandez-Truyol (Ed.), *Moral imperialism—a critical anthology* (pp. 229–240). New York: New York University Press.

Siegel, H. (2006). Epistemological diversity and education research: Much ado about nothing much? *Educational Researcher, 35*(2), 3–12.

Stewart, G. (2005). Māori in the science curriculum: Developments and possibilities. *Educational Philosophy and Theory, 37*(6), 851–870.

Sutherland, D. (2002). Exploring culture, language and the perception of the nature of science. *International Journal of Science Education, 24*(1), 1–25.

Tobin, K. G. (2008). Contributing to the conversation in science education. *Cultural Studies of Science Education, 3*(3), 535–540.

Tuhiwai Smith, L. (1999). *Decolonizing methodologies—research and indigenous peoples.* Dunedin, New Zealand: University of Otago Press.

Young, R. E. (1989). *A critical theory of education: Habermas and our children's future.* New York: Harvester Wheatsheaf.

IV
Critical Multiculturalism
in Humanities and Social Science

12

Discussing Race and Culture in the Middle-School Classroom
Scaffolding Critical Multiculturalism

JILL EWING FLYNN

Can the messy, elusive, and often taboo topics of race and culture be fruitfully discussed in a secondary classroom? Glazier and Seo (2005) declare that subjects like social class, politics, religion, culture, and race are generally "silenced," seen as dangerous "hot lava topics" that teachers avoid raising, fearing the difficult and complex dialogues that they may bring about (p. 687). Given the pervasiveness of racism and prejudice in U.S. society and the persistence of the achievement gap, it is clear that avoiding these hot lava issues serves only to perpetuate the status quo. Teachers and teacher educators must come to a greater understanding of how productive conversations about race and culture can happen in classrooms.

This chapter examines how one teacher structured a critical multicultural curriculum, using the following questions as a guide: How can issues of race, power, and culture be productively taken up in a diverse middle-school Social Studies class? What are some of the possibilites as well as the challenges resulting from this pedagogy?

Background to a Case Study of Mr. Evans

This chapter is a piece of a larger qualitative study that I—a white,[1] female, middle-class, heterosexual, able-bodied, graduate student and former secondary teacher—recently conducted. From October 2007 until June 2008, I was a participant observer an average of three days per week in eighth-grade classes at Metro Arts School. I audio-recorded class discussions, took ethnographic field notes, interviewed students and teachers, collected school documents and curriculum materials, and examined student work throughout the year. This chapter presents a case study of Mr. Evans (all names are pseudonyms), a white, married, able-bodied man in his late 20s, who was in his fifth year of teaching Social Studies at Metro Arts School, a public arts magnet school housing grades four through eight. The eighth-grade students I studied were approximately 60% white, 35% African American, and 5% Latino or Asian American (field notes, 10-15-07); they also came from socioeconomically diverse backgrounds.

Through district staff development programs, school personnel at Metro Arts were strongly encouraged to reflect on their own racial identities and the ways in which they impacted their work with students (cf. Bishop, this volume). Administrators supported teachers who addressed issues of race and culture in the classroom. The school has had considerable success closing the achievement gap. According to the school principal, by eighth-grade, 80% of African American students test proficient on state tests; the state average is a woeful 40%.[2]

Sociocultural and multicultural education learning theories provide useful lenses for examining the work of Mr. Evans and his students. Sociocultural theory conceptualizes learning as a primarily social activity. Drawing from the work of Vygotsky (1978), this framework asserts that all learning is socially and culturally determined and needs to be supported by a community. Vygotsky (1978) wrote of the "Zone of Proximal Development" (ZPD), a structure in which an expert guides a novice through learning, helping the learner to understand and assimilate increasingly complex ideas and concepts. While Vygotsky himself did not use the term "scaffolding," other educational theorists developed it in applying the ZPD to educational contexts (Balaban, 1995).

Multicultural education and critical theories are also important for understanding Mr. Evans' curriculum. Banks and Banks (2004) explain that the chief aim of multicultural education is to achieve educational equity. Effective multicultural education serves an important purpose in a diverse society, country, and world, helping students cultivate the knowledge, dispositions, and attitudes necessary to work productively with "people from diverse groups to create a civic and moral community that works for the common good" (p. xi). While multicultural education in the United States has often been conceptualized as a pedagogy for students of color, Banks and Banks (2004) show that the skills and attitudes fostered in effective multicultural education are essential for all students, white and non-white, to "function effectively in a pluralistic democratic society" (xiv).

However, as the introductory chapter to this volume discusses, the field of multicultural education has struggled with defining itself and maintaining focus, resulting in the emergence of a new term: "critical multiculturalism." The work of Freire (2000), McLaren (1998), Delpit (1995), and many others speaks to the need for critical examination of systems of power in classrooms, particularly in regards to race and culture. Ukpokodu (2003) defines teaching from a critical multicultural perspective as a

paradigm in which teachers and students consciously engage in the construction of knowledge, critique the various forms of inequities and injustices embedded in the educational system, and strive to gain the empowerment needed to engage in culturally responsive and responsible practice.

(p. 19)

Other theorists highlight the need to center issues of racism and white privilege. May (1999) explains that:

a critical multiculturalism needs both to recognize and incorporate the differing cultural knowledges that children bring with them to school, *while at the same time* address and contest the differential cultural capital attributed to them as a result of wider hegemonic power relations.

(p. 32)

Educators who seek to implement critical multiculturalism must confront substantial obstacles. One problem for classroom teachers is the gap between theory and practice. Sleeter and Bernal (2004) note that critical pedagogy has been explored most deeply at the theoretical level, "often leaving practitioners unclear about what to do" (p. 244). Other barriers facing teachers who strive to realize such work include the sensitive nature of race and the difficulty white students have in acknowledging and understanding the role of their culture, as well as the unearned privileges they receive as a result of their skin color (McIntosh, 1990). Finally, the larger sociopolitical context of American education affects teachers' perceptions of the feasibility of discussing race and culture. Teachers in the United States often have a sense that these issues are somehow peripheral, that the focus on standards and accountability reflected in (and created by) the high-stakes standardized assessment system, exemplified in *No Child Left Behind,* leaves no room in the curriculum for multicultural matters (cf. May & Sleeter, this volume). Despite the impediments, it is vital for teachers and teacher educators to address these issues with their students. Thus it is important to examine how teachers like Mr. Evans have successfully implemented a critical multicultural curriculum (see also Fitzpatrick, this volume).

Scaffolding Critical Multicultural Curriculum

Research has documented the difficulty white people have talking about race and culture. For example, much of the literature on teacher education students' examination of their own racial privilege (Florio-Ruane, 2001; LeCompte & McCray, 2002; Gay & Kirkland, 2003) shows that white students resist the work. Students frequently rely on the discourses of colorblindness, meritocracy, and individualism to defend their views and avoid acknowledging white privilege. Many white teachers, too, struggle to understand the role that race plays in their identities. LeCompte and McCray (2002) observe that they often "struggle with the notion that their Whiteness affords them privilege and power and threatens oppression for their students of color" and fail to recognize the racism inherent in institutions such as schools (p. 26). Yet it is vital that white students and teachers come to understand the racist sociocultural forces in the United States and, by extension, other contexts.

Helping white students see their own race and making all students aware of institutional racism were among Mr. Evans' major goals. He structured his course around the somewhat more "safe" notion of culture, a concept that was easy to map onto state standards and one that would likely not immediately alienate or threaten students. However, the curriculum took up more thorny issues of power, race, and privilege at multiple points. It is clear that Mr. Evans made careful, reflective choices about how to scaffold the curriculum in order to center culture in a meaningful, critical way. He organized the four quarters of the academic year into evolving themes: (1) defining culture; (2) cultural collision; (3) cultural conflict; and (4) cultural resolution.

Defining Culture: Building Community and Introducing Race

Mr. Evans started the year by building a positive, collaborative classroom community in order to lay the groundwork for delving into "hot lava" topics (see also Fitzpatrick, this volume). A tall, thin, energetic man, he welcomed laughter into his classroom with gentle teasing and self-deprecating humor. Besides working to connect with each of his students, Mr. Evans spent the first quarter developing a foundation for students' understanding of culture and modeling the importance of self-reflection. In the first two months of the school year, students defined culture and discussed at length the many influences cultures had on their lives, including the role played by race.

For the major project of this quarter, students created collages that identified the cultures that they were part of and the relationships between those cultural identities and their individual identities. To present their work, students gathered in a circle of chairs and spoke about elements of their collages. Mr. Evans displayed prompts for students to answer during the presentation, such as, "If you really knew me you would know…" and "Tell us what we need to know in order to interact/be around you." He modeled responses to the prompts, sharing information about his relationships with his father and stepfather. These "culture collages" were displayed in the classroom and referred to for the rest of the year.

The sharing structure and format of "circle" was important as well. Mr. Evans gave explicit instruction about the behaviors and practices expected during this time, which included active listening and complete focus on the speaker. "Circle" was used for both serious academic topics and "check-in" time—a chance to hear how each classmate was doing that day and why. Mr. Evans typically implemented "circle" once or more per week throughout the school year, continuing to build and emphasize classroom community.

Another of Mr. Evans' purposes for the culture collage project was the acknowledgment of race as a topic that was open to discussion. As Mr. Evans noted, "When you ask kids to talk about themselves, this stuff [race] just comes up. You don't have to force it" (field notes, 10-2-07). A number of students self-identified as bi- or multiracial; these students' culture collages and presentations reflected the influences and conflicts between the racial worlds in their backgrounds. Mr. Evans explained how he used this first quarter to signal cultural responsiveness:

> [I]t builds credibility with black students … in the first week or so when we're doing the culture collage … we say "Race is on the table here, we're going to talk about it," it's a sense of relief to black students because they know all of a sudden … that you're culturally aware. … You know that it

exists and you're not going to be standing in front saying, "I treat every-body the same!" and they, they know that that's not true ... so I think it does help with our relationship with our black kids.

(Interview, 3-14-08)

Mr. Evans noted that his students of color saw through so-called colorblind phi-losophy; in his experience, these students can and do want to talk about race. With issues like these typically silenced in school (cf. Lea, this volume), finding a meaningful way to bring up the topic is paramount. For white students in Mr. Evans' class, defining and centering culture helped them begin to understand how their race was a key aspect of their identity.

During this quarter, some white students began to see that they were not just "nothing" or "American," that their race as well as their region, family status, and other identity markers shaped their experiences. After reading "Body Ritual Among the Nacirema" (Miner, 1956) a satirical look at American grooming habits, students discussed how what they took for granted as normal—shaving, brushing teeth, plucking eyebrows, wearing deodorant—could be viewed as strange or deviant from another perspective. Quarter one ended with an explo-ration of ethnocentrism, including a debate on whether one's individual or cul-tural identity was more powerful. Students' beginning examinations of culture and race, as well as the safe space created in the classroom, were necessary prerequisites for the discussions to follow.

Cultural Collision: Examining Marginalization and Colonization

In quarter two, students examined the patterns of contact that tend to emerge when cultures collide, as colonizing forces enter the territories of indigenous people (cf. Bishop, this volume). They analyzed articles and pictures from sources ranging from their own textbook to *National Geographic* to the film *The Gods Must Be Crazy* (Uys, 1980) in order to see the ways that indigenous peo-ple were portrayed as exoticized Others and marginalized visually as well as his-torically. They read accounts by Native writers regarding the history and impact of colonization. Other major texts of the unit (which Mr. Evans co-taught with Mr. Ramsey, the English teacher) were short stories and a film by Spokane/Coeur D'Alene author Sherman Alexie. As the teachers articulated in the permission slip that went home to families, they used Alexie's work to investigate "racism, stereotyping, and marginalization ... the broader idea of what it means to be misrepresented" (Alexie permission slip, 1-14-08).

Students also studied facts about reservation life and debated the use of American Indian mascots by sports teams. The latter activity sparked a great deal of discussion and argument, with conversations and disagreements spilling over into passing time, lunch, and recess. Mr. Evans relished the passion with which students engaged with this issue, commenting to me after class one day, "I love it when kids are coming up to me to talk and debate this stuff—I love teaching this!" (Field notes, 1-16-08).

Still, not all students participated fully. From time to time, Mr. Evans expressed frustration over students who seemed to be tuning out. He worked to get them engaged without negatively judging them, calling them to action by warning them about the dangers of indifference. During one discussion, he implored, "These are important things that we're talking about and they build on each other. … We're missing out on the community piece of how we can better understand this as a group" (Field notes, 1-16-08). Rather than asking students to participate to facilitate their personal advancement, Mr. Evans emphasized the ways that the students could—and needed to—learn from one another, "to get smarter as a class" (Field notes, 1-25-08). Unlike the individualistic ethos emphasized in most classrooms, this teacher often worked to focus on the ways people should work together to learn.

During this unit, Mr. Evans also mentally prepared the class for the work ahead. Mindful of the distractions of an eighth-grader's day, he asked students to put their heads down and "wind down" for one minute at the start of the period. Reminding them that the subject matter was "tough stuff," he helped students make transitions from the excitement of recess or the intellectual challenges of another subject to the serious work around culture, race, and power in his class (Field notes, 1-18-08). Mr. Evans used this type of quiet time as well as individual journal writing to foster metacognition and reflection.

Further, he was explicit in his instruction to ask students to think critically; as they watched a scene from a film for the second time, he asked, "You got your critical lenses on?" As some students pretended to put on imaginary glasses, he urged, "Focus 'em" (Field notes, 1-30–08). Many students took Mr. Evans' advice to challenge and be critical seriously. For example, in May, one student engaged the class in a lengthy discussion of why they studied primarily Europe, the United States, and Africa in their Social Studies curriculum, neglecting South and Central America. This discussion was encouraged and extended by Mr. Evans (Field notes, 5-13-08).

Throughout the second quarter, Mr. Evans and his students continue to raise issues of race, considering how skin color difference played a role in colonization and exploitation. Such examinations helped students continue to stretch and grow in their critical and cultural understandings.

Cultural Conflict: Discussing White Privilege and "Othering"

"Race Discussions"

Quarter three focused on cultural conflict, issues of power and privilege that emerge as a result of racial and religious difference. The heart of Mr. Evans' curriculum was the week of "Race Discussions," a unit that he again co-taught with Mr. Ramsey. The teachers' stated goals for this unit were as follows:

- Have students test out talking about race and racism inside and outside of a classroom;
- Give students of color a voice and forum for sharing their experiences with racism;

- Facilitate students' understanding of white privilege—particularly, but not solely, white students;
- Help students develop the language and skills of antiracism (Interview, 12-18-07).

These goals reflect the ways Mr. Evans and his colleague believe discussions about race should happen. They value student voices as a testimony to the pervasiveness of racism. They recognize the difficulty students have, especially white students, in talking about these issues, and seek to provide a safe space for such discussions. They also have explicit goals of having students understand and ultimately work to combat sociocultural forces such as institutional racism.

After coming together to share and discuss these definitions of racism gleaned from books, websites, and personal interviews, students read and discussed "White Privilege: Unpacking the Invisible Knapsack" (McIntosh, 1990). Mr. Evans and Mr. Ramsey next went over "Four Agreements" that guided discussion:

- Stay engaged
- Experience discomfort
- Speak your truth
- Expect and accept non-closure.[3]

By working through these agreements—discussing what they mean and what they look like in a classroom—the two teachers again prepared students psychologically for the difficult work ahead. The teachers used "circle" check-in and reminded students of the guidelines each day before diving into discussions (Field notes, 2-5-08, 2-6-08). While these agreements were not perfect, they nonetheless did provide some important principles to guide discussion. Mr. Evans pointed out the structure needed to facilitate difficult conversations, particularly with white students.

> [T]hat conversation too is about educating white students. About the reality of it. And—and I believe that part of the problem of racism is that white people don't talk about it …. So I think it gives them some language and some words, and an ability to enter into conversations and that's why we keep going back to … the agreements.
>
> (Interview, 3-14-08)

Next, students examined their own skin color privilege; filling out a chart called "Because of my Race or Color," students responded to questions about things like how easily they saw their race positively represented in mainstream media, how likely they were to see someone of their skin color in power in everyday situations, how often they could count on their race to work in their favor when shopping or traveling, and so forth. Students and adults in the room—the teachers, myself, the principal (who participated several times during the week), and educational assistants—sat in a circle according to their scores, which ranged from 115 (those with the most skin color privilege, which ends up being the score for almost all whites) to the low 30s (those with the least).

Mr. Evans and Mr. Ramsey began the discussion by asking students to respond to the "color line" that was formed as a result of the survey, with white students around one part of the circle, Latino and Asian students following, and African American students on the other side. As the week's conversations continued, students delved into personal stories of bias, the notion of reverse racism, the role of institutions in perpetuating racial injustice, the black-white dichotomy, the difficulty that people (particularly white people) have discussing race, feelings of guilt and responsibility, and other weighty topics. The teachers ended the "Race Discussions" by having students write in their journals and publicly state to the class one commitment they could make regarding racism moving forward. Mr. Evans put forth a challenge:

> [N]ow, once you're armed with that information, that there is something wrong out there, what are you going to do? … you guys, the only thing you can do is to continue to educate yourselves, and to work against it. And especially being white, it's not about saying, "Well, I just want to get rid of these privileges that I have." You can't! In fact what's happened is somebody has handed you a megaphone in your life, without asking for it … your skin color works for you in all these different situations. And if you're using that? To work against the system of racism? Only *then* are you not contributing to racism.
>
> (Field notes, 2-7-08)

While students displayed a range of reactions, the class largely took these challenges seriously. Many students identified the race discussions as an influential experience. One girl noted that she "loved" the experience: "I felt like I [finally] got to say what I have been wanting to say for years!! I feel very proud of myself" (Student work sample, 6-1-08). Another called it "powerful," explaining that afterward "I felt much more comfortable talking about racism with my family, friends, and many people who I didn't really know" (Student work sample, 6-1-08). As evidenced in their class participation, interviews, and work samples, black and bi/multiracial students tended to respond positively, valuing the chance to discuss race with their white peers and share personal stories of discrimination. The response of Latino, Asian American, and white students was more varied, ranging from resistance to the idea of white privilege; to feelings of exclusion and guilt; to a sense of racial awakening, including the acceptance of responsibility and empowerment to act. While there was an array of responses, it is clear that the teachers' goals for the unit were met in many cases. Twenty-three out of 38 students identified their newfound knowledge of racism and white privilege as the most or one of the most important ideas that they would take away from the class (Student work samples, 6-1-08).

World War II and the Holocaust

Quarter three continued with a return to a more "traditional" history curriculum, a unit on World War II. Teaching about the Holocaust, Mr. Evans emphasized the effects of "othering," the ways in which dehumanizing a person or group of people can lead to violence. Material from the textbook, his own PowerPoint presentations, and films about the war facilitated students' deep understanding of this era. Mr. Evans also connected the historical period to the present, insisting, "we have to look at where otherness is happening in our world right now and act" (Field notes, 4-14-08). As he told me in an interview,

> [W]hen we start doing the Holocaust ... I want to really teach them about that idea of otherness, and I have that as a theme ... otherness vs. understanding. ... trying to get that idea that it's the racial other, or the religious other, or ... the other in the middle school, like the way humans—the way we do that.
>
> (Interview, 3-14-08)

Mr. Evans sought for students to understand not only the historical implications of dehumanizing, but the seemingly small ways such processes persist in middle-school life.

Concurrent with the World War II unit, students worked on a combined English–Social Studies assignment that extended into quarter four, a research paper on a topic of their choice related to cultural conflict. Writing inquiry questions, taking notes from both online and print sources, writing thesis statements and outlines/thinking maps, formatting the paper, and documenting sources, students practiced traditional research skills. They also reflected on the emotional impact of their research topics through creating digital collages on the subjects they investigated—topics including children in the Holocaust, genocide in Rwanda, Jewish gangsters, racism in music, Malcolm X—and the feelings it evoked in them. This approach to the research paper allowed students to continue to make personal connections to the curriculum.

Cultural Resolution: Studying Africa and Concluding the Year

Quarter four focused mainly on Africa, including the ways in which the diamond trade shaped politics and the reconciliation of apartheid in South Africa. Students continued to explore issues of race, exploitation, and power along with culture. However, with the last eight weeks of school disrupted by testing, field trips, performances, holidays, and other schedule irregularities, it proved difficult for Mr. Evans and the students to follow a curriculum that built on itself as logically and meaningfully as the rest of the year had. Mr. Evans commented that, like most teachers, there were times he got tired and could not put the effort into preparation that he would have liked to. He himself felt that the idea of cultural resolution got short-changed.

In the last week of school, though, Mr. Evans asked his students to reflect on their five years at MAS and what they learned in eighth grade in particular. After they laughed, talked, and reminisced about their experiences, he finished class by reading a poem and then issuing a final challenge: "You guys, my final thoughts for you all. Think about those conversations we had. Think about being critical, challenging things. Not accepting status quo. Looking out for others" (Field notes, 6-2-08).

Concluding Thoughts

Teachers need to learn to implement critical multiculturalism in order to teach in relevant and responsive ways. Yet this work does not come easy. In an interview, Mr. Evans noted that each group of students responded differently to his curriculum; he also explained that he sometimes got frustrated about having to make connections for some students. Far from being satisfied with how things progressed, Mr. Evans saw room for improvement, demonstrating the reflective practice that marks good teachers.

Moodley (1999) comments on the importance of the teacher's stance, explaining that students must be "allowed to work through their own stereotypes without being embarrassed or silenced from the outset. All too often antiracist advocates display a self-righteous superior morality that by definition exempts the speaker from the sins of racism" (p. 141). By modeling and fostering self-reflection and acknowledging his own and students' struggles with these issues, Mr. Evans created a safe space for his students to explore issues of race, power, and culture together with him (see also Fitzpatrick, this volume). Structuring experiences that lead to meaningful examination of one's own cultural identity therefore takes time, sensitivity, and careful design.

In her list of guidelines for critical multicultural practice, Nieto (1999) writes that "[c]ritical multicultural education affirms students' culture without trivializing the concept of culture itself"; it "challenges hegemonic knowledge" (p. 206); it "complicates pedagogy" (p. 207); and it "encourages 'dangerous discourses'" (p. 209). While the work is messy and uncertain, Mr. Evans' curriculum and pedagogy largely followed these principles. The efforts of Mr. Evans, like other critical teachers and their students, contributes to a growing and important research and teaching dialogue around the successes and dilemmas of critical multicultural practice, helping us to consider how we may—that we must—enact this work in our own ways, in our own classrooms.

Notes

1 Even while using racial identity markers, I remain cognizant that race is a socially and culturally constructed term. Despite the fluid and hybrid nature of identity categories, it is still nonetheless useful to use such designations to describe the study participants, including myself. While I will not take up many of the methodological issues related to identities here, I do recognize that these positionings—of myself, the teachers, the students, and the rest of the school community—significantly impacted the way I experienced this work and the way I write about it now.

2 This figure comes from an article on the school published by a local newspaper. To maintain confidentiality, I have chosen not to provide the citation for the article.

3 These guidelines come from the staff development program that all Metro Arts School staff participate in, led by Pacific Educational Group.

References

Balaban, N. (1995). Seeing the child, knowing the person. In W. Ayers (Ed.), *To become a teacher: Making a difference in children's lives* (pp. 49–57). New York: Teachers College Press.

Banks, J., & Banks, C. (2004). Introduction. In J. Banks & C. Banks (Eds.), *Handbook of research on multicultural education* (pp. xi–xiv). San Francisco, CA: Jossey-Bass.

Delpit, L. (1995). *Other people's children.* New York: New Press.

Florio-Ruane, S. (2001). *Teacher education and the cultural imagination: Autobiography, conversation, and narrative.* Mahwah, NJ: Lawrence Erlbaum.

Freire, P. (2000). *Pedagogy of the oppressed* (30th anniversary edition). New York: Continuum.

Gay, G., & Kirkland, K. (2003, Summer). Developing cultural critical consciousness and self reflection in preservice teacher education. *Theory Into Practice, 42*(3), 181–187.

Glazier, J., & Seo, J. (2005). Multicultural literature and discussion as mirror and window? *Journal of Adolescent and Adult Literacy, 48*(8), 686–700.

LeCompte, K., & McCray, A. (2002). Complex conversations with teacher candidates: Perspectives of whiteness and culturally responsive teaching. *Curriculum and Teaching Dialogue, 4*(1), 25–35.

May, S. (1999). Critical multiculturalism and cultural difference: Avoiding essentialism. In S. May (Ed.), *Critical multiculturalism: Rethinking multicultural and antiracist education* (pp. 11–41). Philadelphia and London: Falmer Press.

McIntosh, P. (1990, Winter). White privilege: Unpacking the invisible knapsack. *Independent School, 49*(2), 31–36.

McLaren, P. (1998). *Life in schools: An introduction to critical pedagogy in the foundation of education.* New York: Longman.

Miner, H. (1956). Body ritual among the Nacirema. *American Anthropologist, 58,* 503–507.

Moodley, K. (1999). Antiracist education through political literacy. In S. May (Ed.), *Critical multiculturalism: Rethinking multicultural and antiracist education* (pp. 138–152). Philadelphia and London: Falmer Press.

Nieto, S. (1999). Critical multicultural education and students' perspectives. In S. May (Ed.), *Critical multiculturalism: Rethinking multicultural and antiracist education* (pp. 191–215). Philadelphia and London: Falmer Press.

Sleeter, C.E., & Bernal, D.D. (2004). Critical pedagogy, critical race theory, and antiracist education. In J. Banks & C. Banks (Eds.), *Handbook of Research on Multicultural Education* (pp. 240–258). San Francisco, CA: Jossey-Bass.

Ukpokodu, O.N. (2003). Teaching multicultural education from a critical perspective: Challenges and dilemmas. *Multicultural Perspectives, 5*(4), 17–23.

Uys, J. (Writer, Director). (1980). *The gods must be crazy.* United States: Sony Pictures.

Vygotsky, L. (1978). *Mind and society: The development of higher psychological processes.* Cambridge, MA: Harvard University Press.

13

A Critical Multicultural
Approach to Physical Education
Challenging Discourses of Physicality and Building Resistant Practices in Schools

KATIE FITZPATRICK

Introduction

Physical education is the only school curriculum subject that focuses on the study of movement, bodies, physicality, and sport. As such, it provides opportunities for embodied curriculum learning as well as exploration of critical issues associated with racialized and gendered bodies in a variety of cultural contexts. Physical education, then, is a unique and potent context for the exploration of issues close to the heart of critical multiculturalism, antiracist education, and critical race theory.

And yet, discussions of physical education as a specific site for the articulation of a critical multicultural practice remain rare. While physical education has strong traditions of critical theory and pedagogy (for example, see Fernandez-Balboa, 1997; Kirk &Tinning, 1990; Wright, MacDonald, & Burrows, 2004), the majority of this work focuses on bodies, gender, sexuality, (dis)ability, class, and inclusion. With a few notable exceptions (for example, Azzarito & Solomon, 2005; Hokowhitu, 2008; Oliver & Lalik, 2000, 2004), scholars in the field largely ignore "race," racism, ethnicity, and racialization, despite these having a significant place in sport sociology (Entire, 2000; Hoberman, 1997; Palmer, 2007).

So what might a critical multicultural pedagogy of physical education look like? What discourses need it address and how does it differ from other critical approaches to physical education? In this chapter, I aim to answer these questions in four parts. I first explore physical education as a key but contradictory space for critical multicultural practice because it is often conflated with two discourses: the privileging of thin white bodies, and the devaluing of the physical in opposition to the intellectual. Such discourses have racialized and gendered consequences for participants and must, therefore, be a central focus of a critical multicultural approach to this subject. In part two, I share an example of a critical multicultural approach to physical education. Drawing on a critical ethnographic study of a multiethnic working-class suburban school in New Zealand, I share the pedagogy of one physical education teacher, Dan. After briefly introducing the ethnographic study, I focus on five key aspects of Dan's teaching, arguing that his approach can be viewed as a critical multicultural pedagogy of physical education. In the third part of the chapter I discuss the importance of context in any critical multicultural program and provide further background to Dan's classes. I end by reflecting on what I have learnt about the potential of critical multicultural practice in physical education.

Narrow Discourses: Gendered and Racialized Notions of the Physical

As we shall see, physical education is potentially a key site for critical practice but it is also aligned with problematic racialized and gendered constructions, two of which I focus on here. The first concerns oppressive body norms privileging thinness and whiteness. The second locates physical bodies and physical education as non-academic.

Thin White Bodies: Physical Education and Body Control

Thin white bodies are highly valued in western societies, at least in recent historical terms. Read as attractive and sexy, the slender form in particular is privileged in popular media and the fashion, fitness, and beauty industries, and is internalized by communities as desirable (Garrett, 2004). In addition, moral panic about the increase of fatness in western countries, termed the "obesity epidemic" in popular and media discourse, has created a frenzy of body awareness and action. Health professionals and government agencies in many western countries now consider obesity a pressing national health problem. The notion that the population is getting fatter is generally accepted, as are the plethora of physical activity and nutrition-related initiatives aimed at reducing people's weight. Critical analysis of this discourse (for example, Campos, 2004; Gard & Wright, 2005) is largely ignored, and many of these initiatives directly impact schools in the form of imposed restrictions on canteen foods and increased physical activity and sports programs for students.

The overt focus on body size and shape in the obesity discourses encourages the view that there is a correct and "healthy" type of body, one linked directly to physical size and weight (Gard & Wright, 2005) and usually related to a white ideal. Brown and black bodies are routinely cited as problematic in this discourse. Working-class Māori[1] and Pasifika[2] peoples in New Zealand, and African Americans in the USA, for example, routinely appear in media releases dealing with national obesity statistics and are attributed blame for contributing to the "problem" (Campos, 2004). For young people, in the midst of development, body norms are highly problematic, especially when conflated with the aggressive promotion of unrealistically slim white bodies as desirable (Burrows & Wright, 2004; Oliver & Lalik, 2004). Physical education in Western countries is often blamed in media and policy discourses for creating the so-called "obesity epidemic" while also being charged with providing the solution (Gard, 2004).[3]

The Physical as Lower Order and Devalued

Physical education is frequently elided with sport and charged with producing elite athletes, or judged simply as "play time" or "time out" from classes. As a training ground for sport and the maintenance of the body, and as a relief from "work," rather than a discipline of study, physical education is presumed to be non-academic and relegated in school subject hierarchies far beneath ostensibly "elite" subjects such as mathematics and science. The hierarchy, of course, extends outside of schools: play and leisure are dichotomized with work, physical jobs rank more lowly than studied professions, and sport is viewed as neither a job nor a serious activity at a non-elite level (Shivers & deLisle, 1997). In many nation-states, sport is part of national identity and viewed as a positive, character building activity for young people and one which acts as an "intervention" for "wayward" and delinquent (read: Black, Brown, and poor) youth (Collins & Kay, 2003). New Zealand's top Māori and Pasifika athletes are often held up as role models and charged with the responsibility to inspire young people. Sport for Brown youth in New Zealand is touted as "a way out" of poverty and educational failure, much like basketball in the United States (Entire, 2000).

A racialized perception abounds that Māori and Pasifika athletes in New Zealand and Black athletes in the USA, are "naturally" talented. Sports commentators, television personalities, and people from a range of cultures continually reinforce this position (Bruce, Falcous, & Thorpe, 2007; Entire, 2000). The "natural talent" label in both countries has specific effects, such as a perception that success in sport requires little effort of Brown and Black athletes, and is not the result of hard work, training, and commitment (Entire, 2000; Hokowhitu, 2008). While White athletes are praised for their discipline, stamina, and determination, Māori, Pasifika, and Black athletes are more likely noted for their "flair" and instinct (Hoberman, 1997; Palmer, 2007). Success in sport reinforces the social Darwinian view of the brown body as "naturally physical," lower order and non-intellectual (Banton, 1998). The assumption that Māori, Pasifika, and Black students are "naturally" physically talented implies that they are not naturally academically talented and reinforces the Cartesian notion that the mind and body are separate (Hoberman, 1997). This dualism is hierarchical, with the lower-order, instinctual and anti-intellectual human traits defined as physical and positioned in the body, while higher-order, academic and spiritual development are mental, and inhabit the mind (Arnold, 1979; Descartes, 1988). Physical education's relegation to the former category reinforces the social Darwinian racial hierarchy in relation to Māori, Pasifika, and Black youth (Hoberman, 1997).

Physical education is thus problematically located in relation to racialized and gendered discourses of the body. If teachers ignore such constructions, hierarchies will continue to be reinforced in physical education classes. These discourses, however, also provide a starting point for a critical multicultural approach to physical education. How one teacher, Dan, approaches such issues in his practice is the subject of the second part of this chapter. I first introduce the study from which this is drawn and then outline five aspects of "Dan's" teaching that contribute to a critical multicultural practice of physical education.

A Critical Approach: Dan's Pedagogies of Physical Education

During 2007, I conducted a critical ethnographic study (Thomas, 1993) of young people in health and physical education classes in one school. Situated in the southern suburbs of New Zealand's largest city, Auckland, Kikorangi High (a pseudonym) is a multiethnic suburban high school. I had taught health and physical education at the school between 1999 and 2003. The students who attend are almost all from Māori and/or Pasifika cultural backgrounds. The area surrounding the school, known as South Auckland, is one of the most poverty-stricken in New Zealand. It is also known, especially in media discourses, for crime, drugs and gang activity (for example, Collins, 2008; cf. Locke, this volume).

Although I spent time in a range of health and physical education classes during 2007 (over 300 hours), I spent the most time (150 hours) with a Pākehā[4] (European) teacher in his mid twenties, Dan. I joined Dan's class of 16 young people (all aged between 16 and 17 years old), participating in classes along with the students (not as a teacher) and focusing on building relationships (Fine, 1994; Fine, Weiz, Weseen, & Wong, 2000). During this time, I journaled my experiences and thoughts and engaged students (in groups and individually) in recorded research discussions about topics that concerned them.[5] During my participation in Dan's classes, I noted several aspects of his pedagogy that, I believe, contribute to a critical multicultural practice.

I have organized Dan's pedagogical approach into five key practices: building the environment; deconstructing power; playfulness; studying critical topics, and embodied criticality. I will discuss each of these in turn, using a mixture of stories and conversations with Dan and the students.

Building the Environment

A foundational aspect of Dan's approach to teaching was building relationships and trust within the class, which permeates the four other pedagogical aspects below (see also Flynn, this volume). Dan focused his classes on questions about relating to others and experiences which brought students into teams and required problem solving and discussions. The class attended a week-long outdoor education camp together at the beginning of the school year and experienced hiking, camping, and problem-solving activities. During many of his classes, Dan would constantly steer student discussions back to relationships, highlighting the significance of listening skills, encouragement, and trust. Significantly, he took a facilitative rather than a directive attitude to teaching. He allowed students space and time to negotiate and solve problems, resisting stepping in with directions and solutions. Drawing on several physical education pedagogies that highlight relationship building (for example, sport education and social responsibility),[6] Dan structured many of his classes around teamwork and problem solving.

As a result, students saw physical education as a space where they learnt about relationships. Ben, a student from Dan's class, commented repeatedly during discussions that physical education "helps us to get to know each other ... we didn't know anyone before, but now we're tight." At moments like these, one of the others would usually add triumphantly, "like undies [underwear], we're tight like undies!" One of Dan's students, Harriet, believed that the willingness of students to relate to others is "part of our culture." She went on to explain that, "even if we don't know, or like someone, we don't want them to feel left out ... it's not our way." Harriet later attributed this behavior to Māori and Pasifika values and experiences, saying that people with "brown skin" knew what it was like to be discriminated against and, therefore, had more empathy with others. In this sense, Dan was also connecting with students' own cultural worlds, allowing their cultural practices and values to become a central part of the class (Bishop & Glynn, 1999). While an important pedagogical approach in itself, building a strong network of relationships within the class became a platform upon which Dan established a critical approach, which he introduced by first deconstructing aspects of his own power with the students.

Deconstructing Power

Year 12 students spill into the gym through three different doors. Many are already changing clothes, as they walk across the gym floor they shed clothes, revealing shorts and t-shirts below their uniforms. Others strip off school shirts in the middle of the floor, flex their muscles and then pull t-shirts over their heads. The atmosphere is noisy and the students are ready to play, the room is buzzing. Dan beckons students into the middle of the gym and they sit in a circle. He starts a discussion about leadership by asking: "Why are we sitting like this?" Harriet offers "So we can all see each other," and then Sione, "So we are all on the same level sir." "Yeah, so what difference does that make," asks Dan, now getting up, "how do things change when I talk to you from up here?" "You're talking to us like you're all that and we're nothing sir, it makes you, like, not one of us."

Led by Dan, the students then discuss how teachers and leaders affect the class atmosphere even with their body language. The first activity is a game of "crash," a simple two-team game where points are scored by placing a ball on a big crash mat at the end of the gym. Dan changes the game, adding new rules during natural game pauses. First, only students wearing certain colored shirts are allowed to touch the ball, then boys and then girls. The students get angry when they're left out of play. The class ends with discussion of how some students dominate games while others are left out, and how teachers' choices of activities and rules affect participation. Dan reminds his class that soon they will be teaching junior students and, as leaders, they are powerful and responsible for including everyone.

During discussions like this, Dan consciously made students aware of power relationships and how even simple interactions are inscribed with discourses of power. During all his classes Dan gave students choice about lesson content, topics, and activities. He used questioning to stimulate thinking, but did not dictate the answers. Rather, he allowed students to discuss and debate until a resolution was found. Dan frequently communicated that teachers are less powerful than students think, that he could not force them to do anything, that they had many choices.

Dan also made specific references to his "whiteness" during classes. He would joke about himself being "just a Palagi" (European) and encourage students to question inequities, such as which ethnicities were most prevalent in the New Zealand parliament. Important here is Dan's interrogation of both teacher power (McLaren, 2003) and his own cultural positioning as a White teacher. By acknowledging and discussing teacher power and racial inequities he laid the foundation for students to be able to discuss and contest issues of power, including racism and gender (see below). Such a sharing of power and acknowledgment of power relations is not always straightforward. Allowing students to have choice during lessons and to unpack issues of power is messy and, at times, disrupts normative notions of a "controlled" school environment. Dan's classes could appear at times to be disrupted and "out of control." As schools are often key sites of surveillance (Foucault, 1977), students and teachers who disrupt power relations in classes may find themselves monitored.

In addition to building relationships and reflecting on his own power, a culture of playfulness in Dan's classes also allowed students to engage with critical issues.

Playfulness

Dan set up an environment where playfulness was valued and encouraged. By modeling a playful attitude, making jokes, acting "goofy" and avoiding an authoritative approach, Dan allowed students to interact with him and others in playful ways. Experimentation, games without rigid structure, input from all of the class, and a lot of laughter and pastiche, were hallmarks of Dan's lessons. Lugones (1994) defines playfulness as intentional activity, open to uncertainty and surprise. Playfulness, she explains, is partly "an openness to being a fool." Such openness combines "not worrying about competence, not being self-important, not taking norms as sacred and finding ambiguity and double edges a source of wisdom and delight" (p. 636). Noting that different cultural worlds have different values and boundaries, Lugones argues that an ability to be playful is a signal of an embracing world. People exhibit playfulness when they are fully part of the society and community. New Zealand's cultural Eurocentrism means Māori and Pasifika youth have less opportunity and less potential for playfulness.

A focus on the playful in classes depends on the milieu created by teachers and the interactions between students and teachers. While Dan models a playful attitude, the students are able respond in kind because of the deep relationships formed. Thus, the foundation of relationships creates greater potential for playfulness. The level of competition is also key—the more competitive the environment, the less likely is playfulness. Dan constantly provides comic relief for his classes; he joins in games and often "acts out" amusing and ironic moves. He rejects the staunch male physical education teacher stereotype (see below), and the students take his lead. One of Dan's students, William, for example, is an elite rugby player with outstanding coordination, confidence, and competence. He rarely plays aggressively during classes or with a serious competitiveness. This isn't to suggest that he doesn't play to win, it's just that winning is almost never the focus of classes. At the end of vigorous and energetic games, no one seems to know the score, and there's never a referee. William plays with a mischievous, rather than a competitive, attitude; he "plays around" with the rules and extends the boundaries of games. Running with the ball, he catches people's eye, makes a face, invites them to laugh, and makes a joke about his finesse or his mistakes. He performs exaggerated, almost comic, side steps, rolls on the ground to lob a "miracle ball" pass under his legs to a teammate. William takes his performance seriously but it is not serious. Playfulness is, indeed, the opposite of antagonism (Lugones, 1994).

In addition to valuing playfulness and relationships, Dan also explicitly studies critical topics in his program.

Studying Critical Topics

Dan's class is discussing body image. The students are given a set of photos from fashion magazines and asked to respond to a series of questions about the pictures. Some photos are highly sexualized images of women advertising cars, perfume, and underwear. Others are male models displaying the latest "trendy" clothing, while others are seemingly androgynous youth posed in the street. A group of boys in the class ridicule the "skinny white" male models in the pictures. William laughs and calls them "gay" before attending to the questions. Dan picks this up and questions William about why the pictures suggest "gayness." William explains, "Oh, I didn't mean like gay gay sir, you know homosexual, I just meant these guys are sad." The class then discuss how "gay" shouldn't be used in a negative way and one student affirms "yeah, I mean it's cool to be gay or whatever, we need a different word [to mean sad]."

Dan then focuses their attention on the pictures, asking what messages are given about gender and sexuality. The students struggle to answer at first so he helps by explaining an advertisement for makeup. In the photo is a woman's face. She is pouting at the camera with red lipstick and has "perfect" skin. "What does this woman look like?" asks Dan. One of the girls replies, "pretty" then whispers to her friend "I wish I had skin like that." "Nah, she looks fake," replies Sofia "no one really looks like that". "You're right Sofia, this image has probably been altered, but what does she actually look like, what message does this picture give about women?" "That you have to look perfect and have no acne," offers Harriett. "Yeah, and that pale skin is nice, with lipstick and all that" adds Ema. "That's right," affirms Dan, "we get messages from these pictures; a certain image is being portrayed here." Dan gets the students into groups to assemble a list of what the advertisements promote as attractive and discussion turns to why magazines want to promote such narrow forms of beauty. "Do we listen to these messages though?" asks Dan. "I don't," states Sepela, "I don't care about those stuck up prissy pictures." "Do you care how you look though?" Dan pushes her. She mumbles "Nah, I jus' do what I want." "What about you guys, what do you want to look like," asks Dan. "Pretty sir," mocks Sione and the others laugh. "We don't want to look like these ones Sir," laughs William, "they look dumb, weak." He flexes his muscles and grins.

This is a short example of how Dan introduces critical topics to the students. He challenges dominant notions of gender and racialized images of beauty, but in gentle ways, asking students to identify personally with the discourses and the critique. The lesson above comes from a series of lessons on body image, looking at how racialized, sexualized, and gendered bodies are represented in the media, and how such images affect young people. This study extends to examining sporting images, how athletes' bodies are sexually commodified in the promotion of sport. Dan uses a critical inquiry approach to such topics. Prominent critical physical educator, Jan Wright, explains the difference between "critical thinking" and "critical inquiry." The former she suggests is based on "logical reasoning," while the latter is concerned with "assisting students to examine and challenge the status quo, the dominant constructions of reality, and the power relations that produce inequalities" (Wright, 2004, p. 7). Wright argues that, while logical reasoning and evaluation are useful skills for young people, only critical inquiry will enable them to interrogate the workings of power. Dan explicitly engaged his students in critical inquiry in a range of topics during the year. Such studies included: racism and sport, gender, body image and media, leadership, and outdoor education. The final part of Dan's approach is his embodied critical orientation.

Embodied Criticality

I have left this section until last because I think it is the most radical of Dan's approaches to teaching. I use Bourdieu's notion of "habitus" (see Bourdieu & Passeron, 1990) here to understand how Dan disrupts dominant notions, especially of gender and sexuality. Bourdieu's theory of habitus is often used to analyze and describe how people live and reproduce culture through their bodies and subsequently how social group boundaries (including those of class, culture, gender) are maintained. David Brown (2005), for example, describes the habitus of the male physical education teachers in his study:

> a suitable (predominantly mesomorphic) physique; demonstrations of specialised practical ability; a strong competitive disposition; highly contextualised and codified emotional displays; a willing acceptance of physical contact, pain and effort in sport; and, perhaps above all, an orientation towards dominance and control over others.
>
> (p. 10)

The silent assumption in Brown's description is that the male physical educa-tion teacher is also definitively heterosexual. Brown (2005) and others (Evans, Davis, & Penney, 1996) suggest that physical education teachers learn these embodied qualities as children and adolescents. These dispositions are later reinforced and normalized through teacher education and school practice. The embodied dominant or "hegemonic" masculinity of Brown's (2005) teachers is an established theoretical position in physical education and sport-ing contexts (Messner & Sabo, 1990) but is also highly contested. Pringle and Markula (2007) argue, for example, that a greater diversity and continuum of acceptable masculinities exists, even in the most aggressive sports (see also Francis, 2008). It is reasonable at least to assume that many physical education teachers do not conform to these dispositions, even if they are still highly visible (Webb & Macdonald, 2007).

Dan, for example, embodies a different kind of physical education teacher habitus, and a different kind of masculinity than the heteronormative model identified by Brown (2005). He consciously uses this difference as a teaching pedagogy to subvert dominant notions of sex, gender, and sexuality. Dan does this in several ways. Instead of asserting control and valuing performance in physical education, he encourages play and undermines competitiveness. By dressing in a range of colors, including pink clothing that could be labeled "fem-inine," and by explicitly discussing his emotions and thoughts about gender, he "shakes" people's assumptions about what it is to be a man. He challenges het-eronormative assumptions through inclusive language and by questioning stu-dents' heteronormative comments during formal teaching and in casual conversations. Dan's embodied critical approach directly disrupts students' assumptions about the relationship between gender, sex, and sexuality, what Deborah Youdell (2003) calls the "sex–gender–sexuality constellation." This con-stellation describes the inextricable link between the three areas so that:

> the female body is already feminized, the feminine is already heterosexual, the hetero-feminine is already female. Sex–gender–sexuality, then, are not causally related; rather, they exist in abiding constellations in which to name one category of the constellation is to silently infer further categories.
>
> (p. 256)

In Dan's case, the constellation invoked is the hetero-masculine male, which, according to Brown (2005) is reproduced by the physical education teaching profession in specific ways. Dan's embodied dispositions, as well as his class-room pedagogies, are a direct challenge to the gender–sex–sexuality constella-tion. His embodied and critical approach undermines the silence, or at least extreme discomfort, around sexuality in schools (Epstein & Johnson, 1998) and overt homophobic and heteronormative discourses (Youdell, 2005).

Dan's ability to disrupt normative gender expectations with his class is based on all of the preceding approaches discussed. Without an inclusive class atmosphere where relationships and teamwork are valued, playfulness would not be possible. The way Dan's raises critical issues, both in everyday conversations and as explicit topics of study, enables students to begin to engage with issues of power in their own ways.

Notes on the Context: New Zealand and Physical Education Curriculum Policy

The context Dan is operating within is a specific one. Critical multicultural practice must heed the subtleties of context in order to be effective (McLaren, 1995). While I contend that any teacher can apply aspects of Dan's practice in their own context, the social, historical, and political landscape of education in any location is important to consider. One particular aspect of the context is significant here, the Health and Physical Education curriculum policy in New Zealand.

New Zealand Curriculum Policy

Like other colonial societies, New Zealand's history contributes to ongoing social and political inequalities between Europeans, Māori, Pasifika peoples, and other migrants (cf. Bishop; Stewart, this volume). Such inequalities, of course, play out and are reproduced by schools and other social institutions, which rarely implement critical approaches or explicitly address issues of power (Hokowhitu 2004a, 2004b; Bishop & Berryman, 2006). Dan's approach to teaching is, however, supported in New Zealand by current national curriculum policy in health and physical education. Recent national curriculums (New Zealand Ministry of Education, 1999, 2007) are based on what has been referred to as a "socially critical" view (Tinning, 2000; Penney & Harris, 2004) of physical education and, its partner subject in policy, health education. In the case of physical education, such a policy allows teachers to move away from individualized, sport-based, competitive and hierarchical forms of physical education, towards more critical and inclusive pedagogies, including the type of critical inquiry Dan employs.[7] Recent health and physical education curriculum policy in New Zealand (Ministry of Education, 1999, 2007) includes a range of sociocritical concepts and terms, three of which I'll mention here. The first is termed "a socio-ecological perspective." This concept encourages teachers to contextualize physical education activities within interpersonal and wider social contexts. "Critical thinking" (based on critical inquiry, see above) is also included, as are opportunities for students to develop critique of sporting cultures and media messages. Significantly, the curriculum also includes a concept from the indigenous Māori world, termed *hauora*.[8] *Hauora* includes recognition of physical (*tinana*), spiritual (*wairua*), mental and emotional (*hinengaro*), and social (*whānau*) aspects of wellbeing (cf. Bishop; Stewart, this volume). This holistic concept provides a challenge to Eurocentric views of physical education, which tend still to focus on the physical in isolation from other dimensions.

Final Thoughts

The time I spent with Dan taught me a great deal about teaching young people. It taught me, or rather reminded me, that context is important, and relationships are everything. It also taught me that "doing" critical pedagogy, while challenging and, at times, uncomfortable, can also be playful. Too often in my own teaching with high-school and tertiary students, critical topics would go badly. After engaging in critical discussions about gender, racism, or sexuality, my students would get angry, engage in personal and defensive debates and my "positive and inclusive" class atmosphere would be lost (cf. Hanley; Lea, this volume). I refuse, however, to spend classes ignoring the very real critical issues in my subject area and pretending that as long as we "get along" then power hierarchies don't impact. Building relationships with and between students and reflecting on how we enact teacher power may be a good starting point before more focused critical inquiry. The playfulness in Dan's classes and his own personal challenges to dominant masculinities provide opportunities to expose and critique discourses of power in more embodied ways.

The young people Dan works with are from Māori and Pasifika backgrounds; they live in a poor and abject suburb in New Zealand's largest city (see also Locke, this volume). Their peers rarely appear in any of the country's universities or in the top achievement statistics. The pedagogies of one teacher cannot change the overwhelming social and political circumstances these students face (McLaren, 1995) but they *can* make a difference. By helping students to engage critically, Dan is creating an environment where the workings of power can be exposed. Academic texts encouraging critical approaches are common but too often these fail to provide concrete examples of critical practice. In this sense, Dan provides us all with some hope.

Notes

1 New Zealand's indigenous peoples.
2 Pasifika is the now commonly accepted pan-ethnic term to describe Pacific migrants to New Zealand, principally from the islands of Samoa, Tonga, Cook Islands, Niue, Tokelau, and Tuvalu. (For further discussion, see MacPherson, Spoonley, & Anae, 2000; Spoonley, MacPherson, & Pearson, 2004.)
3 The obesity epidemic is the subject of much scholarly debate. Most of the work questioning the tenets of this supposed epidemic is not represented in media debates, which tend to reinforce simplistic relationships between nutrition, physical activity, and body weight. In addition, such media reporting tends to reinforce the normativity of slim white bodies and marginalize non-slim bodies, deeming the latter "unhealthy." A critical approach to physical education requires closer study of these assumptions. (For extended discussion see Gard & Wright, 2004.)
4 Pākehā is the Māori term for European or Non-Māori. The equivalent Pasifika term is Palagi.
5 It is beyond the scope of this chapter to discuss methodological approaches and issues in this study. (For a fuller discussion see Fitzpatrick, 2010.)
6 See Siedentop, Hastie, and van der Mars (2004); Hellison (2003).

7 For further discussion of the critical aspects of physical education curriculum policy in New Zealand, see Fitzpatrick (2009).
8 Space here precludes any in-depth engagement with this concept (for this and subsequent debate see, for example, Durie, 1994; Fitzpatrick, 2006; Hokowhitu, 2004a).

References

Arnold, P. J. (1979). *Meaning in movement, sport and physical education.* London: Heinemann.
Azzarito, L., & Solomon, M. A. (2005). A reconceptualization of physical education: The intersection of gender/race/social class. *Sport, Education and Society, 10*(1), 25–47.
Banton, M. (1998). *Racial theories* (2nd ed.). Cambridge, England: Cambridge University Press.
Bishop, R., & Berryman, M. (2006). *Culture speaks.* Wellington, New Zealand: Huia.
Bishop, R., & Glynn, T. (1999). *Culture counts: Changing power relations in education.* Palmerston North, New Zealand: Dunmore Press.
Bourdieu, P., & Passeron, J-C. (1990). *Reproduction in education, society and culture* (R. Nice, Trans., 2nd ed.). London: Sage.
Brown, D. (2005). An economy of gendered practices? Learning to teach physical education from the perspective of Pierre Bourdieu's embodied sociology. *Sport, Education and Society, 10*(1), 3–23.
Bruce, T., Falcous, M., & Thorpe, H. (2007). The mass media and sport. In C. Collins & S. Jackson (Eds.), *Sport in Aotearoa/New Zealand society* (pp. 147–169). Melbourne, Australia: Thomson.
Burrows, L., & Wright, J. (2004). Being healthy: Young New Zealanders ideas about health. *Childrenz Issues, 8*(1), 7–12.
Campos, P. (2004). *The obesity myth: Why America's obsession with weight is hazardous to your health.* New York: Gotham Books.
Collins, M., & Kay, T. (2003). *Sport and social exclusion.* New York: Routledge.
Collins, S. (2008). Mayor urges focus on drugs. *New Zealand Herald,* 2 December.
Descartes, R. (1988). The real distinction between the mind and body of man. In W. J. Morgan & K. V. Meier (Eds.), *Philosophic inquiry in sport* (2nd ed., pp. 70–72). Champaign, IL: Human Kinetics.
Durie, M. (1994). *Whaiora: Māori health development.* Auckland, New Zealand: Oxford University Press.
Entire, J. (2000). *Taboo: Why Black athletes dominate sports and why we're so afraid to talk about it.* New York: Public Affairs.
Epstein, D., & Johnson, R. (1998). *Schooling sexualities.* Buckingham, England: Open University Press.
Evans, J., Davis, B., & Penney, D. (1996). Teachers, teaching and the social construction of gender relations. *Sport, Education and Society, 1*(1), 165–184.
Fernandez-Balboa, J. M (Ed.). (1997). *Critical postmodernism, human movement, physical education and sport.* New York: SUNY Press.
Fine, M. (1994). Dis-stance and other stances: Negotiations of power inside feminist research. In Andrew D. Gitlin (Ed.), *Power and method: Political activism and educational research* (pp. 13–35). New York: Routledge.
Fine, M., Weiz, L., Weseen, S., & Wong, L. (2000). For whom? Qualitative research, representations and social responsibilities. In N. K. Denzin & Y. S. Lincoln (Eds.), *Handbook of qualitative research* (2nd ed., pp. 107–131). Thousand Oaks, CA: Sage.
Fitzpatrick, K. (2006). The dangers of minimalism: Health and physical education in the draft New Zealand curriculum. *Teachers and curriculum, 9,* 11–18.
Fitzpatrick, K. (2009). Indigenous perspectives in HPE curriculum: Contradictions and colonisation. In M. Dinan-Thompson (Ed.), *Health and physical education: Contemporary issues for curriculum in Australia and New Zealand.* Melbourne, Australia: Oxford University Press.
Fitzpatrick, K. (2010). Stop playing up! Physical education, racialisation and resistance. *Ethnography,* forthcoming.

Foucault, M. (1977). *Discipline and punish: The birth of the prison* (Trans. A. Sheridan). New York: Random House.

Francis, B. (2008). Teaching manfully? Exploring gendered subjectivities and power via analysis of men teachers' gender performance. *Gender and Education, 20*(2), 109–122.

Gard, M. (2004). An elephant in the room and a bridge too far, or physical education and the "obesity epidemic". In J. Evans, B. Davis, & J. Wright (Eds.), *Body knowledge and control: Studies in the sociology of physical education and health* (pp. 68–82). London: Routledge.

Gard, M., & Wright, J. (2005). *The obesity epidemic: Science, morality and ideology*. London: Routledge.

Garrett, R. (2004). Gendered bodies and physical identities. In J. Evans, B. Davis, & J. Wright (Eds.), *Body knowledge and control: Studies in the sociology of health and physical education* (pp. 140–156). London: Routledge.

Hellison, D. (2003). *Teaching responsibility through physical activity* (2nd ed.). Champaign, IL: Human Kinetics.

Hoberman, J. (1997). *Darwin's athletes: How sport has damaged Black America and preserved the myth of race*. Boston: Houghton Mifflin.

Hokowhitu, B. (2004a). Challenges to state physical education: Tikanga Māori, physical education curricula, historical deconstruction, inclusivism and decolonisation. *Waikato Journal of Education, 10*, 71–84.

Hokowhitu, B. (2004b). Physical beings: Stereotypes, sport and the "physical education" of New Zealand Māori. In J. A. Mangan & A. Ritchie (Eds.), *Ethnicity, sport, identity: Struggles for status* (pp. 192–218). London: Frank Cass.

Hokowhitu, B. (2008). Understanding the Māori and Pacific body: Toward a critical pedagogy of physical education. *Journal of Physical Education New Zealand, 41*(3), 81–91.

Kirk, D., & Tinning, R. (1990). *Physical education, curriculum and culture: Critical issues in the contemporary crisis*. London: Falmer Press.

Lugones, M. (1994). Playfulness, "world" travelling, and loving perception. In D. S. Madison (Ed.), *The woman that I am: The literature and culture of contemporary women of color* (pp. 626–638). New York: St Martin's Griffin.

MacPherson, C., Spoonley, P., & Anae, M. (2000). *Tangata o te moana nui: The evolving identities of Pacific peoples in Aotearoa/New Zealand*. Palmerston North, New Zealand: Dunmore Press.

McLaren, P. (1995). *Critical pedagogy and predatory culture: Oppositional politics in a postmodern era*. New York: Routledge.

McLaren, P. (2003). *Life in schools: An introduction to critical pedagogy in the foundations of education*. Boston: Allyn & Bacon.

Messner, M. A., & Sabo, D. F. (Eds.). (1990). *Sport, men and the gender order: Critical feminist perspectives*. Campaign, IL: Human Kinetics.

New Zealand Ministry of Education. (1999). *Health and physical education in the New Zealand curriculum*. Wellington, New Zealand: Ministry of Education.

New Zealand Ministry of Education. (2007). *The New Zealand curriculum*. Wellington, New Zealand: Ministry of Education.

Oliver, K. L., & Lalik, R. (2000). *Bodily knowledge: Learning about equality and justice with adolescent girls*. New York: Peter Lang.

Oliver, K. L., & Lalik, R. (2004). "The beauty walk": Interrogating whiteness as the norm for beauty within one school's hidden curriculum. In J. Evans, B. Davis, & J. Wright (Eds.), *Body knowledge and control: Studies in the sociology of physical education and health* (pp. 115–129). London: Routledge.

Palmer, F. (2007). Treaty principles and Maori sport: Contemporary issues. In C. Collins & S. Jackson (Eds.), *Sport in Aotearoa/New Zealand society* (2nd ed., pp. 307–334). Melbourne, Australia: Thomson.

Penney, D., & Harris, J. (2004). The body and health in policy: Representations and recontextualisation. In J. Evans, B. Davis, & J. Wright (Eds.), *Body knowledge and control: Studies in the sociology of physical education and health* (pp. 96–111). London: Routledge.

Pringle, R., & Markula, P. (2006). *Foucault, sport and exercise: Power, knowledge and transforming the self.* London: Routledge.

Shivers, J. S., & deLisle, L. J. (1997). *The story of leisure: Context, concepts and current controversy.* Champaign, IL: Human Kinetics.

Siedentop, D., Hastie, P. A., & van der Mars, H. (2004). *Complete guide to sport education.* Champaign, IL: Human Kinetics.

Spoonley, P., Macpherson, C., & Pearson, D. (2004). *Tangata Tangata: The changing ethnic contours of New Zealand.* Palmerston North, New Zealand: Dunmore Press.

Thomas, J. (1993). *Doing critical ethnography.* Newbury Park, CA: Sage.

Webb, L., & Macdonald, D. (2007). Dualing with gender: Teachers' work, careers and leadership in physical education. *Gender and Education, 19*(4), 491–512.

Wright, J. (2004). Critical inquiry and problem solving in physical education. In J. Wright, D. MacDonald, & L. Burrows (Eds.), *Critical inquiry and problem solving in physical education* (pp. 3–15). London: Routledge.

Wright, J., MacDonald, D., & Burrows, L. (Eds.). (2004). *Critical inquiry and problem solving in physical education.* London: Routledge.

Youdell, D. (2003). Sex–gender–sexuality: How sex, gender and sexuality constellations are constituted in secondary schools. *Gender and Education, 17*(3), 249–270.

14

The Arts and Social Justice in a Critical Multicultural Education Classroom

MARY STONE HANLEY

My 40-year journey as an educator has always directly or indirectly included some form of the arts, as I worked in public schools, higher education, community centers, libraries, and in summer schools and theater programs. I learned the value of the arts from experience. My earliest and most pleasant memories as a child include the arts. Growing up in the middle twentieth century in a Black urban community, the arts were a source of culture, pleasure, and agency. Black secular and religious music represented a standard of excellence during a time when little of Black excellence was represented in the mass media and was an alternative space we proudly claimed in opposition to White claims of superiority. Many poets, particularly Black poets like Dunbar and Hughes, were regularly recited in my home. Participation in drama became a means of creative expression and critical thought. I carried many of these memories and skills into teaching.

I have used the arts in teacher education courses on critical multicultural education, and at the same time I have worked with adolescents in drama projects in various community sites with the goal of empowering them as artists, learners, and citizens. In critical multicultural education classes, the emphasis is on the process rather than the product to tap into the intrinsic motivation (Csikszentmihalyi & Schieffle, 1992) and empowerment (Hanley, 2002) of artistry. The goal is to use the arts to help students become metacognitive about their capacity for imagination, creativity, conceptualization, and transformation.

This chapter presents my pedagogical and theoretical reasoning for arts integration, along with examples of how I engage adults and adolescents in critical multiculturalism through the use of the arts. Although my work has been predominately with adults and adolescents much of the ideas presented here can apply even in elementary school classrooms.

Critical Multicultural Education

Sleeter and McLaren (1995) assert that critical pedagogy and multicultural education:

> Bring into the arena of schooling insurgent, resistant, and insurrectional modes
> of interpretation and classroom practices which set out to imperil cultural life,
> and to render problematic the common discursive frames and regimes upon
> which "proper" behavior, comportment, and social interaction are premised.
>
> (p. 7)

Teaching educators about the multiple and complex dimensions of critical multicultural education (Banks, 2007; Sleeter, 1996) requires attention to the multifaceted nature of its aims and means. The term critical implies criticism, an act of analysis used to examine society. Leonardo (2004) describes the process of criticism as a means to "cultivate students' ability to question, deconstruct, and then reconstruct knowledge in the interest of emancipation" (p. 12), which firmly embeds critical theories and pedagogy in the discursive realm. However, social change is physical and emotional, as well as intellectual, and critical multicultural pedagogy should reflect that.

It can be daunting to deal with the notion that everything you formerly believed to be unquestionable truth is open to question and may even be part of a system of oppression for many. It can be frightening to know that you must unlearn and relearn what you thought you knew, and since you will never know all, you will have to walk on ambiguous shifting sands of culture and change and never again claim to know the definitive answer.

Many students initially resist transformative learning because they are overwhelmed, frightened, or angry. The emotional terrain in the critical multicultural classroom is rutted with surprisingly deep holes where participants can get trapped, never to reemerge unless carefully attended. In the final analysis, the work of students and teachers needs to be in a context of support, caring, and hope (Freire, 1994; Wink, 2000; cf. Fitzpatrick, this volume).

To navigate this minefield, I often use the arts, because opportunities to engage in imagination, creativity, somatic, and affective learning enable dialog and also foreground hidden beliefs and feelings.

Teaching Adolescents

Urban youth involved in critical multicultural learning through the arts have additional emotional responses. Many swim in feelings of powerlessness that sap their energies and drive resistance, which entangles them in violence and failure. Their response to the arts and critical multicultural experiences is very often relief—relief that someone is interested in their stories, that their cultural knowledge is worthy, and when they understand themselves as change agents and artists there is relief that they are not powerless after all. In response to a ten-week drama program one girl wrote:

> I like the [drama] program because it made me have more confidence in myself. It made me believe in myself because I was so use to people putting me down, telling me you can't do this, you can't do that. It was never to try and you will succeed, so I gave up on myself. Thank you. You helped me a lot …

She found empowering support in a community of peers and caring adults involved in drama in which she and her fellow performers, who thought of themselves as the bottom rung of significance, repositioned themselves as creative and powerful artists with much to teach others in their communities, including teachers, about who they were and what they dreamed.

Artists are agents of change; they transform media, themselves, and audiences through the expression of their worldview. For students who suffer alienation because of passive learning and the perpetual regurgitation of others' thought, the pleasure of power and ownership through the arts can be a life-changing experience. However, a caveat about teaching the arts to adolescents is that they must be relevant in some way to the young people's lives. Teachers who put the canon of the arts before the culture and prior knowledge of the students are liable to find the same resistance that a teacher of any subject will find. My pedagogical project has always been to conceptualize, layer, and construct an instructional experience that positions students, regardless of their level of education or social power, so that they can overcome fears and resistance and become transformed learners and transformative agents of change, in effect to become conscious of their consciousness, an act of conscientization (Freire, 1993; Wink, 2000).

Framework of Instruction

In teacher education, we begin with a theory of imagination (Egan, 1992; Sigurdardottir, 2002) as the human faculty to conceive of possibilities with which to envision multiple perspectives, culture, social change, and social justice. One of our first activities and discussions is to imagine a just world; what would it be like? We use the definition of social justice presented by Bell (2007), "Social justice includes a vision of society in which the distribution of resources is equitable and all members are physically and psychologically safe and secure" (p. 1). We imagine the possibilities and contradictions in such a life. Is it possible, or desirable? What role does imagination play in creating and reaching that vision?

I open similar discussions on imagination and social change with adolescents after orchestrating a choral reading of the poem, *Question and Answer*, by Langston Hughes (Hanley, 1999). The last lines of the poem are "Dreams kicked asunder, Why not go under? / There's a world to gain / But, suppose I don't want it, Why take it? / To remake it." We discuss their visions of the world; sadly many do not have a very positive vision. The discussion must include hope, a historical perspective on the legacy of social change, and their power as change agents.

We also examine creativity (Cornett, 2007; Csikszentmihalyi, 1996) as an extension of imagination and as the human proclivity to adapt and problem-solve. Understanding imagination and creativity positions students as agents of change from an anthropological perspective, in which social justice is an ongoing adaptation for human survival. Another concept explored in every critical multicultural education course is culture (Bruner, 1996; Geertz, 1973; Nasir & Hand, 2006) as a social construction of meaning. We discuss how culture, identity, and social power are derived from the human imagination and creativity as humans work to construct an ideological world.

Other pedagogical values and practices that I have found to be essential are described by Shor (1992), as he depicts an empowering education which is "participatory, affective, problem-posing, situated, multicultural, dialogic, desocializing, democratic, researching, interdisciplinary, and activist" (p. 17). Therein the student is an active and inquiring learner who uses a creative process to investigate the world of self and other. Of the values and practices Shor describes, I have found that the affective, dialogic, and democratic activities are those which stimulate creativity and curiosity and which can facilitate openness to critical consciousness. An actively engaged class, as Nieto (2004) points out, is a feature of critical pedagogy that also supports multicultural education. For students to claim a critical consciousness, the learning must be theirs and not passively absorbed from a dominant ideological leader. Thus, imagination, creativity, and culture provide a framework for the theories and practices of critical multicultural education as we examine the dimensions of multicultural education, content integration, equity pedagogy, prejudice reduction, knowledge construction, and an empowering school culture (Banks, 2007; Sleeter, 1996), and the practices of critical pedagogy as a social reconstructionist project in a multicultural world (Sleeter & Grant, 2003).

Arts Integration

The arts in education have two approaches, art production and aesthetic education; arts integration involves both. Aesthetics provides opportunities for viewing the arts to explore cultural symbols, forms, and meanings. Through art production, the artist engages in a transformative meaning-making process that has imagination and creativity at its core and in every step. Even inexperienced artists shape the social construction of meaning using their socially situated imaginations and create a means for those who interpret the art form to suspend what is normal, explore other possibilities, and create alternate realities. Eisner (2002) describes the imaginative work of artists in the process of artistic conceptualization when he states:

> Concepts are distilled images in any sensory form or combination of forms that are used to represent the particulars of experience. With concepts we can … imagine possibilities we have not encountered, and we can try to create in the public sphere, the new possibilities we have imagined in the private precincts of our consciousness. We can make the private public by sharing it with others.
>
> (p. 3)

One student expanded on Eisner's point when she reflected on an in-class activity, in which students visually mapped their identities in overlapping shapes with multiple colors, sizes, widths, and textures that represented the relationships of race, class, gender, sexuality, religion, and other ways in which they identify themselves. She wrote:

> When art goes into a public moment, as opposed to the private experience, it carries new responsibilities .... For an introvert like myself, it was both creative and invigorating while also being an act of exposure and vulnerability. And isn't that a place we need to go before we can genuinely be open to others?

Voice and Expression

Another way to view the use of the arts in teaching and learning is that they enable student voice, which Giroux and McLaren (1986) define as self-expression, or the ways in which students confirm their own class, cultural, racial, and gender identities. Voice is both an internal and external process. Internal voice is the way that students order and understand their reality. Submerged ideas that are tinged with powerful and inhibiting emotions may emerge to be examined and expressed through an art form. The following quote is an example of the internal voice of an African American female student involved in a game, Australian Hypnosis (Boal, 2002), in which students in pairs alternately lead each other through a space. She reflected,

> I recall feeling a deep tension when we were asked to lead our partner with our hand about 5 inches from our partner's nose. My partner was a white female, and I felt considerable tension with being led by her hand, and a different kind of intense tension when I was leading her with my hand. (I also remember feeling guilty for feeling the tension.) I recall that I was not the only person who felt this way and we were able to discuss this in class. It moved us to literature on multicultural conflict and even the ways bodies are disciplined in the classroom (and in systems of power/ oppression).

External voice is a vehicle for the exchange and construction of ideas and feelings. Thus, the use of the arts gives students a means to wrestle with and represent ideas and feelings with which other students and the teacher can engage, which leads to more dialog, and provides an excellent vehicle for assessment as well.

Attributes of the Arts

In general, the arts present a wealth of pedagogical possibilities. The list in Table 14.1 was developed with the help of colleagues, artists, and students. In various settings I have asked "What do you think is the value of the arts?" Or "What have you learned about the arts from doing this learning activity?" I also have added attributes from my own experience and study. The list pertains to producing and viewing the arts and is a partial list because I continue to get answers that had not been included previously. Each characteristic makes a valuable contribution to critical multicultural teaching and learning. Critical thinking, imagination, creativity, research skills, hypothesizing, and higher-order thinking skills are essential to develop a critical consciousness and problem posing. Risk-taking is necessary to deconstruct long-held

Table 14.1 Attributes of the Arts

Imagination	Active learning	Self-discipline
Creativity	Affective learning	Hypothesizing (what if?)
Problem-solving	Risk-taking/vulnerability	Mental and physical agility
Higher-order thinking skills	Sensory awareness	Research skills
Collaboration	Community building	Aesthetics: study of beauty
Intrinsic motivation	Alternative symbol systems	Multiple perspectives
Communication	Pattern & rhythm	Language
Interdisciplinary thinking	Harmony, balance, &	Disciplinary knowledge
Structure	composition	
Observation skills	Critical thinking	*Artistic Agency:*
Connection of mind, body,	Social change	Perception
emotions, & spirit	Cultural knowledge	Conceptualization
Cultural history	Pleasure (fun)	Expression
Empowerment	Concentration/focus	Transformation
Flow	Empathy	

worldviews constructed by distortions and untruths and induces vulnerability that comes with critical self-reflection about the many ways that privilege and subordination affect perspective and experience and oppress others. Vulnerability connotes the disequilibrium created by new learning. Collaboration in artwork builds community that supports participants in the risky endeavor of the construction of a critical consciousness. Integration of mind, body, emotion, and spirit helps participants to understand their own complexities and the densities of difference and context. Work in the arts in which these points are explored may help students to metacognitively understand the importance of the arts in learning and agency.

Aesthetic experience, the perception of the arts by those who view the work, also integrates cognitive and affective ways of knowing and doing, and provides opportunities to activate the subtleties of intuitiveness, human relationships, and the feelings necessary to care about social change (Reimer, 1992). Structure, composition, form, patterns, and rhythm can inform understanding of the dialectical character of change. There are rhythms and patterns in nature and human social constructions like culture or relations of production. For example, students and I discuss the patterns and rhythms in works of art like Picasso's *Guernica*, or the pattern of social critique emerging in "conscious" hip hop, compared with the patterns in the social construction of White supremacy as presented in Horsman's (1981) *Race and Manifest Destiny: The Origins of American Racial Anglo-Saxonism*, or the patterns of the divide-and-conquer technique as presented in Zinn's (2001) *A People's History of the United States: 1492–Present*. The aesthetic experience has the possibility of helping us to see the familiar in unfamiliar ways and to introduce the viewer to new ideas and feelings.

Artistic Agency

The experience of making art is replete with creative demands that engage learners intellectually and affectively on the levels of perception, conceptualization, expression, and transformation (Eisner, 1980). The interaction of these processes is the agentive act of the artist as he or she employs curiosity, imagination, creativity, surprise, and self-efficacy while producing an art form. In the realm of psychology, Bruner (1996) posits agency as thinking for oneself in a problem-solving and decision-making process in order to arrive at responsible and successful choices. In philosophy, Martin, Sugarman, and Thompson (2003) state that agency is "the freedom of human beings to make choices in ways that make a difference in their lives" (p. 15). Artistic agency is the power to transform through the arts. Students in my classrooms integrate mind, body, emotion, and spirit, cultural knowledge, emotion, rationality, and intuition to conceptualize, make hypotheses and choices, to try solutions, to transform the art medium, themselves, and those who view and interpret their work.

Specific Arts-Based Activities—Theater, Hip Hop, and Film

One of the first arts-based activities in my teacher education courses is autobiography (cf. Vavrus, this volume). After examining whatever memories and artifacts that they can gather students use any art form that they choose to represent their lives, particularly their experiences with race, class, gender, and sexual orientation. Presentations of their autobiographies in an art form provide a layered expression of self through story, image, rhythm, rhyme, and other alternative forms of signification. Below are examples of how we have used theater, hip-hop, and film.

Theater

Writing plays (Chapman, 1991) is an exciting multifaceted activity that can enable critical dialog about students' world views, some of which is informed by internalized oppression and powerlessness. It also immerses students in experiences of literacy, strengthens reading skills, and taps student agency as they transform themselves and their audiences.

Plays written by students are inherently culturally responsive because they are created from the culture of the writers. The most inclusive approach is to write a theme play (Bray, 1994). I begin the process by telling students that plays inform people about what the writer understands of the world; I ask them what they would like to teach their audiences. They then generate themes for the play. Past examples include: I believe I can fly; Do your best, forget the haters; Follow your dreams; Be somebody, be yourself. After what is usually a heated discussion, they choose one theme for the whole play. The next step is for the students to write, improvise, and revise characters, dialog, conflict, and scenes about the theme. Finally, the performance of the play includes the scenes or character monologs connected by music, poetry, dance, etc.

Augusto Boal's (1979, 2002) Theater of the Oppressed techniques are appropriate for critical multicultural work. Schutzman and Cohen-Cruz (1994) describe the goals of the techniques: "Boal's vision is embodied in dramatic techniques that activate passive spectators to become spect-actors—engaged participants rehearsing strategies for personal and social change" (p. 1). Through the use of the body and story, participants engage in games and performance that engage participants' critical consciousness.

I have used improvisational games, Image Theater, and Forum Theater (Boal, 2002) to explore critical and multicultural concepts, social change, activism, transformation, and problem-solving. Image Theater uses the physicalization of ideas to explore the essence of experience and discourse. Using the body as clay, without the use of language, participants sculpt and are sculpted into representations of relationships, concepts, emotions, and experience to touch conscious and unconscious meaning and emotion. Participants also find a multiplicity of perspectives and positions through imaging. Jackson (2002) explains, "a group of individuals will perceive a whole range of different, but often intriguingly related, meanings within a single image, often seeing things which the sculptors had no idea were there" (p. xxiii). Thus, Image Theater helps students and instructor to grapple with the complexity of social connections by distilling the essence into a still life image and relating meaning across images.

Forum Theater (Boal, 2002) is a mode of performance in which the audience plays an active role in the resolution of oppressive life experiences. Students perform a scene, based on the lives of the class members, about marginalization, exploitation, racism, sexism, etc. in an unsolved form, and the audience as spect-actors are invited to enter the scene to enact effective change and to positively transform the situation for the protagonist—the oppressed—in the scene. Forum Theater is a problem-solving rehearsal of social change. Multiple ideas for solutions are examined to prepare students for real life situations: "the result is pooling of knowledge, tactics, and experience, and at the same time what Boal calls a 'rehearsal for reality'" (Jackson, 2002, p. xxiv).

Improvisational theater games (Rohd, 1998; Spolin, 1983) present an opportunity to play in a classroom. In fact, although games are valuable for risk-taking, trust building, and sensory awareness (cf. Fitzpatrick, this volume), an important result is the rupture that games make in the notion of what is acceptable format for learning. Games present multiple possibilities as experience and metaphor of experience. Somatic and intuitive knowledge are given credence, relationships of people and ideas can be explored in the moment rather than in a text, and they build a supportive community.

Hip Hop

Hip hop is a contemporary culture for many youth, and the use of poetry to express experience and critique is a valuable tool in a critical multicultural classroom. We have had really heated discussions in teacher education classes when we did a content analysis of commercial and underground rap lyrics and videos about of race, class, gender, and misogyny. Exploration of the political economy of hip hop can be the basis for a historical analysis of the context that can help students understand the contours of capitalism, by examining the exploitation of young people in the industry, consumerism, and the control of meaning and the art form for the marketplace.

Another use of hip-hop culture in the classroom is to share the spoken word poetry that students have written for the class and for other situations. Spoken Word has become a democratic soap box among youth that they write and perform in community centers, churches, clubs, at poetry slams and open mics where everyone is encouraged and no one is denied the right to "represent." I invite the culture of hip hop into the classroom to access the creative and democratic impulse already in youth culture. At times we write together, at other times we read our work, and still other times we bring the work of favorite lyricists and poets who speak about the topic we are discussing. The performance aspect of spoken word also adds to everyone's vulnerability, which needs the encouragement of the community, thus building support to deal with difficult and challenging issues in the critical multicultural curriculum.

Film

Film is also a powerful medium that can be used for content analysis and examination of context (cf. Lea; Sharma, this volume). *Rabbit Proof Fence* (Noyce, 2002) is a true story of the effects of the early twentieth-century Australian policy of racial cleansing. Mixed-race children were taken from their Aboriginal parents to be trained in a school for mixed-race children, never to see their families again. Three little girls defied the power of the state and traveled thousands of miles to return to their families. The film supported our study of the social construction of White supremacy and the resistance that erupts, as exemplified by the children, when confronted with oppression. *Smoke Signals* (Eyre, 1998), based on short stories by Native American writer Sherman Alexie, is the first feature film made by a Native American crew and creative team that provides an example of insider perspectives. We pondered cultural aspects that are outside of our realm of knowledge, as well as asked the question of who is not represented in this film to think about the diversity within and outside of a culture. The film also presents an opportunity to acknowledge our collective ignorance and assumptions about Native culture in order to talk about the concept of partial knowledge as a part of prejudice and the human condition. There are, of course, innumerable films that can be used to teach and highlight, using a film's virtual experience and narrative to precede or follow readings and foment discussions.

Conclusion

Imagination and creativity are central aspects of agency; they are mental abilities used in constructing human meaning and institutions, and are thus necessary for the transformation of culture and society. They must be evident in social justice curricula. How can we build a new world without imagining it? What good is a curriculum of critique without the hope, empathy, and support that creativity evokes? With the arts, students tap into the transformative power of creativity in the search for meaning. The arts also integrate affective learning, acknowledging that there is no cognition without affect, and no affect without cognition.

Among the rewards of teaching critical multicultural education using the arts is my students' use of the arts in working with students in their own classrooms. A former doctoral student, who now teaches preservice teachers, points to the dialogic nature of the use of Boal theater techniques in her teaching when she states:

> image theatre and forum theatre brought people into an active relationship with events and issues, opening a space for dialogue .... It is a reminder that our role must not be always at the head of things, leading people to their own freedoms, but in the midst of things, working with people, striving to understand their world and their need, ally and not enforcer.

After experiencing the arts in my courses, a first-grade teacher began using arts with her students. She described an arts-based project in her multicultural classroom:

> [M]y students were highly motivated to learn . . . to work together . . . to think and create! They literally skipped throughout the classroom while working on the project (which took several days) saying how much they loved school. I have a classroom with children of all ability levels and they all actively participated in the ... project.

In higher education, K-12 classrooms, and informal educational settings, the arts support respect for student agency, multiple perspectives, and expression that motivates active and dialogic learning, releasing the wonder that should always be in learning.

References

Banks, J. A. (2007). Multicultural education: Characteristics and goals. In J. A. Banks & C. A. M. Banks (Eds.), *Multicultural education: Issues and perspectives* (pp. 242–264). Hoboken, NJ: John Wiley & Sons.

Bell, L. A. (2007). Theoretical foundations of social justice education. In M. Adams, L. A. Bell, & P. Griffin (Eds.), *Teaching for diversity and social justice* (2nd ed.) (pp. 1–14). New York: Routledge.

Boal, A. (1979). *Theater of the oppressed.* New York: Theater Communications Group.

Boal, A. (2002). *Games for actors and non-actors.* London: Routledge.

Bray, E. (1994). *Playbuilding: A guide for group creation of plays with young people.* Portsmouth, NH: Heinemann.

Bruner, J. (1996). *The culture of education.* Cambridge, MA: Harvard University Press.

Chapman, G. (1991). *Teaching young playwrights.* Portsmouth, NH: Heinemann.

Cornett, C. E. (2007). *Creating meaning through literature and the arts: An integration resource for classroom teachers* (3rd ed.). Upper Saddle River, NJ: Pearson.

Csikszentmihalyi, M. (1996). *Creativity: Flow and the psychology of discovery and invention.* New York: HarperCollins.

Csikszentmihalyi, M., & Schiefele, U. (1992). Arts education, human development, and the quality of experience. In B. Reimer & R. Smith (Eds.), *The arts, education, and aesthetic knowing: Ninety-first yearbook of the National Society for the Study of Education* (pp. 169–191). Chicago: University of Chicago Press.

Egan, K. (1992). *Imagination in teaching and learning: The middle school years.* Chicago: University of Chicago Press.

Eisner, E. (1980). Artistic thinking, human intelligence and the mission of the school. *The High School Journal, 63*(8), 326–334.

Eisner, E. (1998). Aesthetic modes of knowing. In *The kind of schools we need: Personal essays* (pp. 32–43). Portsmouth, NH: Heinemann.

Eisner, E. (2002). *The arts and creation of mind.* New Haven, CT: Yale University Press.

Eyre, C. (Director). (1998). *Smoke signals* [Motion picture]. New York: Miramax Films.

Freire, P. (1993). Pedagogy *of the oppressed.* New York: Continuum.

Freire, P. (1994). *Pedagogy of hope.* New York: Continuum.

Geertz, C. (1973) *The interpretation of cultures.* New York: Basic Books.

Giroux, H., & McLaren, P. (1986). Teacher education and the politics of engagement: The case for democratic schooling. *Harvard Educational Review, 56*(3), 213–238.

Hanley, M. S. (1999). A Culturally relevant lesson for African American students. Retrieved April 1, 2009, from http://www.newhorizons.org/strategies/multicultural/hanley2.htm

Hanley, M. S. (2002). Learning to fly: Critical multicultural education through drama. *Arts and Learning Research Journal, 18*(1), 75–98.

Horsman, R. (1981). *Race and manifest destiny: The origins of American racial Anglo-Saxonism.* Cambridge, MA: Harvard University Press.

Jackson, A. (2002) Translator's introduction to the first edition. *Games for actors and non-actors.* London: Routledge.

Leonardo, Z. (2004). Critical theory and transformative knowledge: The functions of criticism in quality education. *Educational Researcher, 33*(6), 11–18.

Martin, J., Sugarman, J., & Thompson, J. (2003). *Psychology and the question of agency.* Albany, NY: State University of New York Press.

Nasir, N. S., & Hand, V. M. (2006). Exploring sociocultural perspectives on race, culture, and learning. *Review of Educational Research, 76*(4), 449–475.

Nieto, S. (2004). Critical multicultural education and students' perspectives. In G. Ladson-Billings & D. Gillborn (Eds.), *The RoutledgeFalmer reader in multicultural education* (pp. 179–200). London: RoutledgeFalmer.

Noyce, P. (Director). (2002). *Rabbit proof fence* [Motion picture]. New York: Miramax Films.

Reimer, B. (1992). What knowledge is of most worth in the arts? In B. Reimer & R. Smith (Eds.), *The arts, education, and aesthetic knowing: Ninety-first yearbook of the National Society of the Study of Education* (pp. 20–50). Chicago: University of Chicago Press.

Rohd, M. (1998). *Theatre for community conflict and dialogue: The hope is vital training manual.* Portsmouth, NH: Heinemann.

Schutzman, M., & Cohen-Cruz, J (Eds.). (1994). Introduction. *Playing Boal* (pp. 1–16). London: Routledge.

Shor, I. (1992). *Empowering education: Critical teaching for social change.* Chicago: University of Chicago Press.

Sigurdardottir, B. (2002). Imagination. *Thinking, 16*(2), 34–38.

Sleeter, C. E. (1996). *Multicultural education as social activism.* Albany, NY: State University of New York Press.

Sleeter, C.E., & Grant, C. A. (2003). *Making choices for multicultural education: Five approaches to race, class, and gender.* New York: John Wiley & Sons.

Sleeter, C. E., & McLaren, P. (1995). Introduction: Exploring connections to build a critical multiculturalism. In C. E. Sleeter & P. L. McLaren (Eds.), *Multicultural education, critical pedagogy, and the politics of difference* (pp. 5–32). Albany, NY: State University of New York Press.

Spolin, V. (1983). *Improvisation for the theater.* Evanston, IL: Northwestern University Press.

Wink, J. (2000). *Critical pedagogy: Notes from the real world.* New York: Addison Wesley Longman.

Zinn, H. (2001). *A people's history of the United States: 1492—present.* New York: Perennial Classics.

15

Breaking Through "Crusts of Convention" to Realize Music Education's Potential Contribution to Critical Multiculturalism

CHARLENE A. MORTON

Music, like other art forms, has been extolled as a vehicle for transformative education and social change. Music has also been criticized as a cultural form that helps sustain social inequities, in part, by leaving them unquestioned. While affirming the emancipatory and transformative potential of arts education, Maxine Greene calls upon arts educators to pay more attention to the need "to break through some of the crusts of convention, the distortions of fetishism, the sour tastes of narrow faiths" (Greene, 1995, p. 146). There is "no question," she continues, that the distortions and omissions in arts curricula, shaped by the meta-narrative of Eurocentric aesthetic sensibilities, must be corrected to welcome multiple worldviews (p. 162; see also Hanley, this volume). She adds that "we need openness and variety, as well as inclusion . . . avoid[ing] fixities, even the stereotypes linked to multiculturalism" that essentialize differences (pp. 162–163).

How much progress has music education made opening up the Eurocentric music curriculum to welcome, study, and celebrate diverse musical sensibilities? How well is music education taking up the challenge to expose, critique, and disrupt biases and stereotypes sustained through musical arts? As a Canadian university instructor and former school music specialist in Canada since the early 1980s, I have witnessed an increase of interest in social justice and multicultural education among a small community of music education scholars.[1] Similarly, I am aware of pockets of committed school practitioners exploring musical projects in world musics and for social change. For the most part, however, efforts to expand the musical repertoire of classrooms and concert stages can best be described as musical tourism—a token form of multicultural education that showcases soundscapes from around the world, but fails to provide spaces to foster intercultural understanding, critical dialog, or sociopolitical action. For example, repertoire for classroom and ensemble use include many arrangements of film scores, originally composed to accompany stock Hollywood narratives and invariably reproducing racial and gendered tropes. Joseph Abramo (2007) points to a band arrangement for the film *King Kong* (2005), describing how the ABA format of the music score uses familiar Western orchestration techniques in the two A sections in contrast to ethnic or exotic tropes for the B section, highlighting the music publisher's claim that "This ... tune will really bring out the 'ape' in your band [requiring] some African drums, a tribe, and lots of bananas to feed the monkeys!" (p. 7). He also describes students pretending to be Asian by hitting a gong followed by a low bow with clasped hands. Similarly, he recounts music students mimicking African dancing by improvising "pulsating, repetitive, yet enticing rhythms of African drums" (p. 6). He concludes that, by failing to critique stereotypes and their ubiquitous sonic props that flourish in all media formats, music education is serving to "reify racial symbolic violence," ultimately reinforcing rather than challenging the "destructive side" of formal as well as hidden curricula (p. 21).

Many curricular and education policy documents give music education a sociopolitical mandate to both promote cultural diversity and redress social inequities. Clearly, it is not a given that positive changes in policy translate into music curriculum objectives or classroom practice. A case in point is the Fine Arts Integrated [Curriculum] Resource Package for the Canadian Province of British Columbia (BC Ministry of Education, 1998). Its mandate for multicultural and antiracist education is tucked away *at the end* of the long document in "Appendix C: Cross-Curricular Interests," along with other transdisciplinary themes such as Aboriginal studies, English as a second language, environment and sustainability, and gender equity (pp. C–3). Furthermore, none of these themes is directly addressed in the Music Kindergarten to Grade 7 Curriculum section, except with a few general comments in the introductory pages, where teachers are reminded that "shared experiences in music significantly contribute to the development of a healthier society through activities that respect and reflect the diversity of human experiences" (BC Ministry of Education, 1998, p. 120).

Another case in point is the recently revised arts curriculum for the Canadian Province of Ontario. Initially, it looks more promising. The official arts curriculum guide begins by describing a rationale for four organizing ideas, including "making a commitment to social justice and dealing with environmental issues" (Ontario Ministry of Education, 2009, p. 6). Accordingly, one of the first introductory chapters begins with instructional strategies, including an analysis of problems with Eurocentric and patriarchal curricular traditions relevant to repertoire and performance choices:

> [T]eachers should avoid focusing on art forms from only one place or that reflect only one style; avoid judging some art forms as "better" than others; avoid teaching by artistic movement or period; and avoid choosing only male artists' work or only European works for study. To put this in positive terms, teachers should include consideration of arts from around the world and from a variety of times, including contemporary works by living artists; comparisons of a variety of art works by theme, topic, and purpose; and study of both male and female artists.
>
> (pp. 37–38)

Also included is a substantial analysis of bias and stereotypes, statements about systemic discrimination and inequities, and a section on anti-discrimination education (pp. 49–50). Nothing, however, is presented in terms of social justice, exploitation, cultural imperialism, or (critical) multiculturalism. Furthermore, the new arts education document offers few, new practical insights for music educators. It simply reiterates the need to select music from a broad representation of musical traditions and genres and to encourage students to play any band instrument rather than, for example, assigning flutes or violins to girls and trombones and double bass to boys. Similarly, it suggests that children should be encouraged to sing songs in support of, for example, "antibullying and violence-prevention programming" (p. 50). For the most part, these issues or topics were identified 30 years ago, and, I believe, are being attended to, at least as far as they go. More to the point is that the learning outcomes have remained fundamentally the same. In other words, while philosophical frameworks for arts education curriculum continue to develop a stronger mandate to investigate and challenge social injustices, curriculum learning outcomes do not reflect these changes, providing little pedagogical leadership to break open "crusts of convention" (Greene, 1995, p. 146).

The purpose of this chapter is to expose the serious challenges posed by these crusty conventions so that music education can better contribute to transformative education and social change as part of the educational enterprise of critical multiculturalism. In the first section of this chapter, I examine the priority afforded *music literacy* and its impact on curricular reform in multicultural music education. After briefly explaining the concept of literacy and reviewing its status in elementary music programs, I discuss its significance for high-school programs, its impact on multicultural societies and oral music traditions, and my own efforts to shift away from conventional elements of music literacy in teacher education classes. In the second section, I examine the tension between the need to provide or perform more inclusive musical choices and a lack of confidence in presenting authentic repertoire from diverse musical traditions. I offer a critical review of a professional music teacher's early and post-secondary training as an explanation of why many hesitate to embrace multicultural education and, consequently, consume, uncritically, the resources prepared by music-publishing industries. I conclude with a recommendation for music educators to move beyond their marginalized position in the development of school curricula, becoming full partners in a collaborative effort to challenge "crusts of convention" and to build cross-curricular networks for critical multiculturalism.

Music Literacy and Music as Music Notation

Teaching students how to read and write music is a fundamental aspect of musicianship training, often described as being able to hear what you see (written in the musical score) and to see what you hear (that is, to visualize heard sounds in notation). In keeping with literacy as a resilient standard of achievement across the curriculum, music literacy remains a curricular priority for the assessment of students' musicianship and musical knowledge. Although I cannot and would not argue against the importance of literacy in anyone's education, including my own, such a "narrow faith" (Greene, p. 146) in the significance of literacy so defined neglects the responsibility to include, celebrate, and learn from oral traditions, which are often struggling to be heard or to survive. The continuing emphasis upon literacy also ignores the need to attend to musical insecurities related to the fear or (gendered) disdain of singing, prevalent among North Americans, even musicians, and often exacerbated by school music programs (Pascale, 2002).

A case in point is the Kodály method, best known among music educators for its pedagogical attention to music literacy in elementary school programs. It is a cornerstone of curricular design in Canada, as well as abroad.[2] Believing that "music belongs to everyone," Zoltan Kodály (1929) assembled strategies for teaching music literacy as a way to make "good" Hungarian music accessible to its people, freeing them from a Germanic cultural legacy and "trashy" music in general (p. 119). This plan for reviving Hungarian nationalism was heavily invested in developing musical literacy through the singing of folk songs that moved to the linguistic rhythm of the Magyar language. Critics have pointed out that, because Hungarian music reflects a relatively homogeneous culture, this monolingual and monocultural approach cannot be successfully adapted to multicultural or hybrid societies. This case illustrates how embracing a music-literacy approach makes it difficult to integrate diverse and multiple worldviews, and maintains the elitist and exclusive metanarrative of European classical music.

The impact of a music-literacy focus upon multicultural reform is apparent in a sociological study of high-school music classrooms in Ontario, Canada. In a reissue of this 1983 comparative study, Shepherd and Vulliamy (2007) observe that unlike in England, no overt [multi]culture clash was found in Ontario schools between school music and the music interests of students. They saw Ontario school music programs positively positioned to explore multicultural approaches, reasoning that, because music education is not compulsory in high school, *unlike* in England, it is considerably easier for Ontario (and other Canadian) music directors to implement a more flexible, multicultural approach in designing band and choral programs. Nonetheless, they argue that the pedagogical process, *like* programs in England, is still entrenched in "particular ideologies of the dominant musical culture . . . . What is shared is a conception of music as equatable with musical notation" (p. 210). That is, although school music programs might appear to embrace different musical genres and cultural repertoire, the aesthetic, global, and social lessons were the same as if the music was from the Western canon. In other words, musicianship continues to be defined in large part by the ability of students to read music off the page, omitting any reference to different musical languages and the social/cultural contexts of these new curricular resources.

Mapping Western music methods, such as learning to read Western musical notation, onto the study of non-Western music seriously reinforces "a Western educational hegemony and . . . [will] negate the basis of multiculturalism" (Dunbar-Hall, 2002, p. 67; Robinson, 2002, pp. 223–224). The problem is exacerbated by the commercial relationship between music education and the music industry.[3] What is a band program (which starts as early as Grade Four) without a music score? Music-publishing industries, as well as other music industries that produce instruments and other large ensemble resources such as music stands and band uniforms, all have a vested interest in sustaining school programs that rely on the study of music's structural elements—melody and rhythm. And, although publishing companies and composers of school music have become more diversified in their musical offerings, curriculum objectives dictate that the music be learned from Western notation and performed accordingly. Furthermore, these pseudo-multicultural compositions for large ensembles are usually little more than essentialized misrepresentations of exoticized cultures. The history of these musical misrepresentations is as long as the history of music composition for stage and screen, often evoking "vague," "casual," or simply "careless" images associated with musical Orientalism and other alternative sonic delights (Scott, 1998).

One positive argument for teaching musical literacy is that musical notation is a strategy for preserving musical cultures in danger of extinction. Ethnomusicologist Bonnie C. Wade (2004) observes, perhaps naively, that "touching stories circulate about groups whose traditional music no longer exists for some reason—radical change from international influence or memory loss where no system of reinforcement was in place" (p. 19). She explains that "recovery and revival is possible through recordings" as well as through standardized musical notation, which "constitutes a kind of international musical language" and "can be a great help as a tool for musical communication" (pp. 19–24). Quoting Mantle Hood, a former teacher of hers, she adds that "a written tradition is only as strong as the oral tradition it supports" (p. 24). Hood's adage might be more useful if applied to questions about the status and success of music education in fostering music literacy. In North America, the curricular status of oral and aural skills—listening and singing—is secondary at best, making music education a curriculum for those motivated to read Western music notation. Furthermore, although music programs spend a large portion of curricular and extra-curricular time devoted to reading music notation, success is sketchy and short-lived. In other words, the adage that "a written tradition is only as strong as the oral tradition it supports" helps explain why music education has not been able to produce a music-literate population. Here, then, is a problem with the potential for a win–win solution: By shifting the curricular focus from reading music to the development of oral (and aural) sensibilities, music education can nurture a broader understanding of music(al) literacy that will also better accommodate world-wide music traditions—especially those that integrate different dimensions of music-making such as playing instruments, singing, dancing, narrative, pageantry, ritual, and a multitude of other cultural functions.

In contrast to the expectation that music notation will preserve and sustain oral cultures, there are many examples where the introduction of musical notation and other forms of Western cultural practices have weakened marginalized cultures. Drawing on interviews in the 1980s with Zulu music students, Elizabeth Oehrle (2002) explains how students' music making as a way of life is greatly diminished after attending university music schools:

> Thus we have swung full circle. We brought Africans to America and discouraged their traditional ways of making music. We initiated a process of music education based on singing and music notation literacy, and then these notions and others were transmitted back to parts of Africa. Music making in parts of Africa stands to lose more than it could hope to gain, because today these notions are [still] incorporated into music education.
>
> (p. 79)

Greene (1995) explains that the process of developing literacy should "provoke critical questions around the many *modes* of literacy, the preferred languages [scripts and notation systems], the diversity of languages, and the relation of all of these to the greater cultural context" (p. 111). Unfortunately, in British Columbia, like other North American jurisdictions, the singular *mode* of musical literacy is the curricular category "Structural Elements: Melody and Rhythm," fundamental for learning to read and write musical notation. To foster other musical modes of literacy, I have skewed my introductory music education courses for (generalist elementary) teacher-candidates to focus on the second and third categories, "Thoughts, Images, Feelings" and "Context: Personal and Social, Historical and Cultural." I remind my *generalist* teacher candidates that private, public, and post-secondary education for music education *specialists* is focused almost exclusively on developing music literacy and, subsequently, performance skills. That's what specialists do best as trained musicians. To compensate for this narrow understanding of music education, I encourage future *generalist* teachers to attend to the other two important but neglected categories, adding that is what they can do best—and perhaps do better. I set up activities and assignments for them to practice exploring and articulating feelings, thoughts, and images, using musical artifacts from a wide range of cultures and cultural practices. These in turn become platforms for critical dialog about, for example, their lack of confidence to teach music and their fear of presenting themselves as musically illiterate, non-singers, unmusical, or non-performers. These activities also allow for exploring alternative views about what constitutes *good* or *not-so-good* music in creative, social, or political terms. Finally, when listening to music matched with images so common in contemporary multimedia entertainment, these exercises can help students name and discuss social issues in context.

My initial explanations to my student teachers about why my music education course does not focus on the structural elements of music (literacy) have not (yet) satisfactorily disrupted ideological assumptions that music equals music notation. Feedback indicates that some student teachers want more opportunities to learn to read and perform from musical notation.[4] My prediction is, however, that as long as music education is configured to develop music literacy, defined as reading music notation, music education will not be able to uphold its responsibility to give voice, literally and figuratively, to under-represented cultures and diverse worldviews. Furthermore, given the tenacity of literacies across the curriculum, projects for critical multiculturalism in music education must be supported by curricular partners in other subject areas investigating "the sour tastes of narrow faiths" (Greene, 1995, p. 146) that have a negative impact on adopting a more open and inclusive study of aural and oral dynamics of knowledge (re)creation.

Music Education as Authentic Performance, Authentic Practice

In this section, I examine another crust of convention in school music programs: preoccupation with performance—and, in the context of multicultural music, *authentic* performance. After briefly explaining the concept of and professional fixation on authentic performance or practice,[5] and exploring potential reasons for this fixation on cultural purity, this section proceeds with a critical examination of how to resolve the tension between, on the one hand, an acknowledged need for more inclusive and representative music repertoire and, on the other hand, a lack of confidence in locating and presenting repertoire from unfamiliar and diverse musical traditions.

The issue of authentic performance "is perhaps the most discussed ontological issue of interest to philosophers, musicologists, musicians, [music educators], and audiences alike" (Kania, 2007, sec. 2). Using a harpsichord rather than a piano, for example, to perform J. S. Bach's *English Suites* is a topic of discussion enjoyed by musicologists, musicians, and audiences of Baroque music. The cultural or sociopolitical significance of the piano-versus-harpsichord debate, however, is relatively benign. That is, although a piano does not provide an accurate recreation of the Baroque sound or performance practices, its use does not jeopardize, exploit, or substantially misrepresent harpsichord keyboard traditions in particular or Baroque musical communities in general. In contrast, some ethnomusicologists and anthropologists in their research among marginalized music communities struggle with ethical issues when trying to balance academic interests with cultural preservation on the one hand and potential exploitation on the other (Nettl, 2005). Moving to the school context, using Orff accompaniment (for example) to introduce Navajo cultural practices to young music students raises similar dilemmas. In this case, however, a balance between pedagogical interests and cultural understanding is not apparent. Because Navajo music is essentially vocal music with no history of using barred instruments played with mallets, the rationale to use Orff accompaniment in this classroom and other musical arrangements of Native American music makes little sense as authentic performance. It is not difficult, therefore, to appreciate the criticism that "nothing could be less authentic or less illuminating" than "perverting the style" of Navajo culture by using Orff xylophones and other percussion instruments (Leonhard, 1989, p. 6). More troubling, though, is the exploitation of a marginalized cultural practice for pedagogical purposes in the name of multi-cultural education.[6]

A major factor contributing to the importance placed on authentic perform-ance by music educators stems from their early and professional training as musi-cians. Most music education specialists study vocal or instrument music in European classical music traditions where performers recreate masterworks through the careful study of authentic practices. Although musicologists and his-torians may present Baroque, Classical, and Romantic music as evolving tradi-tions, the reality is that musicians are educated to recognize distinctive musical characteristics for each and to recreate authentic interpretations accordingly. Having experienced this kind of training, I believe that the temptation to fix—as well as fixate on—music as a set of static rather than fluid cultural traditions sets up a psychosocial disposition among music educators to essentialize difference, especially in unfamiliar musical traditions.[7] Complicating the capacity for music educators to disrupt an understanding of (multicultural) music education *as* authentic performance, "one may also argue that an observer [or student] is inca-pable of perceiving a complex phenomenon except in its static form, change being a rapid succession of stable states, and that therefore if culture is something con-stantly changing, one can deal with it only as an abstraction (Nettl, 2005, p. 222). Furthermore, although "the idea that one makes or listens to music to show who one is . . . has been around a long time . . . , [the politics of] identity hasn't been recognized until the last two decades as a major function of music" (p. 257).

Perhaps no musical cultures are the focus of identity politics more than Aboriginal cultures. And, perhaps no musical cultures are so under-represented in music education.[8] Active in the search for, maintenance of, and development of traditional and hybrid identities, culturally grounded in ecological and spir-itual ways of knowing, and fighting a history of oppression and assimilation, indigenous musics/cultures appear ontologically and epistemologically counter to Western notions of music and virtually impossible to understand or recreate as authentic performance. Their creative and cultural survival is evident in the revival of traditional practices alongside the mix of contemporary Aboriginal as well as non-Aboriginal practices such as Métis fiddle music, Aboriginal hip-hop, blues and country music, and, of course, intertribal pow-wows. For music edu-cators heavily invested in the development of (conventional) musical under-standing based on authentic performance, exploring Aboriginal music is a troubling prospect. However, if the preoccupation with authentic performance—fixing it in time and space for study and unconnected to the study of identity politics—was acknowledged, then music educators could better understand and critique their attachment to essentialized notions of both music and culture.[9] They could subsequently question music's role in cultural imperialism and exploitation, as well as music education's responsibility to help foster under-standing of and solutions for social injustices.

Music educators are nonetheless aware of the importance of representing multicultural school populations and the need to rejuvenate a mostly irrelevant Eurocentric curriculum. At the same time, they generally have legitimate concerns that either their own music education has left them unprepared, or that no amount of education could adequately train anyone for the task of multicultural music education. Ironically, and perhaps because of their awareness about the importance of multicultural education, concerns about misrepresenting authentic practices often dissipate when they are offered world-music workshops and materials for classroom or ensemble use. The music industry seems always posed to attend to consumer needs, producing materials that combine the development of musicianship through performance and music literacy with adventures in musical tourism through familiar but often racist musical narratives such as *Persian Prelude, Indian Dance, Asian Suite,* and, of course, *King Kong.* How, then, might music education shake its preoccupation with curricular crusts of convention and its uncritical exploitation of musical stereotypes and cultural hierarchies, and reinvest its professional energy in the educational enterprise of critical multiculturalism for social change?

Realizing Potential Contributions to Critical Multiculturalism

To insiders in music education, these crusts of convention might appear secondary. Specifically, music educators have a very visible and long-standing preoccupation to secure or raise the status of school music programs in general. In their advocacy work, music educators often present a host of conflicting rationales, exposing the "tension between the pluralistic foundation of multiculturalism and the subtle but deep-seated monism of aesthetic ideology" (Bowman, 1993, p. 24). So, when music educators argue that "music embodies an 'ineffable' [aesthetic] essence that is common across all cultures, in all contexts, [this] argument functions well to justify a universal commitment to music education; [but] it does not do the work needed to bring issues of social justice and various political locations into view" (Vaugeois, 2007, p. 178). Furthermore, "while developing an appreciation of cultures other than one's own may encourage students to think more broadly about music, it does not require that [students] consider the social and political situatedness of people and therefore neglects potentially important material concerns" (Vaugeois, pp. 182–183). Scott Goble (2008) concludes that it is almost impossible to explain why music education should be in the official curriculum at all when it continues to focus on aesthetic sensibilities and other "intra-musical meanings, [making] no important connections to anything outside itself" (p. 67).

So, what can music education scholars, curriculum developers, and practitioners do "to break through some of the crusts of convention, the distortions of fetishism, the sour tastes of narrow faiths" (Greene, 1995, p. 146), perhaps also improving music education's self-serving need to improve its curricular status? Trained, as Bryan Burton (2002) concedes, to be "the world's greatest band [orchestra or choir] director" and in the image of the Great White Father (p. 162), music educators often have to find and sustain their own motivation to pursue professional development in critical multiculturalism. Given this lack of support, as well as the pressure to perform on stage and to attend to the development of music literacy, would it not be prudent to leave the inherently ethical and practical demands of critical multiculturalism to the subject area best prepared to explore sociopolitical issues—that is, social studies? I say no! Unexamined feelings of incompetence, and a general failure to explore political issues associated with the "creation, production and consumption" of music (Haynes, 2005, p. 366), are not pedagogical issues to leave to one curricular corner of student or teacher education.

I recommend that, in order to realize music education's potential contribution to critical multiculturalism and social justice, we engage in transdisciplinary professional development and dialog. Music educators should join discussions about the overstated importance of literacy and cultural authenticity uncritically cultivated across the curriculum. No cross-curricular imperative or ethical enterprise in public education—whether it be Aboriginal or antiracism education, social or eco-justice, or democratic or moral education—can take hold as long as curricular silos remain singularly invested in subject-based content. A case in point are the two themes identified in this chapter—literacy and authentic performance. Both are themes that run through the collection of seminar papers published in *World Musics and Music Education: Facing the Issues* (Reimer, 2002). Missing from most of the seminar dialogue, however, is a discussion about power issues, historical exclusion, and other forms of oppression that musical practices are subject to or sustain. More promising, in theory, are the contributions to *Action, Criticism, and Theory for Music Education.*[10] Nowhere, though, is there attention given to cross-curricular solutions for supporting oral traditions, community outreach, inclusive practices, critical media literacy, social activism, democratic responsibilities, and eco-centric traditions—many not easily brought inside institutional walls for study, critical inquiry, or even to enjoy.

Finally, we cannot underestimate the tendency for many music education specialists, as well as generalists who enjoy teaching music, to embrace the age-old assumption that the implicit healing and harmonious powers of music alone can still save the day. Teachers, like the general public, (want to) believe that "Music has charms to soothe the savage breast / To soften rocks, or bend a knotted oak."[11] So, it is not surprising that music educators leave implicit lessons about power and oppressive relationships to the magic of subconscious pedagogical osmosis. Given this inclination, music education could easily continue as simply a curricular platform to showcase music literacy, performance skills, and musical tourism. I believe that the profession would be better served if it grappled with its attachment to curricular conventions, including its pedagogical practices, and explore what it is willing to let go, modify, or introduce. The project is huge—no less so than the scope of transdisciplinary obligations now appearing in federal, state, and provincial education policy documents. To find the impetus, support, and ideas to fulfill these social responsibilities, music education needs to be more active in transdisciplinary conversations about curriculum development, mentorship, practice, and scholarship. It should be clear that I have made these critical observations not to single out music education or music educators. Rather, my observations are presented to encourage *all* educators to participate in collective projects for critical multiculturalism and to welcome and mentor music educators as important partners in this transformative process.

Notes

1 The first two North American conferences focusing on music education and social justice were organized in 2006 and 2008.
2 See http://kodaly.eu/index.php?option=com_content&task=view&id=20&Itemid=35
3 See http://www.musicounts.ca
4 Interview data collected by Vetta Vratulis, a UBC doctoral student, reveals that former teacher-education students equate music education, music literacy, and performance. Although some acknowledge that their online multicultural playlist assignment are interesting or "cool," most view it as a secondary learning experience compared to the mechanics of how to teach music skills.
5 I use *authentic performance* and *authentic practice* interchangeably. *Practice* in this context does not mean practicing, for example, to play piano.
6 Like exoticized settings and musical scores for tired Hollywood film narratives, these kinds of inauthentic interpretations are probably motivated more by desire rather than attending to cultural understanding, preservation, or inclusion (Scott, 1998, p. 328).
7 In fact, concerns for authenticity in classroom practice seem to be given more priority by music educators than by "indigenous musician[s]" (Robinson, 2002, p. 231). Similarly, cultural intermediaries in the world music industry see "the desire for authentic performances of music . . . as a potential limitation for [world music artists] who wish to expand their repertoires" and disrupt essentialist or racialized notions of culture (Haynes, 2005, p. 377).
8 Because Aboriginals "are the most legally differentiated people in the United States [and in Canada], the only group granted formally special status and rights by the federal government, [they] represent the *arche*-difference" (Young, 1990, p. 181). For a helpful text that explores musical and political themes of indigenous cultures, see Diamond (2008).
9 A case in point is Bruno Nettl's advice to music educators expressing concerns about identifying authentic practice. Out of frustration, he "reminded the participants that the only constant . . . is change" (McCullough-Brabson, 2002, p. 133).
10 The e-journal for the MayDay Group, in particular Vol. 6(4), at www.mayday group.org
11 William Congreve (1697). *The Mourning Bride*, Act 1 Scene 1.

References

Abramo, J. (2007). Mystery, fire and intrigue: Representation and commodification of race in band literature. *Visions of Research in Music Education, 9/10.* Available at http://www. usr.rider.edu/~vrme/

Bowman, W. (1993). The problem of aesthetics and multiculturalism in music education. *Canadian Music Educator, 34*(5), 23–30.

British Columbia. Ministry of Education. (1998). Fine arts kindergarten to grade 7: Containing curricula for dance, drama, music, visual arts. Integrated resource package. http://www.bced. gov.bc.ca/irp/fak7.pdf [Revised edition in progress, 2008–2009]

Burton, B. (2002). Weaving the tapestry of world musics. In B. Reimer (Ed.), *World musics and music education: Facing the issues* (pp. 161–185). Reston, NJ: National Association for Music Education.

Diamond, B. (2008). *Native American music in Eastern North America: Experiencing music, expressing culture*. New York: Oxford University Press.

Dunbar-Hall, P. (2002). The ambiguous nature of multicultural music education: Learning music through multicultural content or learning multiculturalism through music? In B. Reimer (Ed.), *World musics and music education: Facing the issues* (pp. 57–67). Reston, NJ: National Association for Music Education.

Goble, J. S. (2008). Music education curriculum, new media policies, and the next generation: A philosophical opportunity. In C. Leung, L. Yip, & T. Imada (Eds.), *Music education policy and implementation: International perspectives* (pp. 63–71). Hirosaki, Japan: Hirosaki University Press.

Greene, M. (1995). *Releasing the imagination: Essays on education, the arts, and social change*. San Francisco, CA: Jossey-Bass.

Haynes, J. (2005). World music and the search for difference. *Ethnicities, 5*(3), 365–385.

Kania, A. (2007). The philosophy of music. Retrieved from E. N. Zalta (Ed.), *The Stanford Encyclopedia of Philosophy*: http://plato.stanford.edu/entries/music/

Kodály, Z. (1929/1974). Children's choirs. In F. Bonis (Ed.), *The selected writings of Zoltan Kodály* (Trans. L. Halápy & F. Macnicol). London: Boosey & Hawkes.

Leonhard, C. (1989). Music education: A unifying force with social significance. In T. Rice & P. M. Shand (Eds.), *Multicultural music education: The "Music Means Harmony" workshop* (pp. 3–7). Toronto, ON: Institute for Canadian Music, University of Toronto.

McCullough-Brabson, E. (2002). Passing the cultural baton of music. In B. Reimer (Ed.), *World musics and music education: Facing the issues* (pp. 119–137). Reston, NJ: National Association for Music Education.

Nettl, B. (2005). *The study of ethnomusicology: Thirty-one issues and concepts* (new edition). Urbana: University of Illinois Press.

Oehrle, E. (2002). A diverse approach to music in education from a South African perspective. In B. Reimer (Ed.), *World musics and music education: Facing the issues* (pp. 71–90). Reston, NJ: National Association for Music Education.

Ontario Ministry of Education. (2009). *The arts: Grades 1–8* (revised). Retrieved May 2009. http://www.edu.gov.on.ca/eng/curriculum/elementary/arts18b09curr.pdf

Pascale, L. (2002). "I'm really NOT a singer": Examining the meaning of the word *singer* and *non-singer* and the relationship their meaning holds in providing a musical education to schools. In A. Rose & K. Adams (Eds.), *Sharing the voices: The phenomenon of singing III* (pp. 164–170). St. John's, NL: Memorial University.

Reimer, B. (Ed.). (2002). *World musics and music education: Facing the issues*. Reston, NJ: National Association for Music Education.

Robinson, K. (2002). Teacher education for a new world of musics. In B. Reimer (Ed.), *World musics and music education: Facing the issues* (pp. 219–236). Reston, NJ: National Association for Music Education.

Scott, D. B. (1998). Orientalism and musical style. *Musical Quarterly, 82*(2), 309–335.

Shepherd, J., & Vulliamy, G. (2007). A comparative sociology of school knowledge. In L. Barton (Ed.), *Education and society: 25 years of the British Journal of Sociology of Education* (pp. 209–227). London: Routledge.

Vaugeois, L. (2007). Social justice and music education: Claiming the space of music education as a site of postcolonial contestation. *Action, Criticism, and Theory for Music Education, 6*(4), 163–200. http://act.maydaygroup.org/articles/Vaugeois6_4.pdf

Wade, B. C. (2004). *Thinking musically: Experiencing music, expressing culture*. New York: Oxford University Press.

Young, I. M. (1990). *Justice and the politics of difference*. Princeton, NJ: Princeton University Press.

Contributors

Lilia I. Bartolomé is Professor of Applied Linguistics at the University of Massachusetts at Boston, USA. As a teacher educator, Bartolomé's research interests include the preparation of effective teachers of minority second language learners in multicultural contexts. She has published the following books: *Ideologies in Education: Unmasking the Trap of Teacher Neutrality; The Misteaching of Academic Discourses; Immigrant Voices: In Search of Pedagogical Equity* (with Henry Trueba), and *Dancing with Bigotry: The Poisoning of Culture* (with Donaldo Macedo).

Russell Bishop is Foundation Professor for Maori Education in the School of Education at the University of Waikato, New Zealand. His research experience is in the area of Kaupapa Maori research and culturally relevant and inclusive pedagogy. His recent books include *Pathologising Practices* (2005), co-authored with Carolyn Shields and Andre Mazawi, and *Culture Speaks* (2006), co-authored with Mere Berryman. He is currently the project director for Te Kotahitanga, a large New Zealand Ministry of Education funded research/professional development project that seeks to improve the educational achievement of indigenous Māori students through the implementation of a culturally responsive pedagogy of relations.

Jill Ewing Flynn is an Assistant Professor of English Education at the University of Delaware, USA. A former middle-/high-school English teacher, Jill earned her Ph.D. in Curriculum and Instruction: Literacy Education from the University of Minnesota in 2009. Her research and teaching interests include culturally relevant pedagogy, multicultural literature, and critical literacy.

Katie Fitzpatrick is a Research Fellow in Health and Physical Education in the School of Critical Studies in Education, Faculty of Education, University of Auckland, New Zealand. A former high-school health and physical education teacher and Head of Department, her research interests include critical approaches to health and physical education, issues of gender, sexuality, ethnicity and culture, youth perspectives, and critical ethnography.

Eric (Rico) Gutstein teaches Mathematics Education at the University of Illinois-Chicago. His interests include teaching mathematics for social justice, Freirean approaches to teaching and learning, and urban education. He has taught middle- and high-school mathematics. Rico is a founding member of Teachers for Social Justice (Chicago) and is active in social movements. He is the author of *Reading and Writing the World with Mathematics: Toward a Pedagogy for Social Justice* (Routledge, 2006) and an editor of *Rethinking Mathematics: Teaching Social Justice by the Numbers* (Rethinking Schools, 2005).

Ryuko Kubota is a Professor in the Department of Language and Literacy Education in the Faculty of Education at the University of British Columbia, Canada. She has worked as a language teacher and teacher educator in Japan, the USA, and Canada. Her major research interests include culture and politics in second/foreign language teaching, second language writing, critical multiculturalism, and critical pedagogies. Her articles have appeared in such journals as *Canadian Modern Language Review, Critical Inquiry in Language Studies, English Journal, Journal of Second Language Writing, TESOL Journal, TESOL Quarterly, Written Communication*, and *World Englishes*.

Virginia Lea is currently an Associate Professor at Gettysburg College, Pennsylvania, USA. She received her Ph.D. in social and cultural studies in education from the University of California, Berkeley. She sees her research and teaching as a means of developing greater understanding of how hegemony works to reproduce local and global inequities. She tries to live a commitment to working with other social and educational activists to interrupt hegemonic practice and create greater socio-economic, political, cultural, and educational equity in our time.

Terry Locke is Professor of Education in the Arts and Language Department, School of Education, University of Waikato, New Zealand. He is a poet, educational researcher, and teacher educator. Recent monographs include *Critical Discourse Analysis* (2004) and *Resisting Qualifications Reforms in New Zealand: The English Study Design as Constructive Dissent* (2007). His research interests include constructions of English as a subject, the impact of educational "reforms" on classroom practice, the teaching of literature, and the impact of technology on literacy practice. He is coordinating editor of the refereed, online journal, *English Teaching: Practice and Critique*. He is currently editing a book for Routledge entitled: *Beyond the Grammar Wars: A Resource for Teachers and Students on Developing Language Knowledge in the English/Literacy Classroom*.

Stephen May is Professor of Education in the School of Critical Studies in Education, Faculty of Education, University of Auckland, New Zealand. He has published seven books and over 70 articles and chapters in the areas of multicultural education, language diversity, language rights, and the wider politics of ethnicity, bilingualism, and multiculturalism. He is a leading proponent of critical multiculturalism and his books in this area include *Making Multicultural*

Education Work (Multilingual Matters, 1994) and *Critical Multiculturalism: Rethinking Multicultural and Antiracist Education* (RoutledgeFalmer, 1999). His book *Language and Minority Rights* (Routledge, 2008) was recognized as an American Library Association Choice Outstanding Academic Title in 2008. He is also a Founding Editor of the interdisciplinary journal, *Ethnicities*, and Associate Editor of the journal *Language Policy*.

James C. McShay currently directs the Office of Multicultural Involvement and Community Advocacy at the University of Maryland, College Park. He is the former director of undergraduate education for the Department of Curriculum and Instruction at Iowa State University, USA. During his tenure at ISU, he taught courses in multicultural education, ethnicity and learning, and antiracist education. His research has a special focus on how technology can be used to support liberatory pedagogies in K-16 education. His work can be found in the *Journal of Multicultural Perspectives; Multicultural Education and Technology Journal;* and *Contemporary Issues in Technology and Teacher Education.*

Charlene A. Morton taught for 10 years in Canadian public schools as an elementary classroom and music teacher before completing her graduate studies at the University of Western Ontario and OISE/University of Toronto, Canada. She was a faculty member of the School of Music, University of Prince Edward Island before moving in 2002 to the Faculty of Education, University of British Columbia. In addition to teaching courses in music education, social foundations, curriculum issues, and global education, she coordinates the Social Responsibility and Environmental Sustainability Cohort for the UBC Teacher Education Program. Her work appears in *Philosophy of Music Education Review; Music Education Research; Action, Criticism, and Theory for Music Education*, and conference proceedings.

Jeanette Rhedding-Jones is Professor in Early Childhood Education at Oslo University College, Norway. She is also Adjunct Professor at Bergen University College and has an honorary appointment at Melbourne University Australia. She is the author of *What is Research? Methodological Practices and New Approaches; Muslims in Early Childhood Education: Discourses and Epistemologies* (2010, forthcoming), and co-author and editor of *Beretninger fra en muslimsk barnehage* (Tales from a Muslim preschool in Norway). Jeanette has guest edited special editions of *Contemporary Issues in Early Childhood* with a focus on Troubling Identities; and *Australian Research in Early Childhood*, with a focus on Gender, Complexity, and Diversity.

Sanjay Sharma teaches in Sociology and Communications, School of Social Sciences, Brunel University, UK. His research is located in the areas of cultural politics, racialization, and difference, which critically consider questions of representation, radical pedagogy, and subjectivity. He is the author of *Multicultural Encounters* (2006), and the co-editor of the online "race" journal *darkmatter* (http://www.darkmatter101.org).

Christine E. Sleeter is Professor Emerita in the College of Professional Studies at California State University, Monterey Bay, USA, where she was a founding faculty member. Her research focuses on anti-racist multicultural education and multicultural teacher education. She has published over 100 articles in edited books and journals such as *Teacher Education Quarterly, Teaching and Teacher Education,* and *Curriculum Inquiry.* Her recent books include *Unstandardizing Curriculum, Facing Accountability in Education,* and *Doing Multicultural Education for Achievement and Equity* (with Carl Grant; Routledge). She was recently awarded the American Educational Research Association Social Justice in Education Award, and the American Educational Research Association Division K Legacy Award.

Georgina M. Stewart holds a research position in the New Zealand Council for Educational Research. She has a Master of Science degree in Chemistry and an Ed.D. In 1992, she was appointed as foundation teacher of *Pātaiao* (Science) and *Pāngarau* (Mathematics) at Te Wharekura o Hoani Waititi Marae, one of the first Māori medium schools in New Zealand. Her Ed.D. thesis, completed in 2007 and entitled *Kaupapa Māori Science,* has been rewritten as a book, *Good Science? Narratives from the Margins of Power* (2010, forthcoming).

Mary Stone Hanley is an Assistant Professor in Initiatives for Transformative Education in the College of Education at George Mason University in the USA, and has been an educator in public schools and higher education for more than 35 years. She received a Ph.D. in Curriculum and Instruction focused on Multicultural Education from the University of Washington in Seattle, in 1998. Her research agenda includes critical multicultural education, the education of Black youth, and arts and equity in education and research. She is also a playwright and poet and has written several plays and screenplays produced for adolescent audiences.

Michael Vavrus is a Professor of Teacher Education and Political Economy at the Evergreen State College in Olympia, Washington, USA, and is the author of *Transforming the Multicultural Education of Teachers: Theory, Research, and Practice.* He is a past president of the Association of Independent Liberal Arts Colleges for Teacher Education and the Washington state chapter of American Association of Colleges for Teacher Education. Most recently, he has authored chapters and articles on teacher identity formation as related to issues of race, sexuality and gender, and culturally responsive teaching. His current research focuses on a multicultural critical pedagogy that incorporates teacher candidate autoethnographies.

Index

Made in the USA
San Bernardino, CA
30 August 2018